THE CHANNEL ISLANDS

A New Study

Uniform with this book

The Cotswolds
    Edited by Charles and Alice Mary Hadfield

Dartmoor
    Edited by Crispin Gill

Mendip
    Edited by Robin Atthill

THE CHANNEL ISLANDS

A New Study

EDITED BY VICTOR COYSH

Contributors:

Victor Coysh
John Renouf
David E. Johnston, MA
John Uttley, MA
Nigel Jee, BSc
Peter J. Girard, BSc
E. J. Leapingwell, RIBA, AA Dip
E. J. T. Lenfestey
Herbert Ralph Winterflood
Michael Marshall

David & Charles

Newton Abbot   London   North Pomfret (Vt)   Vancouver

ISBN 0 7153 7333 1

Library of Congress Catalog Card Number: 77–076089

Set in 11 on 13pt Baskerville
by Trade Linotype Limited, Birmingham
and printed in Great Britain
by Redwood Burn Limited, Trowbridge & Esher
for David & Charles (Publishers) Limited
Brunel House   Newton Abbot   Devon

Published in the United States of America
by David & Charles Inc
North Pomfret   Vermont 05053   USA

Published in Canada
by Douglas David & Charles Limited
1875 Welch Street   North Vancouver   BC

Contents

List of Illustrations

Plates

Figures

Tables

Maps

Introduction

Victor Coysh

Set in the Gulf of St Malo, closer to France than to England, lie the Channel Islands, less than 100 miles (160km) south of Weymouth. They comprise Jersey, Guernsey, Alderney, Sark, Herm and Jethou, together with smaller islands and reefs, including Les Minquiers, Les Ecrehous and the French Chausey Islands. The former group covers about 150 square miles (38,850 hectares) and the latter approximately 100 square miles (25,900 hectares).

It has become commonplace to quote Victor Hugo's words in his romance, *The Toilers of the Sea*, yet, broadly speaking, they are politically factual today. In translation, he wrote: 'The Channel Islands are portions of France which have fallen into the sea and have been picked up by England'. This may be loose geology, but while they were scarcely 'picked up', the islands have been intimately linked with the Crown of England for over 900 years.

Forming part of the Duchy of Normandy at the time of the Conquest in 1066, the association with the British monarchy has persisted, despite the subsequent loss of Normandy by King John, and today the Queen has no more loyal subjects than the Channel Islanders.

Today, the islands are famed as holiday resorts, for their produce (especially potatoes and tomatoes), as 'tax havens' and because, during the Second World War, they were the only British possessions to have been occupied by Germany. They are densely populated—the two major islands in particular—their buildings and motor vehicles are in places too numerous for comfort and the islands' popularity among tourists seasonally increases this congestion. Yet their charm survives these embarrassments of riches for it is easy to escape the crowds and to revel in the matchless coastlines which, down the ages, have faced the might of the sea with almost unyielding resistance.

The presence of industry has to a rather large extent marred the beauty of the Guernsey countryside, for acres are covered by glasshouses. However, some pastoral regions survive and the cliffs are superb. In Jersey, the cultivation of potatoes has by no means affected its rural attractions and as much may be said of Alderney and Sark, where signs of industry are scarce.

11

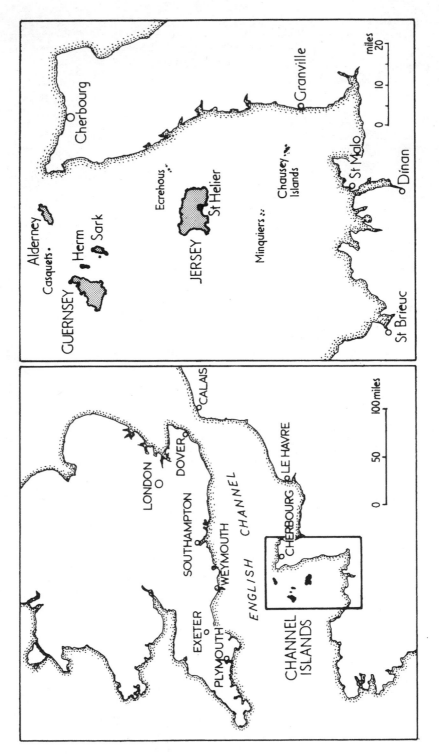

Map 1   The Channel Islands

One of the Channel Islands' most striking features is the degree of contrast one with another. Each is completely different, not merely in physical characteristics, but in atmosphere and outlook. Admittedly, they all have lofty cliffs and rocky shores, but the contrasts outweigh the similarities and this is especially noticeable in the towns. The antiquity and setting of St Peter Port is quite unlike the more modern St Helier, while the diminutive capital of Alderney bears no resemblance to Sark's village.

One of the merits of the two major islands is the fact that they are not entirely dependent for their livelihood upon visitors. True, tourism ranks high in their economy but there are other sources of income and these not only add great interest to the picture but induce an atmosphere beneficial to those who visit Jersey and Guernsey. They meet islanders who find pleasure in the presence of strangers bringing fresh ideas and providing a welcome change to a community which, during much of the year, is compelled to rely on its own company. Yet out of season the islands are not the dead places so often encountered in resorts relying solely on summer guests. Thanks to the benefit derived from horticulture, agriculture and other industries, Jersey and Guernsey enjoy amenities throughout the year and visitors are most welcome to share them with the islanders.

Moreover, the major islands each enjoy their own form of government and while there is some similarity between the States (parliament) of Jersey and Guernsey, the Alderney States and Sark's Chief Pleas each has an unique flavour which enhances the special aura surrounding both islands. These contrasts in home rule are reflected in the way life is enjoyed in all the Channel Islands.

Charm is an elusive word to define, but it is simple enough to discover in these little isles. The visitor finds something of a French atmosphere at once strange and enchanting, a place where the merits of Britain and France combine—almost an English-speaking morsel of the Continent within sight of the French coast. The pace of life in the islands is slower than elsewhere and while progress is not lacking they retain their individualities and refuse to conform, clinging to traditions and a mode of living which, in a troubled world, make them the envy of less favoured lands.

The Jersey Island Development Committee has very wide powers and the scheduling of historic buildings (and the like) is currently taking place. Some years ago those in the town were dealt with and 130 buildings were put in Grade 1. The second grade deals with buildings possessing parts which merit preservation and Grade 3 deals with groups

of buildings. Gorey and St Aubin are to be similarly scheduled and eventually the whole island will be dealt with. The scheduling is the work of the local architects' association.

In respect of conservation in Guernsey, the Island Development Committee Law of 1966 provides for the implementation of a codified policy of planning by way of an outline development plan covering the whole island and detailed development plans for different areas of Guernsey. So far, only the States IDC's detailed plan for an area in the Castel parish has been produced and approved by the States. In 1976 the States accepted the IDC's recommendation that the production of four detailed development plans be suspended as a counter-inflationary measure.

The Ancient Monuments and Protected Buildings (Guernsey) Law of 1967 provides for the listing by the States Ancient Monuments Committee for statutory protection against the demolition and structural alteration of buildings of historical, archaeological, architectural or other special interest. As yet little listing has been done.

The States of Alderney have twice rejected the *Projet de Loi* entitled 'The Historic Buildings and Ancient Monuments (Preservation) (Alderney) Law, 1975' which, had it been enacted, would have empowered the Alderney Building and Development Control Committee to designate for protection not only buildings as being of special historic, architectural, traditional, artistic or archaeological interest, but also whole areas as being of special historical or architectural interest. C. E. B. Brett's book, *Buildings of the Island of Alderney,* published for the Alderney Society, had been intended as a complement to the *Projet de Loi.* He recommended that the whole of St Anne's should be designated as a conservation area.

Sark Chief Pleas, against the advice of the Sark Committee for the Preservation of Natural Amenities, rejected Mr A. G. Jellicoe's plan of 1967, which urged that fewer houses should be built and that any new buildings should be of better quality than hitherto and exclusively for occupation by Sark people. He further suggested that all future development should be concentrated in a few well-defined areas, which should be screened by trees, and that certain areas of agricultural land should be designated as overspill areas for future development. Since then, panic legislation has been produced to curtail development, but only as a temporary measure.

The impact of commerce on the islands is strong, for as well as the chief industries of horticulture and tourism they accommodate merchant banks, important financial concerns, conference centres and the homes

of the ultra-wealthy. The rich settler is made welcome, but such factors are not alone the cause of the islanders' prosperity. Sheer hard work has accomplished this and continues to do so.

What of the future? Such great events as the German occupation and the entry of Britain into the Common Market have not caused fundamental changes in the islands, whose character seems stronger than their history. Essentially they remain as they have been for generations. These tough morsels of territory have survived the forces of Nature and the ways of man and in their immortality lies their strength.

1

Geology

John Renouf

Though the geological history of the formation of the Channel Islands is an interesting story about which we have learned a great deal in recent years, it is a tale extremely difficult to chronicle. The complicated terminology of geology is likely to confuse an uninitiated reader and, in contrast to the recent historical periods discussed in this collection, geological time involves immense periods covering hundreds and thousands of millions of years. Pre-historians are interested in hundreds of years, historians in decades, years and, in some recent studies, minute periods of time, whereas geologists talk in millions of years with ease. Therefore the exact pattern of events is always unclear and indeed there are times when no record exists in the rocks.

Like historians, geologists tend to know more about recent events than those that lie deep in the past and unfortunately the rocks that form the major structural framework of the Channel Islands are very, very old. We must turn to extremely early periods of geological time to understand how this framework was built, though it is the processes that have been active over recent periods, geologically speaking, that account for many surface deposits and for the shaping of the present islands. Between the formation of the basement rocks and the emergence of the Channel Islands as islands stretches a very long period when life evolved from fish to ape and many other events occurred of which no trace or evidence exists in the islands today.

Because of this, one of the popular features of geology, the search for the discovery of fossil remains, is extremely difficult to accomplish in the islands. The basement rocks were formed either deep within the earth under conditions of great pressure and heat, or on exposed and turbulent land masses devoid of vegetation and other life, or in seas virtually barren of life. Yet if the islands did not consist of these hard and ancient rocks, they would not exist in their present form today and many other features so admired by visitors and inhabitants alike would certainly not be found. The rocky cliff lines, the sheltered bays with their golden sands, and even the signs of human usage in the beautifully

17

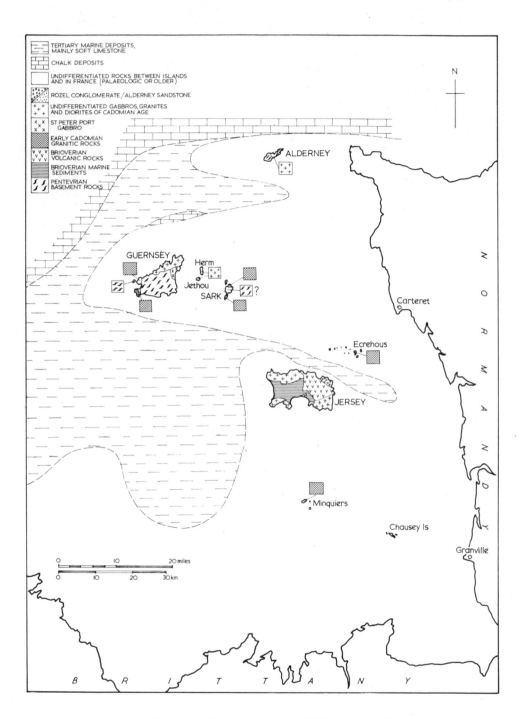

Fig 1 Outline geology of the Channel Islands and adjacent waters

coloured walls of farmhouse and lane, would not contribute towards the scenic splendour of the whole.

But of the time when the Channel Islands were emerging as islands, during our more recent geological past, there are many traces of the processes at work, and indeed the hand of man may be discerned in the latest periods. So, from times of silence and turmoil deep within the earth's past about which we can say little we arrive suddenly in a bustle of life and movement. We have a making and a shaping.

More than 2,000 million years in the making

The Pentevrian: 2,500 – 1,000 my Ago

At least 2,500 million years ago,[1] when the earth was but half its present age, certain rocks along Guernsey's southern coast had been created. They had been formed in the depths of the earth's crust from molten rock called magma which had cooled to become a granite (a plutonic rock). Later the granite was altered by great heat and pressure generated by deep-seated earth movements into a rock called gneiss (a metamorphic rock), this particular one in Guernsey being named the Icart Gneiss[2] after the headland of that name (see Fig 1 and Table 1).

The great age of the Icart Gneiss and a number of other gneissic rocks in the Channel Islands places them among the oldest known in the British Isles and France. The name that geologists give to the times in Armorica when these rocks were being formed is Pentevrian[3, 4] after an ancient name of the St Brieuc area in Brittany. Like all these early geological eras, the Pentevrian covers a vast period of time and in this case encompasses all rocks in Armorica with an age greater than 1,000 million years (see Table 1).

In Guernsey many of the rocks in the southern parts of the island were formed during the Pentevrian, and in Alderney the western half of the island also belongs to these eras. But not all the rocks in these areas were formed deep within the crust; a number were laid down at the surface as sediments (sedimentary rocks). These too, like the plutonic rocks, have been altered into metamorphic rocks known as schists. In Guernsey they occur as dark grey to almost black, banded rocks separating pale-coloured gneisses, and also, typical of Alderney,[5] as dark patches within the gneisses. Rocks of this sort occurring on Sark[6] are probably of Pentevrian age but may be younger.

The rocks of Pentevrian age are best seen on the southern cliffs of Guernsey on either side of Icart Point, while the darker schists are well

Age in millions of years	Rocks and events	
—Present —		
	PLEISTOCENE	
	MESOZOIC AND TERTIARY SEDIMENTARY CYCLES	see Tables 2 and 3
225—		
	PALAEOZOIC SEDIMENTARY CYCLE	not well represented in the Channel Islands but found widely in adjacent Normandy and Brittany uplift and erosion at the end of the Cadomian orogenic cycle. Rozel Conglomerate (Jersey), Alderney Sandstone (Alderney, Burhou, Casquets)
—500 —		
	CADOMIAN OROGENIC CYCLE	intrusion of gabbros (c. 600 my), granites (500–600 my) with formation of diorites: all islands except Sark. Main Cadomian deformation (650–620 my). Early granitic intrusions (Écréhous, Minquiers, Sark, L'Erée in Guernsey)
700—		
	BRIOVERIAN SEDIMENTARY AND VOLCANIC CYCLE	volcanic rocks of Jersey marine sediments of Jersey and of Pleinmont (Guernsey)
—1,000 —		
—1,500 —		
	PENTEVRIAN	the making of the basement rocks of the Channel Islands and the formation of the fundamental framework of the area. All these events occurred more than 1,000 my ago and took more than 1,500 my to happen: granitic gneisses of Guernsey and the western part of Alderney, perhaps the oldest gneisses and altered sediments of Sark
—2,000 —		
—2,500 —		the oldest rocks in the Channel Islands—the Icart Gneiss of Guernsey
—3,000 —		

TABLE 1   The geological story of the Channel Islands—the first 2,000 million years (not to scale)

displayed in outcrops between Jerbourg Point and Castle Cornet, especially at Divette. On Alderney good outcrops occur around Fort Clonque where a further interesting feature of the Pentevrian can be seen. Magma of different compositions forced its way up narrow, almost vertical, partings in the rocks to cool as narrow seams called dykes and give the cliffs opposite the Fort splashes of bright colour.

The Brioverian: 1,000 – 700 my Ago

By about 1,000 million years ago a substantial area of Pentevrian rocks existed in Armorica and the Channel Islands, forming what is known as a basement complex. The upheavals of Pentevrian times had brought very different rock types into contact and erosion had revealed them at the surface, a surface forming land over some regions of Armorica and seas over others. The material eroded from the land areas was swept to the bottoms of these seas where it was reworked by currents and eventually deposited as layers of sediments which steadily built up to considerable thicknesses (see Fig 2A). These lands and seas lasted over Armorica for about 300 million years during the era which succeeded the Pentevrian and which is called the Brioverian, after the ancient name of St Lô in Normandy.

The greatest thicknesses and main outcrops of the Brioverian marine sediments occur in Normandy and Brittany. In the Channel Islands they can be seen principally in Jersey where they occupy a large area of the island (see Fig 1), St Ouen's Bay between La Rocco Tower and L'Etacq offering a particularly fine stretch of low tide exposures. However, at close quarters the rocks form a rather monotonous series of layers of dull-coloured sediments varying in thickness from less than a millimetre to more than a metre. We know that they are marine in origin because a number of distinctive features occur which could only have formed beneath the sea. These seas also contained some very primitive life in the form of 'worm burrows' preserved today as faint traces in the rock.[7] In Guernsey an outcrop of sediments at Pleinmont Point also belongs to the Brioverian but the rocks have been so altered by later meta- morphism that there is little of interest to be seen. It is possible that some of the metamorphic rocks on Sark are of this age.

Towards the end of the Brioverian a new feature appeared to dominate the landscape of this area. Great volcanoes emerged, probably from the sea floors of the time, and spread rains of hot ash and debris over a wide area. (See Figs 1 and 2B and Table 1.) While simple life existed in the seas, all the land was barren and the volcanoes produced an

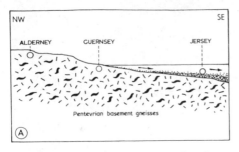

A c 750 my ago—a cross section from
north-west to south-east through Alderney,
Guernsey and Jersey during the Brioverian
some 750 my ago shows currents carrying
sediments from a presumed land area to
the north-west and depositing them far
from shore

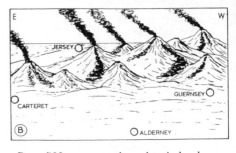

B c 700 my ago—the volcanic landscape
of late Brioverian times some 700 my ago
shows Jersey very close to many active
volcanoes. Other volcanoes lay not far to
the north-east of Carteret but we have no
traces from Guernsey, Alderney or the
other islands at this time

C Between c 650 and 620 my ago the Brioverian sediments, volcanic deposits and early
granitic intrusions (see text) were folded and metamorphosed

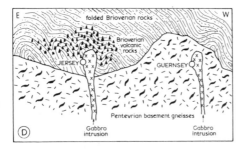

D c 600 my ago—a cross section from
east to west through Jersey and Guernsey
showing the intrusion of gabbros into the
folded Brioverian rocks about 600 my ago.
All the islands at this time were buried
deep within the earth's crust several miles
down

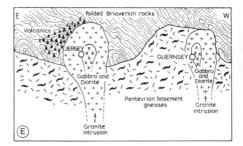

E c 520–600 my ago—a cross section
similar to D but showing the intrusion of
the great granites and the alteration of
much gabbro to diorite

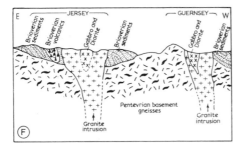

F c 500 my ago—a cross section similar
to D and E but showing the effects of uplift
and erosion which have brought the area of
the islands to the surface

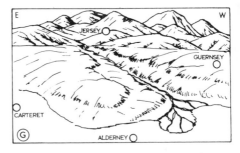

G c 500 my ago—the landscape of Rozel
Conglomerate and Alderney Sandstone
times about 500 my ago showing the
mountain ranges south of 'Jersey' and the
sea covering 'Alderney' and 'Carteret'

Fig 2 (A–G) Past environments of the Channel Islands between 1,000 and 500 million
years (my) ago

additionally desolate landscape. At times of inactivity the air was clear and the ash and lava were eroded by surface waters but at times of eruption the sky was heavy with flying rock debris, ash and smoke and glowing lava plunged down the slopes to end in a spout of steam as it met the sea.

The only volcanic rocks in the Channel Islands are to be found on Jersey[8] where deposits indicate that volcanic peaks lay close at hand but in what direction, or whether one mile or ten away, remains unclear as no actual volcanic vent has been found. Various signs of this volcanic activity can be seen on Jersey where lavas, ashes and mixtures of rocks cemented together all occur. The two best areas to see these rocks are along the east coast between Mont Orgueil and Archirondel and in the north at Bouley Bay. Particularly attractive are the striped multi-coloured rocks of L'Islet in Bouley Bay and the little nut-like pebbles with an internal structure of radiating needles and concentric circles of different colours that can be picked up on the beach. Just north of Anne Port, one of the actual lava flows can be identified by the occurrence of hexagon-shaped columns a little like those of the Giants' Causeway in Ireland, though at Anne Port the rock is a reddish colour.

The Cadomian Orogenic Cycle: 700 – 500 my Ago

Little is known about the convulsions within the earth's crust in the earlier eras of the Pentevrian that caused the formation of the plutonic rocks or their later metamorphism. But from the close of the Brioverian about 700 million years ago for some 200 million years until 500 million years ago, the whole of Armorica was caught up in another series of convulsions and about these we have much information. The events of these 200 million years belong to what geologists call the Cadomian orogenic cycle,[3, 4] Cadomian deriving from the ancient name of Caen in Normandy and orogenic meaning 'earth building'.

The earth consists of a hard crust overlying a more plastic interior. The crust is composed of a number of separate plates[8] which, at their edges, are places of instability and which can be moving apart or coming together. One of these lines of instability—one where plates were being forced together—lay across Armorica and was the cause of the Cadomian orogenic cycle. The plate edges ran in a particular direction ENE/WSW between Normandy and Brittany. Here plates were in collision and the rocks formed during the Pentevrian and Brioverian were driven together and downward by the tremendous energies of the collision.

The friction of the plates as they ground together and drove the

rocks downwards generated enough heat to melt some of the formations of Pentevrian and Brioverian age and to transform others, giving them an entirely new appearance. Those rocks, which were reduced to a molten state, were trapped within the crust and sought release upwards again towards the surface, forcing themselves between, and enveloping, earlier deposits to form massive granites. But many of these granites were not to survive unchanged for long because these movements were only the precursors of a long cycle of destruction, transformation and reformation.

Rocks which have survived from this early episode are abundant in the Channel Islands' area. The rocky outcrops of the outlying reefs of the Channel Islands, especially the Ecréhous and Paternosters and much of the Minquiers, are formed of intrusive granites but altered in later phases of the Cadomian cycle into gneisses similar to that of Icart, formed from granite in a Pentevrian orogenic event. In Sark some of the granites belong to this period and have likewise been changed into gneiss. The most accessible example of the results of this early phase of plutonism, showing also the later transformation into gneiss, is to be seen in Guernsey at L'Erée (see Fig 1 and Table 1).

As the plates continued to force themselves together vast pressures and heat were generated over an ever widening area. The rocks of the Pentevrian and Brioverian throughout Armorica were increasingly affected; they were transformed by the metamorphic processes while also undergoing great folding as the layers were bent and twisted. The main areas of extreme deformation of Brioverian rocks are not, however, found in the islands but in Normandy and Brittany. In the Channel Islands the most severely folded and metamorphosed rocks were those of the Brioverian because the Pentevrian basement was already a rather rigid and unyielding basement.

Those Brioverian rocks, laid down as sediments which we have already noted as occurring in St Ouen's Bay on Jersey, were folded at this time, a feature that can be readily appreciated as the layers of sediment are no longer horizontal but dip at various angles, some being even vertical. The earlier mentioned gneisses of the outer reefs and of Sark and Guernsey owe their alteration from granite to this orogenic phase (see Table 1).

The next series of events involved the emergence of massive swellings of magma, like bubbles forcing their way upward into great domes. The earliest formed were rocks called gabbros (see Fig 2D), which have a 'basic' chemical composition (rich in calcium, iron and magnesium) and nearly all the Channel Islands contain traces of these gabbros. [5, 9, 10]

But these swellings of gabbro were small when compared with the massive domes of granite (see Fig 2E) that were to be intruded a little later. These forced their way upwards not only affecting the existing older rocks (such as at the contact between Brioverian sediment and granite at L'Etacq in Jersey), but also the newer gabbros.

When the granite magma met the gabbro it was a more powerful force; the gabbro still tended to be not quite fully rigid and the granite magma was enormously larger in volume. Consequently the heat it generated was sufficient to change the gabbro in a number of ways. The gabbro was broken up like a jigsaw puzzle (Jersey: Sorel, Elizabeth Castle and near Green Island); the edges of the jigsaw pieces were blurred and rounded as the gabbro was made soft and plastic by the heat (Jersey: as above, Guernsey: Beaucette,[2, 10] Alderney: Roselle Point) and finally the gabbro was reduced back to a molten state when it mixed with the granite magma to form a hybrid rock known as diorite. The considerable quantities of diorite of this period which occur in the islands were formed in this manner. Major outcrops are to be found across central Alderney, along the north and north-east coasts of Guernsey and in Jersey at Sorel and several localities in the south-east. A special form of hybrid feature occurs at Roselle Point in Alderney which has rounded patterns consisting of layers of minerals like a nest of eggs one inside the other.

But some swellings of gabbro were hardly influenced, or not influenced at all, while the massive intrusions of granite cooled to form their own particular domes. The gabbros can be seen particularly well north from St Peter Port harbour in Guernsey (see Fig 1) and there are smaller outcrops at the back of Braye harbour in Alderney and at Sorel Point in Jersey. The largest mass of granite[4] of this age lies outside the Channel Islands, south of Granville in Normandy, where it occupies an area of several hundred square miles. Granites of this age have contributed a vital part to the structure of the islands, forming resistant areas in Jersey and Guernsey and making up the whole of Herm and Jethou (see Fig 1).[1] There is a much smaller outcrop at Bibette Head on Alderney.

We have noted the effects of three major episodes of the Cadomian orogenic cycle, an early phase of granite formation, a climax of pressure and heat causing major transformations of the rocks and a second period of granite intrusion with which earlier gabbro was associated. The forces which had been generated by the plates driving together eventually slackened and all the rocks which had been held down by main force began their upward drive to the surface like a ball that has been pushed below water only to surge up when released. As the mass of Armorica

rose so great mountains, perhaps rivalling those of the Himalayas today, were formed, only for erosion to tear off the surface structures revealing the formations of the Pentevrian and Brioverian beneath. Vast thick-nesses of rock were removed and the roots of the mountains revealed at the surface (see Fig 2F), the gabbros and the granites of the Cadomian, the sediments and volcanics of the Brioverian and the gneisses and schists of the Pentevrian.[4, 5, 12]

The landscape took on a new appearance and we can now say much more about what was happening and what the area around the Channel Islands may have looked like and how it developed. Somewhere to the south of Jersey a mountain range was formed whose foothills lay on Jersey (see Fig 2G).[13] From the high peaks the land fell sharply north-wards across a sloping plain which passed into a shallow sea towards Alderney. Material was eroded out of the mountains by rain, streams and general decay of the exposed rock surfaces; there was no plant cover to secure the bedrock from erosion, only a desolate rocky landscape. Indeed this landscape must have had much in common with some of the arid mountainous ranges of today. Run-off of water down the mountain sides was no gentle affair, great sheets of water rushed rapidly and violently across the surface stripping off the surface rock, wrenching away boulders large and small and sweeping it all down to lower levels. These flash floods, as they are called, often moved many miles before they reached flatter valleys and hollows and spewed their debris over the land, often flooding over into adjacent valleys. The deposit consisted mostly of small debris which was angular, though the larger the pebble or boulder the more rounded it was by its passage in the flood. Some of the boulders were very large up to six or more feet (2 metres) across and bear witness to the wild force of the flooding waters of the time. Eventually all this material was cemented together to form a peculiar-looking mass which, when exposed, gives the appearance of a giant pudding mix. No one can fail to recognise this rock, the pudding mix being known as a conglomerate. The only outcrops in the Channel Islands are those of the north-east of Jersey where they are well exposed at Rozel, hence their name of the Rozel Conglomerate.

The finer debris from the 'Jersey' mountains spilled out northwards towards the lowland seas.[14] Within these seas the gravels, sands and silts, which were all that reached the waters from the highlands, were distributed by currents and eventually deposited. In the shifting sands little life existed but to the east, over what is today parts of the Cotentin peninsula in Normandy, calmer waters allowed early forms of shell life to flourish and to be later preserved as fossils. In limestones at Carteret

some ancient sponge-like animals are preserved as fossils. But the coarser sedimentary sandstones found in the eastern part of Alderney, on Burhou, Ortac and the Casquets contain few traces of life.

The Palaeozoic Sedimentary Cycle and the Variscan Orogenic Cycle: 500 – 270 my Ago

Though the forces of the Cadomian orogenic cycle rended and tore Armorica they were also creative and the final effect was the emergence of an Armorica larger than before and welded together into a unit which was to remain largely intact through all later upheavals. The erosion of the mountain ranges during the final stages of orogeny produced vast flattened plains across which the seas of a new cycle of sedimentation now flooded. This cycle occurred during the era geologists refer to as the Palaeozoic and is the era during which life expanded vigorously. Seas covered much of Armorica much of the time during the Palaeozoic until marine sedimentation was brought to an end during a new orogeny which we know as the Variscan orogenic cycle. The evidence for the Palaeozoic cycle of sedimentation and the Variscan orogeny is meagre in the Channel Islands.[4] Abundant fossils can be found in limestones, shales and sandstones in many parts of Normandy and Brittany, the former denizens of often rather shallow Palaeozoic seas for the thickest sediments were deposited outside Armorica in a new zone of instability across Cornubia (south-west England, see Fig 3).

The Variscan orogeny[4, 15] affected a very large area of north-west Europe and it was during this series of events that Cornubia and Armorica were welded into one unit, though the position of the plate edges that were active at this time remains elusive. One thing is clear for both Cornubia and Armorica, different rocks reacted to the pressures forced upon them in different ways. The softer, more pliable rocks, often desposited as thick wedges of sediment as in Cornubia, were intensively deformed and folded. But the hard core of the older Armorican Massif resisted the forces and only the relatively thin Palaeozoic sedimentary cover was folded. The movements though, were to leave their mark on the basement of Armorica; the points and planes of weakness of the Cadomian orogenic cycle were opened like old wounds while new faults occurred altering levels of rocks, tearing them apart and separating layers.

In the Channel Islands no new rocks were formed as during the Cadomian, only the existing rock structure was altered. But great mountain ranges were once again formed at the end of the Variscan cycle and we

know that some of these mountains lay across northern Armorica, probably over the very site of the Channel Islands. These supplied debris,
also in a sort of replay of the past, to valleys and plains to the north,
though this time lying across southern England.

Only 250 million years in the shaping

*The Atlantic Opens, the Western Channel Forms and the Islands
Begin to Form*

We have seen in the previous section how the basement structure of
the Armorican Massif was built up over an incredible 2,000 million
years; during the next 250 million years, which brings us to the present,
we shall consider how the Massif was sculpted by the forces of marine
and terrestrial erosion into the forms and shapes we recognise today.
But first let us set the scene (see Table 2).

The Cornubian and Armorican Massifs, now welded into one by the
earth movements of the Variscan orogenic cycle, began almost at once
to be sundered apart by downfaulting on the site of the future western
Channel.[9] The major faults often followed the ENE/WSW lines of weakness initiated during the Cadomian orogeny, though new trends and new
faults had been created by the Variscan movements, particularly in
Cornubia. But what was the cause of the tensional downfaulting between
Cornubia and Armorica that persisted long after the close of the
orogeny? The answer in the broadest of terms is the opening of the
Atlantic Ocean as Europe and America began to drift apart, a drifting
that continues today.

The two orogenies that we have discussed, the Cadomian and the
Variscan, were the result of collisions between crustal plates; the opening
of the Atlantic represents the opposite, the drifting apart of two plates,
in this instance those of Europe and America. Where the plates began
to separate down the centre line of the Atlantic, extensive volcanic
activity, drawing upon deep-seated sources, generated enough material
to fill the gap as the two plates of Europe and America moved apart.
Iceland lies on the Mid-Atlantic Ridge and is a creation of this volcanic
activity.

Such movements set up great stresses along the margins of the plates
and one area strongly affected was the north-western edge of Europe
which was rifted by great faults. Armorica today is largely bounded by
such faults. In the north a significant line of weakness with downfaulting
to the north runs from Alderney to Ushant (off Finistère) and this is

Age in millions of years	Eras	
——Present ——		
——	PLEISTOCENE	for the last 150,000 years see Table 3
1.8		the warm, high sea levels of the early Tertiary slowly became cooler. The main plateau levels of the 'islands' above 200 ft (60m) were formed by sea erosion
	TERTIARY ERA	
——50 ——		the Atlantic Ocean continued to open and America and Europe to drift apart
		the early Tertiary seas penetrated deep into and between the emerging Channel 'Islands'. Deposition of rubbly limestones
65——		
		Chalk seas encroached onto the shallow waters of the Normanno-Breton gulf causing the formation of Chalk close to Guernsey. . The 'islands' have begun to take shape
——100 ——		
		the Mesozoic era is not well represented in the Channel Islands' area though there are thick deposits in the downfaulted area of the western Channel
	MESOZOIC ERA	
——150 ——		
		the opening of Atlantic started and America and Europe began their long drift apart. The tension generated in the crust caused extensive downfaulting between Cornubia and Armorica and the western Channel came into being
——200 ——		
225——		
		the Palaeozoic era is not well represented on the Channel Islands though records of the deposits and the events of this era are abundant in nearby Normandy and Brittany
——250 ——	PALAEOZOIC ERA	
		the effects of the Variscan orogenic cycle, though profound, are more evident in Armorica and Cornubia than in the islands. Armorica and Cornubia united
——300 ——		

TABLE 2   The geological story—the middle period, 300–2 million years ago
(not to scale)

complemented by more nearly E/W faulting along the southern margin of Cornubia. Between the two lies the trough-like basin of the western Channel which has considerable thicknesses of Mesozoic, Tertiary and Recent sediments in which oil has been found. To the east, the Paris Basin is largely a down-faulted area and the Bay of Biscay represents a very deep-seated zone of rifting.

Almost by accident the Channel Islands found themselves part of a shallow, gulf-like embayment lying between the higher lands of

Normandy and Brittany on one side and the trough of the western
Channel on the other, with the Alderney/Ushant faults as the line of
separation. We can consider the Paris Basin and the western Channel
as hollows filled with water which sometimes overflowed their bounds
onto the margins of Armorica and sometimes withdrew, these fluctuations
being a response to a variety of geological forces. The shallowness of
the shelf on which the Channel Islands sat was crucial as each small
change of sea level resulted in profound changes around the islands.
The story of the area since the Variscan is the story of sea level changes
and their consequences.

Studies of the Mesozoic sediments of the Paris Basin and below the
bed of the western Channel indicate that Armorica remained a land
mass throughout most of that era. Only the deeper seas of the Cretaceous
period, when the famous Chalk deposits were formed, encroached across
the Alderney/Ushant line for a short distance bringing the Chalk to
within a few miles of the coasts of Guernsey but at a depth of more than
18 fathoms (35m).

Considerable deposits of Tertiary limestones are found on the sea-
floors between the Channel Islands and they define the area of shelf
that lies below 10–15 fathoms (20–30m) (see Fig 1). This is clear evidence
that the main islands and reef masses we know today were already in
existence at this period some 70 million years ago. Moreover, we can go
further and say that the climate was very much warmer than that
of today because the limestones could only have formed in warm conditions (cf the Bermudas at present). North of Jersey, samples of limestone collected by scuba divers prove the early Tertiary existence of the
Le Ruau channel separating the island from the Ecréhous reef (see Fig 3).

Life was abundant in the late Mesozoic and Tertiary seas and the
limestones formed then are prolific in fossils, none more so than the
crumbly limestones of the Le Ruau channel.[16] The sea level changes
that occurred were related to earth movements and the displacements
of plates. The amount of Armorica and the Channel Islands above the
waves varied considerably. At one stage, perhaps during the later Tertiary
some 5–10 million years ago the sea was nearly 400 ft (100 m) higher
than at present and it was then that the summit plateau of Jersey was
planed off. Possibly several different levels of the sea down to just below
200 ft were responsible for the creation of the major, higher plateaux
in the Channel Islands. Certainly by late Tertiary times a visitor from
our time would have had no difficulty recognising the future islands and
reefs, assuming a sea level comparable to that of the present time for
the purposes of the visit.

The Pleistocene – a Time of Climatic Extremes and Sea Level Changes

We have noted the warm climate of the late Mesozoic and early Tertiary and also that sea level changes were caused by earth movements. At the end of the Tertiary several million years ago, a sudden quickening of the pace of climatic deterioration plunged the world into the Pleistocene ice ages. Climate fluctuated from one extreme to another, not once but many times. When great continent-covering ice sheets formed (periods known as glaciations), the sea level of the oceans responded by sinking to unprecedentedly low levels as water was evaporated to nourish the ice build-up. By contrast the sea returned to more usual levels during the intervening warmer periods, known as interglacials, though there is evidence to indicate that an overall relative lowering of sea level occurred during the Pleistocene as a result of earth movements outside our area. This was quite independent of climatically induced variations. Today, if all the world's ice were to melt, the sea level we know would rise as much as 300ft (90m) but this would still be some 200–300ft (60–90m) short of the level of the late Tertiary seas.

Over the comparatively shallow waters of the Normanno-Breton gulf the drops of sea level produced dramatic effects, pushing the sea back over the Alderney/Ushant line far out into the Western Approaches and leaving the Channel 'Islands' as hilly plateaux standing above a vast plain (see Fig 3A).

The climate was not always glacially cold during times of lowered sea level and the Channel Islands area was never actually covered by ice. At different stages during ice sheet formation and decline, a whole range of different climates was experienced locally and the presence or absence of a vegetation cover was often more important in controlling the processes of erosion. A number of distinctive processes operated which were characteristic of most glaciations even though it is the effects of the last (possibly only the latest) which has most affected the present landscape. This glaciation is known as the Devensian in Britain (see Table 3).

Falls in sea level lowered river base levels and increased their erosive power. This was increased still further by the partial or complete loss of vegetation during the colder phases of each glaciation. Where these conditions were also associated with a wet period during the year, conditions were set for maximum erosion. Frost wedged loose large

quantities of rock fragments from exposed outcrops often on cliff and valley sides and this material later sludged down the slopes below, mixing with finer silt and loess (see next paragraph) to form one of the most typical deposits visible round the islands' coasts today, the orange-yellow rubbly deposits known as 'head'. These often form vertical, very unstable cliffs backing the smaller coves of all the islands. Material such as head, which accumulated at the tops of valleys and along the sides, was swept down from the heights of the 'island' plateaux by the turbulent swollen streams of spring and early summer. These streams joined rivers whose courses now lie beneath the seas that surround the islands. During the succession of glaciations in the Pleistocene, the plateaux which now form the islands were slowly but relentlessly dissected by the headward erosion of the small but powerful streams of the time. The final Devensian glaciation, which is taken as ending 10,000 years ago, brought the process virtually to its present conclusion as the basic forms of the 'islands' valleys at this time are also those of today.

However, not all the processes that operated during the glaciations were those of erosion. At times cold dry winds blew across the plains south of the northern European ice sheets (cf the bitter easterlies in winter) carrying with them silt-size material washed out from beneath the ice sheets. This dust was moved vast distances in equally vast quantities and the area of the Channel 'Islands', at this time dry land, received a yellow coating several feet thick (a metre or more). The deposit is called loess and the loesses of the Devensian are very important because they form the basis of the fertile loamy soils of the plateau lands of Jersey, Guernsey and Sark; Alderney is much sandier.

Most of the loess that blanketed the vast plains about the Channel 'Islands' is now drowned beneath the sea and has been redistributed by currents over the sea bottoms. It should be noted, though, that the reefs of the Ecréhous and Minquiers and the extensive tidal expanses of rock around the islands were covered with fertile Devensian loess supporting thick forest up to and including part of the Neolithic less than 6,000 years ago. Remnants of this loess may be seen on Maîtresse Ile on the Minquiers and on other islets such as as Green Island (Jersey) and Lihou (Guernsey).

Between the glaciations, periods of milder climate, often comparable to that of today, and known as interglacials, were characterised by higher sea levels and a strong vegetation cover. The differences in height to which successive interglacial sea levels rose have been referred to earlier. Each level was marked by both erosion and deposition of the sort we see operating about us at present. Most of the evidence of these

Plate 1 La Longue Pierre, *St Saviours, Guernsey* (D. E. Johnston)

Plate 2 *Guernsey's famous statue menhir,* La Grand'mère du Chimquière, *standing at the gates of St Martin's churchyard. This prehistoric figure is still held in some veneration, and certainly affection, by the islanders* (E. Sirett)

Plate 3 (above) Le Trépied, *Guernsey* (D. E. Johnston)

Plate 4 *A Jersey martello tower, one of several built around the coast towards the end of the eighteenth century, when there were fears of a French invasion. In the foreground are islanders gathering* vraic *(seaweed)*

Age in years	Events	Level of sea ref: Ordnance Datum	
		+20–24 ft (6–8 m)	rise of sea level from about 18,000 years ago to reach its present level between 2000 and 1000 BC
10 000 ——	FLANDRIAN		
		−300 ft (100 m)	large quantities of wind-blown dust (loess) accumulated during the later stages of the Devensian, the present basis of the fertile loamy soils of the islands
			very low sea level
−25 000 ——	DEVENSIAN GLACIATION		formation of the main rubbly deposits of orange/yellow material (head) which filled the coastal valleys and often form at present the vertical and unstable cliffs that back many of the bays around the islands
		probable rise to some 10 ft above O.D. (3 m)	the upper deposits of La Cotte cave (St Brelade, Jersey) belong to this glaciation
			there was probably a rise in the sea level to just above Ordnance Datum during a warm intermission of the Devensian
−50 000 ——		low	
−75 000 ——	IPSWICHIAN INTERGLACIAL		raised beaches, marine sands and wave-cut notches are very common around the Channel Islands' coasts. Certain peats (La Cotte de St Brelade, Jersey, etc.) and some animal remains (Belle Hougue Cave, Jersey) are also of this age
−100 000 ——		25 ft (8 m)	
		?–300 ft (100 m)	the oldest deposits of rubbly material (head) and wind blown dust (loess) in the Channel Islands are considered Wolstonian in age
	WOLSTONIAN GLACIATION		the first habitation levels in both La Cotte caves (Jersey) are of late Wolstonian age
−125 000 ——			
		+60 ft (18 m)	formation of raised beaches and wave-cut notches during warm intermission of the Wolstonian

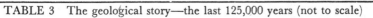

TABLE 3   The geological story—the last 125,000 years (not to scale)

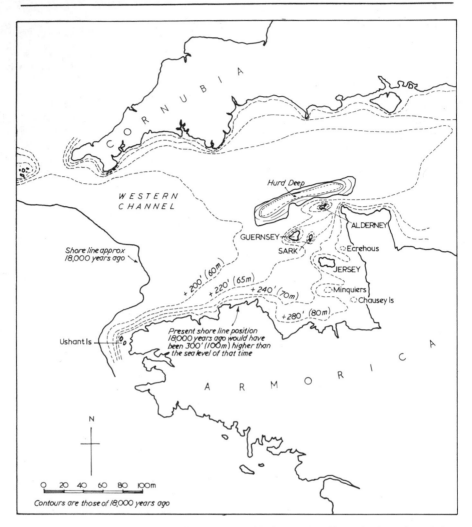

Fig 3 Low sea levels of the Pleistocene. In this figure the effect of a lowering of the present sea level by over 300ft (100m) is vividly shown. The 'islands' were small, hilly plateaux on plains that extended well out into the western Channel of today. Note that the contours indicate that the Hurd Deep would have been a lake. This scene would have been typical of several glaciation phases but was in fact drawn to show the Devensian about 18,000 years ago (see Fig 4)

older sea levels has long since been eroded away but not all; important remnants remain, notably wave-cut notches and abandoned beaches of pebbles. High up on South Hill in Jersey[17] a beach and notch is found above 100 ft (30m) O.D. More abundant are the notches and beaches at 60 ft (18m) occurring at many cliff sites in Jersey but also found in Guernsey and Alderney. But the notches and beaches that have best survived, not surprisingly for they belong to the last interglacial

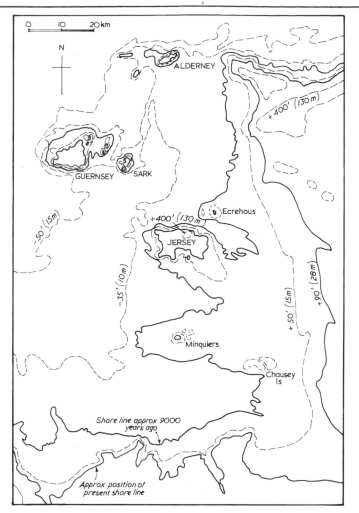

Fig 4   Here a much higher sea level is shown which could represent either a stage in a falling sea level before the peak of a glaciation or a late stage in the subsequent rise towards the normal interglacial levels. Both Figs 3 and 4 represent isolated moments in a continuous process of change

known as the Ipswichian in Britain, are those at 25ft (8m). There are few rocky bays in any of the islands that do not have a notch or ancient beach at this level. They can be easily recognised for they are found at the level of the high spring tides. The beaches are often overlain by the cliffs of head already mentioned (see Table 3).

But there is another interglacial feature the dates for which are uncertain; this is the extensive marine platform which lies between the spring low tide and high tide marks. The most that can be said at present

is that these platforms, of which the Minquiers, the tidal rocks of the west coast of Guernsey and the huge expanses off the south-east coast of Jersey are good examples, have been eroded by seas not so different in level from those of today. However, it is clear from their great extent that they have a history extending back at least hundreds of thousands of years and probably considerably more.

The Final Phases

As our area emerged from the harshness of the Devensian glaciation so the sea level slowly returned towards its interglacial norm and the improving climate encouraged the growth of vegetation. By about 4000 BC, the sea had risen sufficiently to drown most of the land between the islands and the adjacent French coasts. The high tide level of the time was at about the limit of our spring low tides and the waves lapped onto beaches that fringed a landscape thick with mixed oak forest. The sandy bays and tidal expanses of low rock that we know today were still not in existence; they were formed mainly during the Neolithic as the sea moved between present low and high tide marks. In the course of not much more than 2,000 years the soft sands and silts of all the islands' bays and coastal plains were deposited as stream and tide met and competed for mastery. In a strange way neither won this bout because the streams brought down sufficient material from the plateaux to partly fill the larger bays while the sea had to settle for the cliffs. But in places the sea overwhelmed the existing land and the evidence for this lies in the often hidden forests submerged beneath some bays such as those at Vazon in Guernsey and St Ouen's Bay in Jersey. Inland the smaller streams of later post-glacial times were unable to sweep their valley bottoms clear of debris so that all island valleys have flat bottoms from their source to the sea.

In conclusion we can put the book aside and go out and about in the islands to see for ourselves the magnificent coastal scenery in the very process of formation and erosion. We can wander up wooded valleys and enjoy the flat meadowland, adding another dimension to that enjoyment as we appreciate why the stream is such a misfit in its huge valley and the bottom lands are flat. There are few journeys to be made in the islands on which a quarry (sadly now abandoned or filled) will not be passed. From these came the rocks that have given the buildings of each island their characteristic appearance but now we can know something of their origins in the very remote past. And perhaps through all our wanderings there will come a better under-

standing of the ebb and flow of change through time; nothing is still, everything around us is in process of change from what was to what will be, our islands no less than we who look at them.

Notes to this chapter are on pages 241–2.

2

Prehistory and Archaeology

David E. Johnston

The prehistory of the islands (that is, for the purposes of this chapter, up to the end of the Roman period), is part of the prehistory of mainland France. Indeed, for much of its early history, Jersey was a promontory—and today a drop of only eight fathoms in sea level would reunite it to the mainland. For the other islands the record starts with the first Neolithic settlers capable of making the short though hazardous sea crossings. Henceforth, the islands were exposed to any cultural influence that could be brought by sea and modified in an island environment. The later Iron Age, a period of increased cross-Channel communications, doubtless saw their use as staging-points; and we discuss below their possible rôle in the Roman period, a time when piracy was rife and the Channel became a patrolled and fortified frontier between two provinces.

Archaeologically, one is tempted to see the islands as a microcosm of European prehistory, and indeed the cultural unity is evident to any visitor. Each island, however, has an archaeological identity, both in the purely insular developments of their communities and material equipment (the distinctive 'Jersey bowl' for example) (see Fig 6c) and in the way evidence has survived better in some places than others (for example, the open fields of Alderney that are currently under investigation).

Accordingly, we begin with a brief archaeological survey, period by period, to provide a context for the monuments and museum collections, and then pass to a more detailed study of the most notable monuments, island by island. Finally, since archaeology is as much the story of archaeologists as of monuments, we pay tribute to those who laid the foundations of our understanding of the monuments and those who are currently working to save them from the pressures and possible destruction of the twentieth century.

The Old Stone Age

The story of the settlement of early man in the Channel Islands begins, as it does also on the mainland of France, during the third of the three great Ice Ages. Although all the islands were part of the mainland, Jersey alone is known to have been inhabited at this time, and the occupation of the now coastal caves can be proved to belong to the end of the Acheulean phase. Hand-axes of this phase have been found, sea-worn and stained, evidently coming from a fossil beach formed by rising sea-levels in the interglacial. From time to time, then, Jersey was a promontory, and therefore accessible to man and the game he hunted; this included elephant, woolly rhinoceros and other Arctic species. A small deer, *Cervus elaphus jerseyensis* Zeuner, evolved a peculiar island form during isolation in the last interglacial and became extinct with the final glaciation.

Human occupation in the middle phase of the Palaeolithic, the Mousterian, has now been well established by recent excavation in two caves, La Cotte à la Chèvre, and—most importantly—at La Cotte de St Brelade. Between about 150,000 and 100,000 BC, this cave sheltered hunting parties and saw the first accumulation of the deep deposits of wind-blown soil, with some clay and rubble (weathered from the roof and sides of the cave). These contained complex layers of food remains and flake tools. The uppermost (and therefore the latest) levels of this first Mousterian occupation have established La Cotte de St Brelade as one of the most important Middle Palaeolithic sites in Europe. New physical dating techniques are making it possible to correlate the geological and environmental evidence with that from sites on the continent. Moreover, statistical analysis of several thousands of flint and coarse stone tools (and waste) is already showing how rising sea levels cut off the supply of flint for tools (from the mainland and sea-bed), as flint is not native to the islands; the proportion of coarse and stone tools increased, and the now precious flint was used more economically. Thirdly, a welcome surprise was the discovery, in the upper levels of this phase, of a large 'bone heap' in one corner of the cave. Apart from the development of special techniques for recovering this extremely fragile material, the final analysis of these dismembered carcases will give an unrivalled view of Middle Palaeolithic hunting, butchering and feeding habits.

Between 125,000 and 75,000 BC a further warm phase and a con-siderable rise in sea level to eight metres above Ordnance Datum

removed some of the deposits at the cave mouth and a sterile layer formed later, sealing the earlier deposits. Natural weathering deposits began again, and between c.60,000 and 50,000 BC the cave was occupied once more, this time by men of the evolved Mousterian phase, a physical type of *Homo sapiens* close to that of modern man. In 1910 the excavators were rewarded by the discovery of thirteen teeth from both jaws of an individual of Neanderthal type, aged between twenty and thirty. By now, Europe had entered the fourth and last glaciation, Würm, a fluctuating series of cold phases covering the latest developments of the Palaeolithic. In France and Spain these include the flowering of cave art; in Jersey, however, the Upper Palaeolithic is on present knowledge utterly absent, the archaeological record ending temporarily in about 50,000 BC.

The First Settlers

The periglacial conditions meant that Jersey emerged from the final glaciation as an island, smothered with loess and heavy deposits of clayey, rubbly 'head'. The more temperate climate clothed this with denser vegetation, conditions in which man throughout northern France and the British Isles learned to live by hunting smaller game, fowling and fishing. The characteristic microlithic points and blades of this mesolithic phase are largely missing from the islands, though 'pygmy flints' are occasionally found; on the other hand, the mesolithic traits in the rather later neolithic flintwork of all the islands are so marked that it is generally thought that this reflects the background of the neolithic, rather than true mesolithic settlers. However, a challenge to this view may well come from a new site in Guernsey that is producing a more promising assemblage, with microliths. Moreover, the existence of good coastal mesolithic sites on the continent suggests that our missing Channel Islands sites are today under the sea.

The new vegetation can be most dramatically seen at very low tide in St Ouen's Bay, Jersey, in the so-called 'submerged forest' which represents the neolithic land surface. In fact, two peat layers formed by temporarily swampier conditions have been recognised, with neolithic material, in St Helier. By contrast, the 'dark layer' noted in all the islands is generally overlaid by a considerable depth of blown sand, the result of a new climatic phase.

From perhaps 4000 BC the new settlers brought with them the techniques of cereal cultivation, domestication of animals and better methods of forest clearance with polished stone axes. Several settlement

sites are suspected, but only one—the Pinnacle in Jersey—has been excavated. The lowest level produced undecorated pottery of Chassey type and distinctive transverse arrowheads suggesting an origin, ultimately, in Eastern France. Similar pottery from the great stone tombs shows that these settlers were the first megalith-builders in the islands.

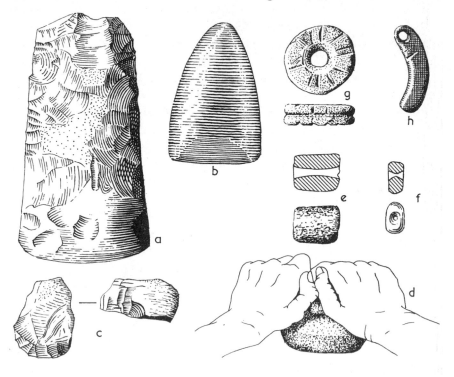

Fig 5 Neolithic tools and adornments: a, b, flaked and polished axes, Alderney: c, flint scraper, Jersey: d, grain rubber in use, Alderney: e, f, stone beads, Sark and Alderney: g, fairy ring (probably a pendant), Sark: h, stone pendant, Jersey (*after N.L.V. Rybot*) (*scale: ½, drawings: author*)

An improvement in technology at this time was the polished stone axe, shaped by flaking and smoothed by rubbing on a coarse stone (see Fig 5 a and b). A really sharp edge is formed in this way, and it can be re-sharpened. Set in a wooden handle (often with an antler sleeve for greater resilience) it was, as recent experiment has proved, a most effective tool for clearing the often dense forest. In the new clearings, simple crops were cultivated, the ground being prepared by burning, digging with digging sticks and hoeing, and animals were herded. More sophisticated arrow-heads, special tools for grinding corn and dealing with shellfish, pottery containers and personal adornments, all these are the clues we find to this more advanced way of life. (See

Fig 5.) Remains of huts and hearths have so far eluded us, apart from one doubtful post-hole; but the search continues.

The megalithic or chambered stone tombs are the most conspicuous feature of the islands' prehistory. Many are box-like cists of stone slabs, containing burials and formerly covered by mounds. But the earlier, and more impressive, are the passage-graves and the gallery-graves. The latter type is rare in the islands, and the two surviving examples are both in Jersey (see Fig 11b). They probably represent a second phase of settlement from Normandy or further afield, where the type is known by its more attractive name of *allée couverte*. It is essentially a parallel-sided cist covered with an elongated mound.

Before discussing the passage-graves, we should note the small structure in Jersey at La Sergenté, named by its excavators the 'beehive hut' but almost certainly a tomb whose corbelled roof was domed by the primitive technique of overlapping the horizontal courses of stone slabs. The significance of this unique site is that it could well mark the beginning of the passage-grave tradition.

The passage-grave (see Fig 11a) is essentially a burial-chamber walled with upright slabs, roofed with even larger slabs and approached by a tunnel-like passage built in the same way. Unlike the chambered long barrows of many parts of Europe, including Wessex, the mounds of passage-graves in the Channel Islands are nearly always circular, without ditches—a feature they share (at a distance) with the better known ones of Brittany. In some cases at least, the mound was revetted with a kerb of upright slabs. One of the finest, the Déhus in the parish of the Vale, Guernsey, has been restored to its original appearance (see Fig 7). The interior (which at the time of writing needs to be explored with a torch) shows two further features. One is the presence of side chambers, four in number (more than one is rare), which also contained burials. These side chambers must be part of the original design, as adding them subsequently would have been virtually impossible. Excavations began in 1837 and found the burials unplundered. They were, however, disturbed in antiquity (parts of the same pot, for instance, being found in both the main chamber and one side chamber), though a polished axe of serpentine lay untouched on a ledge in one chamber. It is quite clear that these tombs were the collective burial places of distinct communities and that they remained open for several centuries as successive burials accumulated in them. Earlier burials were disturbed to make way for new, and the Déhus illustrates well the variety of practice attested by less well preserved sites elsewhere in the islands, Many burials were inhumations, two lying on their sides, knees drawn up

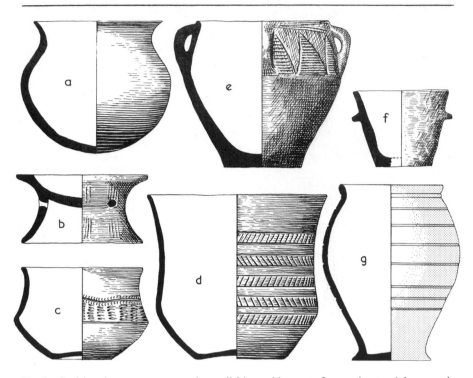

Fig 6 Prehistoric pottery: a, early neolithic cooking-pot, Jersey; b, stand for round-bottomed pots, Jersey; c, 'Jersey bowl', Jersey; d, decorated beaker, Guernsey; e, Bronze Age four-handled urn, Jersey; f, Bronze Age bucket-shaped pot with lug handles, Jersey; g, late Iron Age wheelmade urn, Guernsey *(scale: ¼, drawings: author)*

to the chest in the attitude of the foetus before birth. By contrast, three groups of jumbled bones bespeak the known practice of exposing the corpse until the flesh had disappeared, and then gathering the bones for burial. Most remarkably, the small north-east chamber contained two bodies buried upright, kneeling or squatting, and kept in place by packed earth and shells. In the main chamber, skeletons (of two adults and a ten-year-old child) were mixed with loose bones and cremated remains; here, as in many other sites, there were vast quantities of limpet shells. We do not know whether or not these were food for the next world; nor whether there was food in the cups and bowls that accompanied most of the burials. As in other tombs, burials at the Déhus were in two (or in one chamber, three) layers, separated by paving or layers of pebbles, and the pottery is neolithic in type. Decorated beakers (eg see Fig 6d), however, anticipate the transition to the Bronze Age, and significantly one burial in the main chamber was accompanied by a tanged dagger of copper. Some, perhaps all, the tombs were eventually

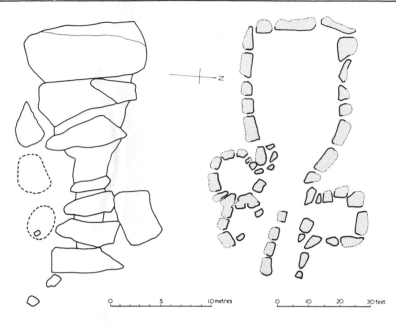

Fig 7   Le Déhus, Guernsey (*source: Kendrick [1928]*)

sealed when funerary customs changed. A few evidently remained open
into the Bronze Age, and even into historic times to judge from Iron
Age and Roman finds in them.

The other feature of the Déhus is something very rare. (See Fig 8b.)
With difficulty one can make out faint carvings on the underside of the
second capstone of the main chamber—the one supported by a pillar.
A knowledge of the better continental examples helps one identify two
eyes, a mouth, two hands and lines across the stone where a human
figure might wear a girdle. Although no breasts can be seen, this is
undoubtedly a female figure—a mother goddess or fertility-figure if one
wishes to speculate. Guernsey possesses a second female figure, also of
the megalithic phase, in the churchyard of Câtel Church. (See Fig 8a.)
In spite of later, possibly Christian, defacement, the breasts can be seen,
with well marked shoulders and a band across the forehead. A U-shaped
'necklace' is represented on the chest and a raised band across the back.
These features can be best matched in the prehistoric carvings of the
Paris basin. She is a statue-menhir, a sculptured example of the menhirs,
or isolated standing stones, that can be seen in many parts of the islands
—for example in the plains behind St Ouen's Bay in Jersey. By analogy
with the famous alignments of Brittany, avenues of these must have
existed in the islands; the only well attested example was salvaged when

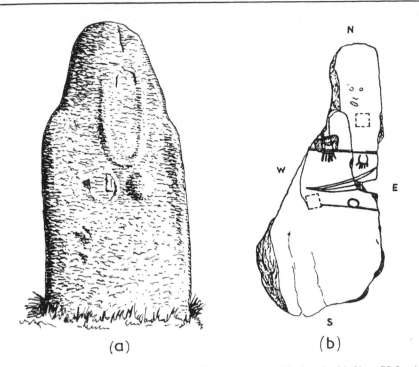

(a)   (b)

Fig 8   Neolithic sculptures, Guernsey : a, Câtel statue-menhir (height 5ft 9in, 175.2cm); b, Le Déhus, underside of principal capstone (length 13ft 6in, 411.5cm) (*sources: a, author, b, Kendrick [1928]*)

the old gasworks was built in St Helier, Jersey, and the stones moved to the Museum gardens.

Bronze and Iron

A neolithic polished axe is a work of art, a joy to handle. We suspect that its creator sometimes thought so, too, judging from the care with which he selected rare and beautiful materials, serpentine, callaïs and jadeite. Even so, this is stone technology pushed to its limits. The coming of a metal technology with the Bronze Age (shortly before 2000 BC in the Channel Islands) provided superior tools, daggers, swords and axes that were prized by the wealthy and probably made by a privileged class of smiths. One such worked in Alderney, to judge from a large hoard of scrap bronze found in 1832; at the time of writing it is not on display, though some recently discovered specimens, probably additions to the main hoard, can be seen in the Alderney Museum. Gold, of course, was rare, but one should not miss the twisted torc, or necklace,

in the Jersey Museum. By the end of the Bronze Age, pots were larger and cruder and used for cremations, often in cemeteries rather than chambered tombs. Some large and formidable specimens are in the Jersey Museum, many of them indistinguishable from those of the Iron Age.

The introduction of iron and its working some time after 1000 BC provided tools and weapons for everyman, and doubtless played its part in accelerating the changes we know were taking place. Traces of Iron Age settlement have appeared in excavations in St Helier, Jersey; and recent excavations in Alderney have provided a glimpse of one community mass-producing and firing its pots on a scale one could almost call industrial (below p 57).

We do not know how extensively the islands were settled at this time; throughout Europe, however, the population was increasing, tribal society was evolving, and the inevitable strains, political and social, were being felt. A symptom of this is the proliferation of hill-forts and promontory fortifications. Of the latter, one is supected in Alderney, and others are known in Guernsey and Jersey. The most impressive is the massive earthwork cutting off the promontory of Le Câtel, in Jersey. A sophistication of the economy is seen in the introduction of coinage, much of it striking in design (see Fig 9), derived from the tribes of Armorica.

Fig 9   Armorican coin, Jersey (*drawing: N.L.V. Rybot, reproduced by courtesy of the Soc Jersiaise*)

The problem of why over fifteen thousand of these coins have been found in several large hoards brings us firmly into the historic period. Even before Caesar's campaigns in Gaul (from 58 to 49 BC) had brought the Roman Empire to the Channel shores, classical influences had been absorbed into Celtic culture, especially art and religion. This coin type, for example, is ultimately derived from a coin of Philip of Macedon. Coin hoards imply panic and insecurity. Whether or not we

regard the Celtic princes who buried their wealth in this way as refugees from the advance of Rome (as Caesar confirms for some who sought refuge in Britain), or from unrecorded dynastic quarrels in Gaul, there is no doubt that the Channel Islands had begun to act as stepping-stones between the Celtic tribes on both sides of the Channel.

The Roman Period

Few parts of Europe remained untouched, even indirectly, by Rome; it is therefore particularly remarkable that these offshore islands of Romanised Gaul have produced little more than chance finds of pottery and coins (and an unproven tradition of a mining interest in Sark). However, the exceptions are important.

The only building certainly of the Roman period now visible is at the foot of the Pinnacle Rock, Jersey, and its purpose is not known. One suggestion is that it was a guard-post for a lookout on the rock itself; the other, more likely, is that it was a Romano-Celtic temple with a central shrine and surrounding verandah. Such isolated rural shrines were not uncommon in the Roman world.

The other is a small rectangular fort with corner bastions, in Alderney (named, doubtless as a joke, the Nunnery). Roman bricks from the nearby settlement were certainly used, or re-used in its masonry. A Roman origin is possible by analogy with other late Roman signal-stations; its first appearance in the written record is 1436, and it has since been a barracks of the Napoleonic era, private house, farm and flats. The final refortification was in 1942, during the German occupation, for small arms and heavy coastal artillery. If it *is* Roman it would form part of the Armorican section of the coastal defences on both sides of the Channel, the 'Saxon Shore Forts'. Until the eighteenth century, Longy Bay was the principal harbour of Alderney and it is possible that Alderney, at least, was a base for the fleet, the *Classis Britannica*, patrolling the Channel to control the piracy which was rife in the fourth century AD.

Longy Common, Alderney, was the site of a substantial Gallo-Roman settlement from as early as the first century AD. Not only have well built buildings and burials been excavated, but the discovery of Alderney stone in Chichester harbour, at Fishbourne, shows that at least one ship discharged its cargo in Alderney and took on ballast before setting off for Britain to load up with fresh cargo. So we are left with two interesting speculations: first, the possibility of a Roman military presence in the islands. And second, the nature of this civilian, Gallo-Roman settlement.

Could it be that we are looking, not at a conventional native settlement, but at the material remains of the very pirates that the fleet existed to deal with?

The Dark Ages

After the Roman period the islands disappear from the record—at least until the coming of the Celtic saints and the events of the next chapter. However, tantalising clues exist: a 'long-house' recently excavated at Cobo, Guernsey, and a fragment of 'bar-lip' pottery of the seventh century, made in Cornwall and used in Alderney. Moreover, one curious site is being excavated at the time of writing, the Ile Agois on the north coast of Jersey. Perched on this tiny offshore rock were several circular, earth-embanked huts and, at the summit, three built of stone. Crowning the rock was a single rectangular structure. The later pottery looks more Roman than anything and the level of subsistence truly prehistoric. However, one crucial sherd puts the site firmly into the Dark Ages and its excavator suggests that this could have been a small community of hermit monks with their chapel, reminding us of the small community that came with St Magloire to Sark in AD 565.

The Monuments

A guide-book to sites in the islands is in preparation but it might be useful at this point to mention those that are most worth visiting. A few are in States ownership, though none of the islands has a Department of the Environment responsible, on the UK scale, for excavation, restoration and maintenance. Many are owned or managed by the relevant Société of the particular island, but most are on private land (an extreme case being the front garden of Mon Désir, Sandy Lane, L'Islet, Guernsey). Public footpaths and rights of way do not exist in the UK sense, so one is frequently obliged to cross private land; in some cases it is courteous to ask permission but generally the visitor who respects the land is unlikely to be challenged. Treasure-hunting with metal-detectors is a reprehensible practice anywhere and in Alderney is illegal.

Jersey

As we have said above (p 41), the only caves inhabited in the Palaeolithic are in Jersey. Today, these are accessible only to the most

intrepid and knowledgeable visitor, and—with the exception of La Cotte de St Brelade—the archaeological deposits are worked out. This last is reached either from the beach or by a steep cliffside path and is at the time of writing in the final stages of a series of excavations that began seriously in 1905. Today the site resembles less a cave than a chasm with an overarching rock bridge, all that remained after a nearly disastrous collapse of part of the cave roof on 3 September 1915, when the nine excavators on the site escaped with their lives. In 1905 the deposits reached almost to the roof; by 1980 a large part of the 50m of deposits will have been removed, concluding the longest and most ambitious excavation undertaken in the Channel Islands.

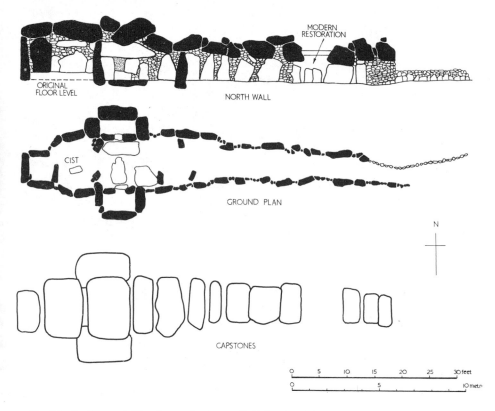

Fig 10   La Hougue Bie, Jersey (*sources: Bull Soc Jersiaise [1925] and Hawkes [1937]*)

Undoubtedly the most spectacular prehistoric monument is La Hougue Bie (see Fig 10), a cruciform passage-grave in a huge mound, both superbly well preserved and among the finest in north-western Europe. The mound is 180ft (54.8m) in diameter, and 40ft (12.2m) high. Until 1924 it was crowned by a remarkable eighteenth-century

'gothic' building, the 'Prince's Tower', demolished to reveal its core, a pair of medieval chapels. Unlike comparable examples in the Boyne valley of Ireland, the mound contains one tomb only. The main chamber, which lies directly below the summit, is accompanied by two rectangular side-chambers and a further small cell at the very end. These form a cross in plan, the shaft being a long passage 32ft (9.7m) long. It grows wider as it approaches the chambers and the headroom averages about 4½ft (137cm). As in the other dolmens the walls are made of upright slabs, roughly paired and roofed with huge rectangular slabs, graduated in size towards the centre of the monument and evidently chosen for their shape. The passage did not start at the circumference of the mound but was approached by a short funnel-like entrance. The neat drystone walling of this, and of that between the uprights in the interior, is original; the mound was originally revetted by a kerb of upright slabs, as was the Déhus, and doubtless others. The mound is composed of earth, limpet-shells and rocky rubble, collected in the neighbourhood; the megalithic slabs, on the other hand, were drawn from many parts of the island (the coastal origin of one being shown by a limpet shell still adhering). The size and unique design of this monument, as well as the fact that in its sources of stone it overrides the well defined zones from which the other tombs derived their slabs, all mark this out as the 'cathedral' of the island. When excavated in 1924–5 by La Société Jersiaise, it was found to have been plundered, either in the Viking period or the early Middle Ages. The finds, of pottery, and flint, with two beads and scattered human bones, are in the Jersey Museum.

Four further fine dolmens are owned by La Société Jersiaise. Les Monts Grantez, in the parish of St Ouen, is a good passage-grave with a single side-chamber. All but two of the capstones are still in position, though most of the mound has perished. This, if the 1912 account is to be believed, was elongated, rather than circular. At least nine burials are recorded, one of them (very disturbed) in the side-chamber. Seven (including a child) were in the main chamber, crouched on their sides, accompanied by limpet shells, animal bones and teeth, and pretty pebbles. What may have been the last burial was found sitting upright against the north wall of the passage, where it joins the chamber, like a sentry asleep at his post.

The second, Mont Ubé (St Clement's parish) should be approached by a woodland path marked at the roadside, not by the drive to a private house. It was saved from the quarrymen in 1848 by F. C. Lukis, who retrieved 10–12 fragmentary pots from the wreckage, with some human remains (burnt and unburnt). Today the tomb is unroofed and

has lost its mound (which Lukis called its 'earthy envelope'). Two surviving uprights at right-angles to the south wall are all that remains of one (or, to judge from an 1869 plan, two) *internal* side-chambers. This very unusual feature recalls another monument whose site on Fort Regent (St Helier) is now occupied by the new Sports Centre. This monument was presented by the grateful townspeople to the then governor, General Conway, who had it transported to England and re-erected in his grounds at Park Place, Henley (where it now is). Its archaeological interest is in its plan, a parallel-sided passage and an exactly circular chamber with five internal chambers recorded out of a possible ten.

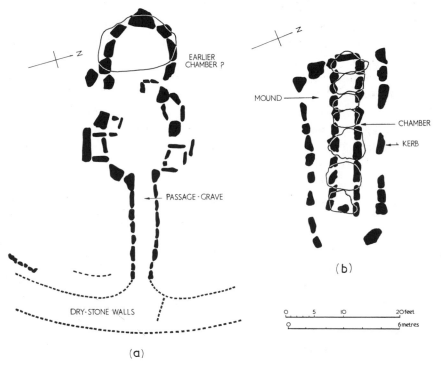

Fig 11   La Pouquelaye de Faldouet, Jersey (left) and Le Couperon, Jersey (right)
(source : Hawkes [1937])

This brings us to the most baffling site of all, La Pouquelaye de Faldouet, (St Martin's parish), a monument much mauled by diggers and restorers who were not archaeologists (see Fig 11a). The plan therefore cannot be trusted in detail; in general, however, it is the only Jersey tomb to show clearly more than one phase of construction. The re-building of chambered tombs, usually by incorporating one or more

simple examples into a more elaborate creation, is well authenticated
in Britain and France, but has not previously been recorded in the
Channel Islands. At Faldouet, the horseshoe-shaped western chamber
with its massive capstone (23–24 tons) presumably survives from an
original passage-grave. Subsequently, perhaps, the passage was dug out
and removed to make way for a second passage-grave like that of Fort
Regent (Mont de la Ville)—though its present restored form may be
largely fictitious. The mound, now vanished, was apparently of more
than one phase to judge from two or three concentric retaining walls
of stone found on the east side. These, too, have been extensively
'restored'.

Of the two surviving gallery-graves, the finer is at Le Couperon (see
Fig 11b), in a beautiful cliffside situation in St Martin's parish. The
outer set of stones is in fact the retaining kerb of the mound, which was
long and straight-sided in this class of monument. The slab with a bite
out of it that now closes the east end was probably one of a pair
forming a 'port-hole' slab athwart the centre of the cist. The other
gallery-grave is only a short bus-ride to the west of St Helier, at Ville-ès-
Nouaux (ask for First Tower); within municipal railings in a park by
the church is a small gallery-grave and beside it a single cist in a stone
circle (which originally encircled the mound).

An hour or two's walk with a map on the grass-covered dunes of
Quennevais will bring the visitor to several good but small menhirs
(some recently defaced, and one destroyed by vandals) and the Ossuary,
a small megalithic chamber that contained, on excavation, the remains
of at least twenty individuals. A mile to the north can be found the
White Menhir in a modern field wall, and the isolated and apparently
aligned Trois Rocques.

Denuded earthworks of the Iron Age are known at Plémont and
Frémont Points, but the finest promontory fort in all the islands is to
be seen at Le Câtel (St Martins). Nearly 20ft (6.09m) high, it owes its
steep unweathered profile to the use of the local loess (a kind of brick-
earth), whose compactness and stability was evidently appreciated in
prehistoric times.

Guernsey

The No 32 bus will take one near many of the ancient monuments
north of St Peter Port. Passing the Château des Marais (see below,
p 66) and Delancey Park, where the monument is built of re-used
dolmen slabs, the traveller should ask for 'The Dolmen' stop. An illegible

signpost directs him along King's Road to the Déhus, 300yd along the lane, adrift in a sea of glasshouses. From here he should travel on to L'Ancresse Common, where a few hours' walk over the golf links will be rewarded by several sites. Two ruined dolmens lie about 100yd sw of the central Martello Tower in L'Ancresse Bay and the map marks the positions of La Platte Mare and especially La Varde. This impressive passage-grave is 41ft (12.5m) long overall, inside a mound 60ft (18.3m) in diameter which has been largely restored. The chamber, in which one can stand upright, has a shallow side-chamber to the north, which shares the largest of the capstones. The burials were in at least two layers, comprising over thirty bone heaps and over 150 urns.

In the south-west part of the island, an equally fine passage-grave is the Creux ès Faies, (parish of St Peter-in-the-Wood) with much of its mound intact, despite wartime disturbance and the truncation of one side in the nineteenth century. A picturesque ruined tomb is Le Trépied, Le Catioroc, overlooking Perelle Bay, in the same parish. (See Plate 3.) It has been restored on three occasions and the granite supports are modern.

The most enigmatic of these burial sites is at L'Islet (see Fig 12), tucked away behind houses in the estate at Sandy Hook (St Sampson parish). Excavated in 1912 it has since been badly vandalised and only recently tidied up by volunteer labour. It seems to be a D-shaped setting of stones, about 45ft (13.7m) in diameter, incorporating six small cists. The best solution to the enigma is to suppose more than one

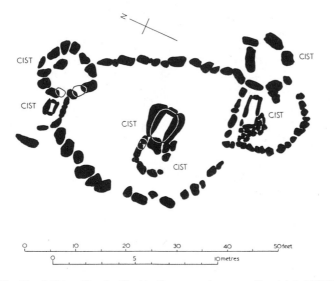

Fig 12   L'Islet (Sandy Hook), Guernsey (*source: Kendrick [1928]*)

reconstruction in antiquity. Perhaps it was originally a revetted mound covering the central twin cists; the flattened side of the D is either original or a subsequent cutting-back, to give a 'façade'. Further cists were then added at the corners, each presumably with its little mound, giving a rough symmetry. This is speculation, of course, and a careful re-examination is badly needed. Only 200yd to the north-west is the oddity of the ruined dolmen in the garden of Mon Désir, Sandy Lane. It is visible from the road.

Menhirs abound in the island; a good specimen is La Longue Rocque (parish of St Peter-in-the-Wood) which is 11ft 6in (3.5m) high; another, 10ft (3m) high is La Longue Pierre (St Saviour's) in an old field wall on the north side of the drive to Fort le Crocq. The reader is invited to consider a second smaller stone 20yd to the west, not mentioned in the available literature. Those who arrive in the island by air should note an inscribed stone, Le Perron du Roi, just outside the airport, opposite the Forest Stores. Cup-markings show that this is a prehistoric stone, either a menhir or part of a lost dolmen. The inscription (best seen in evening light) is no earlier than the eighteenth century and the stone has been a ceremonial mounting-block (*perron*) and a boundary mark of the Royal Fief.

Of the two statue-menhirs, one—that outside Câtel Church—has already been described (p 46), the other (for which the bus stop is 'The Old Post') is at the gate of St Martin's Church (see Plate 2). She is La Grand' mère du Chimquière, head and shoulders carved on a straight-sided granite slab. Other features—breasts, arms and girdle (a band near the base of the statue)—suggest that she was originally a neolithic statue, like that at Câtel; on the other hand the evident remodelling of the face, with its solemn expression, lentoid eyes, triangular nose and slit-like mouth, strongly suggests Celtic work. And the formal braided hair-style would suggest a date in the Iron Age rather than the Dark Ages, as has been sometimes thought.

What must have been a fine Iron Age promontory fort has survived at Jerbourg (by Doyle's column)—by a miracle and in spite of the road, car-park, electricity sub-station, German bunkers and modern beer-garden. It was once a triple earthwork cutting the promontory at this point; its grandeur can best be appreciated where the ramparts emerge on the western cliffs. No finds are known and the stone-faced earthworks at the foot of the monument are attributed to a fourteenth-century fort.

Alderney

Considering its small size, this island has more than its share of fortification and it is interesting to think that the series may begin in the Roman period (p 49). At present, only the exterior of the Nunnery can be inspected, as it is privately owned and closed to visitors.

The prime neolithic monument of the island is the Tourgis Dolmen, formerly known as the Roc à L'Epine, in a clearing in the gorse above Fort Tourgis. Owned by the States of Alderney, it is leased and maintained by the Alderney Society, who recently re-excavated it and conjecturally replaced one end-slab of the cist that was found nearby. It was a small cist under a circular mound and no burials are known. The re-excavation showed that it was built on a flint-working site. At the other end of the island, on the rocky plateau of Les Pourciaux, stood a most interesting tomb, until the war. Its conversion into a German gun-position, and subsequent demolition, have wrecked it beyond recovery.

Below it lies Longy Common, the site of the Roman settlement (p 49) of which no traces survive, though Roman bricks can be picked up on Longy beach by the Nunnery. The hollows here mark the site of the 'Old Town of Longy', which is said to have disappeared in a great sandstorm one night. Recent rescue excavations by The Kennels (the isolated house on the Common) did indeed identify a possibly medieval cultivated layer over-laid by over a metre of blown sand. Below this was a rich Roman layer covering a massive structure of stone blocks with Iron Age pottery.

This pottery was identical to that from Les Huguettes, the other major site in the island, close to it on the west, at the very end of the golf course. Accidentally discovered in 1968, it was excavated and subsequently restored by the Alderney Society. A circular stone wall 30ft (9m) in diameter enclosed an area with a central circular hearth, a semicircular stone platform to the south, and an area with a very thick deposit of ash. Domestic objects included a bronze razor of Bronze Age type, loomwrights, bronze tweezers and a weaving comb. Most remarkable was the quantity of pottery, over forty reconstructable pots, with tools evidently used for shaping and smoothing them. The evidence thus pointed to a communal domestic site, with pot-making and -firing in a large bonfire on an almost industrial scale—a discovery unique in Iron Age Europe. A radiocarbon date gave its age as about 490 BC. This must have been the focus of a small community, as the sites of huts can be made out in the turf around it.

Sark

This island, so interesting in many ways, may be a disappointment
to the visitor in search of prehistoric monuments. In 1874, there were
several 'some of which were large, others of moderate size; others again
are simple cists. Not many years ago the whereabouts of ten cromlechs
could be perfectly distinguished; but all have now disappeared, with
the exception of two nearly entire cists.' Two small cists have been
rediscovered recently by the author. Both are on private land, in Little
Sark, one almost inaccessible on the western cliffs, the other smothered
in gorse at the southern tip of the island. A distant view of this one can
be had looking back from the cliff path to Venus' Pool. Some of the
fine gateposts of the island may well be re-used stones and the large
blocks in the field wall at the SE corner of the crossroads at La Vaurocque
are believed to be from a demolished dolmen.

The northern tip of the island, L'Eperquerie, is traditionally believed
to have been cut off by two earthworks of unknown date. Part of one
can be seen, though hard to make out among the clefts of purely
geological origin and the later construction of a now destroyed battery.

A visit to the abandoned silver mines is dangerous, though forming
part of an interesting story. But whatever Latrobe's authoritative guide-
book may say, there is no reason to believe the causeway of Plat Rue Bay
to be Roman. It may nevertheless be earlier than 1835, when the mines
were so fruitlessly reopened.

Herm and Jethou

Jethou is privately owned and not open to visitors. The owner has
kindly allowed the antiquities to be studied and recorded, and they
include two probable menhirs and a possible burial cist.

Herm, on the other hand, is an attractive day visit from St Peter
Port, and the visitor should have time to inspect some interesting, if
overgrown, monuments. They are mostly in two groups on the two
eminences, Le Grand Monceau (Monku) and Le Petit Monceau, with
some in the Sandy Plain below. Four on Le Grand Monceau comprise
a ruined structure on the crest and a group of three identifiable by their
growth of brambles. The most easterly is a well preserved passage-grave
without capstones in position. When excavated, human bones were found
lying on a bed of pebbles beneath a layer of limpet shells. Those on the
rocky outcrop of Le Petit Monceau are very ruinous and hard to make

out. At least one of the four produced human remains, while another has apparently never been recorded.

In the low ground between these two eminences, north-west of the signpost at Robert's Cross, can be found a peculiar tomb. It is a parallel-sided chamber with a square end to the west and a partition of three low stones (now invisible) forming an almost square western chamber. From this point eastwards the walls converge sharply to a narrow entrance with two capstones. The burials, in at least two layers, were disturbed, probably in Roman times. In the lowest part of the common, in the centre and just to the east of a direct line between the obelisk and the summit of Le Grand Monceau is a slab-lined cist in which pottery and stone tools were found. And on the beach at Oyster Point, the north-west tip of the island, is an unrecorded tomb, revealed by erosion and high tides in the 1950s and becoming covered again in drifted sand. It is empty and no finds are known. But it does demonstrate the relationship between the neolithic ground level and the modern sea level.

Destruction and Rediscovery

This account has been dominated by the megaliths, partly because they strike the visitor so forcefully and partly because nowhere else in Europe, apart from Brittany, are so many so well preserved. They owe their survival in part to a superstitious respect for them as the abode of fairies, who would frequently be seen to dance on moonlit nights. They had more sinister associations, too: at the Trépied. for instance, the witches' sabbaths on a Friday night were so important that the Devil himself attended. The islands have not entirely lost the sense that the supernatural still lingers; in Sark particularly, when the visitors have departed, this can still be felt. It was felt and conveyed by Victor Hugo and by novelists since his day. Most recently this was evoked in a children's novel, *The Grandmother Stone*, by Margaret Greaves, of which Sark is the setting, but the principal object of superstition and eventual destruction was the Grand' mère du Chimquière. A proposal to destroy her is indeed on record and the crack that can be seen doubtless inspired the story. Even today, the occasional small offering can be found at her feet.

In 1837 F. C. Lukis was told a cautionary story which has since been proved to be substantially true. The owner of a great Guernsey monument, La Rocque qui Sonne, resolved to break it up to build a new house, in spite of his neighbours' warnings. Their predictions were

soon fulfilled. For no sooner had the new house been completed than it was burnt to the ground and two of his servants perished in the fire. The remainder of the stone had been broken up as roadmaking material and the two ships carrying it to England were lost at sea. Fate pursued the man to his next home in Alderney, which in turn was promptly destroyed by fire. Finally, when attempting to return to Guernsey, he himself perished on board in an accident as the ship neared land.

By Lukis' day, however, the protecting spirits had taken flight and the tombs were ransacked, 'wantonly thrown down' and used as quarries for building stone. Indeed, many ruined structures still bear the marks of quarrymen's wedges. This, and the widespread spoliation of the islands (especially Alderney) for military fortifications is the setting for the activities of Frederick Corbin Lukis and his four sons, Frederick Collings, John Walter, William Collings and Francis du Bois Lukis. Throughout most of the nineteenth century they devoted their energies to the excavation, recording and even purchase of monuments that were being destroyed. The father, F. C. Lukis, in particular, was a pioneer in archaeological research. Like most of his contemporaries, he was brought up to believe in the great stone structures as Druids' altars, stained with the blood of sacrificial victims. His painstaking examination—and recording—of their contents soon persuaded him that they were communal tombs, that they were all once covered by earthen mounds, and that they were, as tombs, the focal points of ancient communities. In this, as in other ideas, he anticipated much modern research. In contrast with his sons, he published little in the way of learned papers. But his correspondence, and in particular the six great handwritten volumes of notes and drawings, the *Collectanea Antiqua*, form a priceless archive of information, now safely housed in Guernsey and regularly consulted by scholars. All the family collected widely, as their view of antiquity was world-wide, and in 1907 the Lukis Collection was bequeathed to the States of Guernsey. This was displayed first in the family house, then in a separate building, the Lukis and Island Museum. At the time of writing, the collections are on the move again, being packed for transfer to a place of honour in the new museum that is rising in Candie Gardens.

The fame of the Lukis family should not overshadow a number of subsequent scholars, themselves natives of the islands and prominent members of the two great bodies, La Société Jersiaise and La Société Guernesiaise. Of the latter, Major S. Carey Curtis and Col T. W. M. de Guérin should be credited with the excavation of the strange site at Sandy Hook (L'Islet) and the recognition of the Déhus

sculptures, as well as some important papers in early volumes of the *Transactions*. The 'golden age' of Jersey archaeology earlier this century is marked by many names that are well remembered in the island; in particular, those of Fr Christian Burdo, SJ, Major A. J. B. Godfray, Mr E. F. Guiton, Dr R. R. Marett, Mr E. T. Nicolle, Major N. L. V. Rybot and Mr J. Sinel figure prominently in the accounts of major operations at La Cotte, Le Pinacle, La Hougue Bie and elsewhere. Their work is recorded in their own contributions to the *Bulletin* of the Société and in two volumes that are still a basic reference work. Vol 1 of *The Archaeology of the Channel Islands* by T. D. Kendrick appeared in 1928, and Vol 2 by Jacquetta Hawkes in 1937. The basic work of classification and documentary research was done by Kendrick, who was to have written both volumes, while the intervening years enabled Jacquetta Hawkes to reinterpret the material from all the islands in the light of more recent developments in European archaeology. Together these volumes are a landmark in European prehistory.

The Future

It will be clear that the bulk of the research has been done by scholars and archaeologists living and working in the Channel Islands. The archaeology of the islands, however, is of international interest and the monuments, particularly those of the megalithic phase, find their place in any account of prehistoric Europe. The English-speaking reader is referred to the writings of Glyn Daniel (1958 and 1960), P. R. Giot (1960) and Stuart Piggott (1965) to see the neolithic of the islands in its proper European context. But while the Channel Islands material is generally unfamiliar to British archaeologists, our colleagues on the mainland, especially in Brittany, have always seen the islands as coming within their sphere of research. On the other hand, it is over-simple to see them as merely a mirror of mainland cultures. It has been realised for some time that the advance of prehistoric technology in Europe, and the population pressures that gradually built up towards the 'Atlantic Façade' caused peculiar problems at the coastal regions, the ultimate physical barrier. The 'overspill effect', therefore, in the offshore islands is one of the aspects currently being considered by the author of this chapter. Another is the cultural differences between the islands themselves, as it is easy to underestimate their physical and cultural isolation—especially in the earlier prehistoric period when even inter-island communications must have been fraught with danger. For the neolithic, indeed, the differences between the islands are as interesting

as the similarities with the mainland. Finally, the evidence that the tombs provide for the communities that built and used them, and the possibility of envisaging a structure for neolithic society, island by island, places the Channel Islands again in the mainstream of current archaeological thinking. In this connection, it might be appropriate to note the academic support that has been given by the Universities of London, Southampton and Rennes.

Within the islands there has been a renaissance of archaeological activity in recent years. In Jersey, the need to secure the monuments against the inroads of the twentieth century has led to some thorough fieldwork and the compilation of an index of known antiquities. This has been accompanied by a systematic study of field names, many of which include such words as 'hougue' (barrow) and other clues to lost antiquities. For prehistoric Jersey, recent excavations have included a section through a suspected promontory fort, a survey of another, and the re-excavation of a ruined dolmen (at Beauport). La Société Jersiaise has combined with the Jersey National Trust for what will be several seasons' work on the Ile Agois (above, p 50) and with the States of Jersey for the work at Gorey Castle (below, p 66). In all cases, specialist help has been sought from England, while members of La Société have begun the long task of scientific analysis and conservation within the island. Very much the same is true of Guernsey, where La Société Guernesiaise is equally active. In both islands the focus of activity is no longer the prehistoric period, but rather the medieval and post-medieval. Archaeologists in both are facing the problems caused by large-scale redevelopment in St Helier and St Peter Port. In Jersey, the reaction has been an appraisal of the needs and priorities (Finlaison 1975) and rescue excavation, on a voluntary basis. Amateur effort in Guernsey, on the other hand, is currently directed towards the recording of standing buildings that may have to make way for new. This urban archaeology is properly the subject of the next chapter, as are the major excavations at Gorey Castle and the Château des Marais; in both the States are playing an important rôle in the investigation of monuments in their care.

The Alderney Society is very active, and has sponsored four excavations of prehistoric sites in recent years. Its members run the island museum and include archaeological information in their quarterly *Bulletin*.

This chapter is concerned only with those museums in the islands that possess prehistoric and Roman material. Archaeology is one activity which overrides the traditional insularity of the islands. Expertise is

regularly shared informally, while the formal expression of this has been the formation of the Federation of Channel Islands Museums.

We return finally to the one excavation in the islands that is strictly the work of an outside body—that at La Cotte de St Brelade. Since 1960 the work has been carried out by the Department of Archaeology and Anthropology of the University of Cambridge. The final stages, including an important programme of post-excavation analysis and conservation at Cambridge, are a joint undertaking of the University, the British Museum and the Royal Academy; this collaboration is a measure of the international importance of the work.

This account, it is hoped, has shown how far the study of the pre-history of the Channel Islands has come since the eighteenth century and how much in this field the islands have to offer the visitor. As late as the nineteenth century, it could be said (of Jersey) that 'Various remains of Druidical structures are observable on this island'. In the twentieth, Daniel (1960) referred to the culture of the megalith builders as 'rich, brilliant and luxuriant'. One may well wonder what the scholars of the next phase of archaeological activity in the islands will have to say of their own forebears.

Notes to this chapter are on page 242.

3

History

John Uttley

Lying as they do in the Gulf of Avranches, only a few miles from the coast of France, the Channel Islands were on the very outermost fringe of the Roman Empire. Clearly, officials from Constantia, the tribal capital in the Cotentin, would pay occasional visits to collect taxes and issue orders but there is little evidence of Roman occupation. A few coins, handmills, fragments of pottery and a small stone carving have been found but there are only two sites which may safely be attributed to the Roman period, the Nunnery in Alderney and a small rectangular stone building near the Pinnacle Rock, Jersey, a subsidiary signal station. This is a small total of Roman remains and yet the islanders must have been affected by Rome's power even when, after AD 180, it declined. Memories of a more civilised way of life must have remained with the islanders as evidenced by the suffix 'ville' still to be found in many island place-names, eg, Anneville, Leoville, inhabited by the Gallo-Roman lordlings.

The other bequest from the Romans is the tradition of Roman law, which remains as the basis of island law down the centuries, in spite of all the destruction and havoc which were to follow after the final defeat by the Frankish leader Clovis of the Roman general Syagrius in 486. This broke the power of Rome in northern France and left the islanders to eke out a precarious existence on the edge of the known world.

The only other tenuous link with civilisation was the Christian link, for which there is evidence from the names of parish churches in Jersey and Guernsey. St Martin of Tours was the driving force behind the missionary expansion in the north-west in the fifth century and one can assume that the islanders were influenced.

The next visitors to the islands were also good. The struggle between rival Frankish chieftains left Armorica (Brittany) somewhat depopulated and news of this reached the Christian leaders in west Britain, who were hard-pressed by the Anglo-Saxons. They set out with their bishops and priests for this possible refuge and may well have called in on the islands

on their way. Certainly St Sampson gathered a force from them, as the inhabitants were well-known to him, to reinforce him in the Breton struggle. From there missionaries returned to convert the islanders. The first of these whose name was recorded was St Marcouf, who landed in Jersey and founded a religious community in AD 540. He was followed by St Sampson who had risen to be Bishop of Dol in Brittany; he landed in the harbour in Guernsey called after him and built a chapel on the south side of the harbour, with priests to attend it and to spread Celtic Christianity to the island.

At this time St Helier, a disciple of St Marcouf, went to Jersey and founded a hermitage on a rock near the former harbour. Also, St Sampson's successor, St Magloire, founded a monastery in Sark, a little settlement which lasted until 1412, when the French removed the monks.

The Dark Ages

Apart from this sketchy history, there is little record of the islanders during the Dark Ages when Saxon and Viking raiders swept the Channel. Geoffrey of Monmouth records that Prince Cadwalla was driven by a storm to land in Garnareia about AD 630. A hoard of Visigoth coins was found in Sark, and the 'ey' of Guernsey and Jersey is the Norse for 'island'. Wace too, the twelfth-century Jersey historian, refers to a raid by Jarl Hastings on all the islands.

Meanwhile the Viking raiders extended their control of north-western France and in 911 Rollo, the leader, was granted Normandy. By 933 the islands were included in the Duchy and for 300 years they enjoyed comparative tranquility, being organised as parts of various feudal fiefs, the Bessin and the Cotentin in Guernsey, and the Carterets and other families in Jersey. The bishop of Cotentin controlled half of Alderney, and in Herm the Augustinians founded a priory. The tenants, large or small, owed various dues, in money or in services, but there were no serfs, a situation caused by depopulation of the islands so that the dukes had to attract Norman families over to settle. From these dues and services arose a tradition of invoking 'the customs used in the islands time out of mind', which were to play an important part in the story.

By such arrangements the Norman dukes organised the legal, social and economic life of the islands; they allotted the land, the dues were recognised, ducal and seigneurial courts were set up to enforce these and itinerant justices were sent over from Rouen to check that the machinery was working smoothly.

Two elements may be pre-Norman. The office of jurat can be traced

back to John, but it was probably an adaptation of an older office, parish headman, before whom the natives would be tried according to custom. The second organisation was the parish itself, where legal acts of importance took place—in the parish church by an *oui de parois* or parish hearing.

The dukes kept these assemblies going alongside the manorial courts as a jury of presentment or witness for the visits of the justices. The actual parish churches were built in the early eleventh century, of simple but strong granite, but there is no doubt that earlier churches of wood existed, to be burnt down by raiders.

After the strong rule of William the Conqueror, the islands were lucky to pass to Henry as part of the Cotentin and their loyalty was rewarded in the struggle between Stephen of Blois and Geoffrey Plantagenet by Geoffrey's confirmation of their rights and customs. The fief-holders who supported Stephen forfeited their estates, making the king's land more extensive in Guernsey and Jersey. This affected the importance of the royal courts, which came to be administered separately for the two large islands.

Control of the islands passed to John, as Lord of the Isles and later as king. His deputy was Pierre de Preaux, who was to surrender to Philippe of France as the Norman nobles revolted. A confused period followed for the islands, as Eustace de Moine was sent by the French to harry them. But in 1207 they were brought back under John's control by Governor de Suligny. Their customs were confirmed and they were administered by wardens responsible directly to the king, instead of the old centralised government of Rouen.

The French Wars

The islands were now in a key position, firstly because of the road-stead of St Peter Port, offering a safe anchorage for ships plying from England to Gascony, and secondly because, in time of war with France, they were outposts to threaten the French mainland. To secure them de Suligny started on the building of two castles, Gorey and Castle Cornet, with subsidiary outposts in Guernsey of the Chateaux de Marais and Jerbourg. In spite of threats from France, the islands remained secure and well governed for the next fifty years by a succession of able men.

The situation changed at the start of Edward the First's reign. He appointed Otto de Grandison, a busy and important man as Lord of the Isles. Naturally, Otto looked on the islands as an estate from which

Plate 5 *A print of St Peter Port made in 1829, as seen from Fort George. In the foreground is a shipyard and behind it is the town church. The small harbour and old buildings on the hillside present a charming picture of a scene much altered today* (Guernsey Press Co)

Plate 6 *Germans marching past the Royal Hotel, Guernsey, in 1940, soon after they had occupied the island. Crowds of islanders are watching the troops, headed by a band, and the absence of traffic is noticeable* (Guernsey Press Co)

Plate 7 *An ormer, the muscular foot, and sensory tentacles just visible beneath the shell. The ormer is edible* (C. Toms)

Plate 8 *Edible shellfish: spider crabs, their spiny shells encrusted with sponges and the tortuous tubes of bristle worms* (C. Toms)

his officers were to extract the limit of revenue. But the office of warden came to be divided; a bailiff, increasingly a local man, for judicial practices, and a deputy warden for other duties. It was round the bailiff that the islanders gathered to complain of the extortion of the officials and in spite of Edward I's support of the officials and attempts to deny their privileges by sending over judges to hold a general assize, the islanders stubbornly held out for their customs and privileges. The struggle went on into the reign of Edward III, in fact up to the start of the Hundred Years War, when threats from the French caused the king to recognise the islands' privileges *in toto* in 1341. During the constitutional struggle it came to be recognised that each island had its royal court, largely independent of the warden, who had his own officials and men to administer the king's business and guard the royal castles.

Thus, during the long war, the king had the islands as bases and harbours of refuge, manned by his own troops, and backed by loyal islanders. There were many raids by the French—in particular an attack in 1337 which brought all the islands except Gorey Castle under French control. Castle Cornet was only recaptured in 1345, to be taken again in 1356, and it took a combined force from Jersey to regain it before the Treaty of Bretigny brought a lull in the fighting. The war soon flared up again, with a raid on Guernsey led by Owen of Wales in 1372 and, in 1373, a devastating raid on both islands by the famous Bertrand du Guesclin. However, with the appointment of a notable soldier, Sir Hugh Calverly as warden, the French threat declined and the islanders were left to recover from the devastation.

With the accession of Henry V, the islands were affected by the struggle again, as they were by the Papal schism which led to the banishment of the pro-Clement Deans, and by Henry's decision to take over the Alien Priories, which removed the last of the absentee landlords. The period of peace up to Henry's death in 1422 led to prosperity and increased trade with Normandy, from where families went across to settle in Alderney, largely depopulated by earlier French attacks. The islanders contributed armed men and seamen to help in the long rearguard action that the English fought against Joan of Arc, but gradually all French territory was lost except for Calais. The islands escaped the earlier years of the Wars of the Roses, but in 1461 a French force captured and held Jersey for seven years, possibly as a Lancastrian stronghold. Then the Yorkist Admiral Harliston sailed with a strong force from Guernsey and retook the island. As a result of Edward IV's triumph, Harliston was made governor of the islands and managed to arrange an agreement that if war broke out again between England and

France the islands would be neutral. This was guaranteed by a papal bull of Pope Sixtus IV. Thus the islands had struggled through a difficult period but emerged with their privileges intact; in fact they had gained the extra right not to pay English customs dues on their exports. Further, with the central government often weak or anarchic, they had evolved deliberative and legislative assemblies known as the States, in which the bailiff and jurats were joined by other important islanders to form representative bodies, to vote money and give directions to officers. The islands were on the road to self-government.

When the cautious and experienced Henry VII succeeded to the throne after Bosworth Field he inaugurated a strong policy for England and the islands, by which the sovereign and council ordered all affairs of the kingdom, while respecting the rights and feelings of the people. He valued the islands for their strategic position and their link with Normandy and wanted them to be well governed and contented. So he defined the powers of the governor, who was responsible for the general administration and defences but was not to interfere in any judicial procedure; the duties of the jurats were laid down clearly and any dispute between them and the governor was to be referred immediately to the Privy Council. The success of this policy depended on the calibre of individual governors, who had a difficult task. After removing Harliston, a Yorkist, from office in Jersey, the king appointed Thomas Overay, under whom trade flourished. But his next appointment was not so successful, Hugh Vaughan, a masterful and unscrupulous Welshman who laid claim to Trinity Manor, as forefeit to the Crown, and browbeat all opponents. Eventually the bailiff, de Carteret, crossed to England to lay his complaints before the young Henry VIII. Wolsey endeavoured to block his approach but after some time saw that he had been dismissed from office wrongfully. A commission of enquiry, which included two islanders, was set up and this found against Vaughan, for violence and extortion, and he resigned.

The Reformation

From this time, 1529, the personality and policies of Henry VIII dominated the scene, as he defied the Pope and moved to political reformation. His religious measures had little effect on the islands, as Henry V's seizure of the priories had anticipated him, but he was concerned with the defence of the islands against hostile Catholics and had towers added to the defences of Castle Cornet and Gorey Castle. A fort, too, was begun in Alderney, to cover the approaches to Longy Bay.

The threat was shown to be real when a force of 400 Frenchmen landed and took Sark.

The religious measures of Edward VI's council of regency caused little objection; only one or two rectors refused to submit and a few laymen were convicted of attending private masses. By this time the religious views of some of the islanders were outstripping the political reform. The driving force came from north-western France where the advanced reforming views of Jaques le Fevre were popular. Religious tracts and reforming missionaries spread to the islands, and in Jersey this movement was helped by the appointment of Sir Hugh Poulet, an able man and a reformer. By the appointment of his brother, a Catholic, as dean of Jersey, Poulet was able to control any excesses by the pro-Catholic party on the accession of Mary Tudor. But in Guernsey, where the reformers were not so popular, there was persecution; the most terrible deed was the burning of three women and an infant in 1556 on the order of the bailiff and royal court.

With the succession of Elizabeth, the Protestant religion was restored in the islands; a calm transition in Jersey, where Poulet remained as governor, and a change which suited the leading island families, the de Carterets and the Lemprières. But in Guernsey the situation was more difficult. The governor was not respected, the bailiff and the majority of jurats were Catholics, and the islanders were quarrelsome, refusing to contribute to the island's defence. In particular they feared to lose their trade with France. So the English government sent over a commission of enquiry, but though it dismissed the bailiff, the rebellious jurats continued to thwart the commission in every way. At the same time, the Protestant party was turning more and more to Calvinism, the Guise persecution in France having caused a number of Huguenots to flee to the islands where their burning faith soon produced converts.

In both islands a consistory or parish church council was set up. This did not please Elizabeth, as Presbyterianism did not go with her position as supreme head of the church. But the Huguenot case was pleaded before the council by Helier de Carteret, and the council was upset by reports of anti-Protestant riots in Guernsey. So, in 1565, the council dismissed the seven Catholic jurats and this small revolution led to a strong Protestant government in Guernsey and the recognition of Elizabeth by the Calvinist synods in the islands.

One of the most influential Huguenot exiles, Cosme Brevint, went to Sark as minister for the new settlement which Helier de Carteret had started there in 1563. His work so impressed Queen Elizabeth that she presented the island to him as a fief, on payment of a rent and on

condition that the island be inhabited by forty men at least.

By 1570 a fully-fledged Huguenot system was established in all the islands except Alderney, which meant that the Huguenot discipline was now backed by the royal courts. Everyone had to go to church, where they attended the full Huguenot services, including catechising the congregation. This was followed by any secular business, when the constable read out any orders from the royal court. The consistory followed, when any misdeeds were punished according to the very strict Huguenot code which attempted to force the islanders to lead godly and sober lives.

This led to rebellion and a number of cases are reported, followed by fitting punishments. It led, too, to defiance by anti-God sects posing as witches whose covens, if caught, were punished with the utmost severity, one hundred cases being dealt with in Guernsey alone.

During this period the standard of living was comparatively low, but the upper class families started building stone houses of two storeys. The more enterprising went in for trade with France and Spain but the backbone of the population were the small farmers, more or less self-supporting. Some kind of livelihood was provided by two new industries, the knitting or woollen goods and the Newfoundland fishing trade.

The age-old struggle for power between the governors and the bailiff and jurats went on; in Jersey Sir John Peyton fought a long fight, but in the end it was decided that power should be shared co-equally—in effect a victory for the jurats and States. On a second front Peyton fought to secure the frontier of the Anglican church and his right to appoint to livings; backed by James I and his council he appointed a dean over the Jersey church which, by 1623, was thoroughly Anglicised. In Guernsey the lieutenant-governor was a Presbyterian, so that the islands presented a solid front to the demands of the king. As the king's favourite, Buckingham was involved in war with France and Spain, in the course of which it was necessary to secure the islands' loyalty and desperate efforts were made to improve the defences.

The Civil War

With the start of the Civil War the islands went their separate ways. In Jersey the de Carteret clan, royalist and Anglican, held key positions, and although there was quite a strong Presbyterian opposition which confined the royalists to Gorey and Elizabeth castles, George Carteret, a navy officer, landed in 1643 and quickly reduced the island, which remained loyalist until it was forced to surrender in 1651.

Fig 13 Elizabeth Castle, Jersey, from the west, drawn by W. Hollar in 1650, soon after the castle had been built. It was designed by Paul Ivy and one of its first governors was Sir Walter Raleigh

In Guernsey however, Charles I was unpopular as he had forbidden the growing of tobacco, had let the navy decline and had failed to supply money for the island's defence. The island's leaders, led by Pierre de Beauvoir, were appointed parliamentary commissioners and as the governor, Osborne, refused to recognise them, he was confined to Castle Cornet. This fortress dominated the town and roadstead and held out till 1651. Before this Osborne caught the island's leaders by a trick and put them in the castle dungeons, from which they managed to escape. The Presbyterian governor, Warwick, backed them with arms and they established garrisons on Alderney and Sark to protect them from raids by royalist Jersey, where George Carteret was running a successful privateering business.

After the surrender of the castles, military governors were appointed for the two large islands and Guernsey groaned under the expense of paying for the garrison. In Jersey there was trouble between the Presbyterians and the garrison Independents, and also over the claims of returned exiles to the property they had been forced to sell. The island commander too, Gibbon, was an unscrupulous martinet who extorted money from ex-royalists and allowed navy press-gangs to operate, contrary to the island charters.

Charles II's Declaration of Breda was received with joy in Jersey and with relief in Guernsey, where the stubborn islanders waited with apprehension of what his policy might be. He issued a general amnesty, but of course favoured his friends, the de Carterets in Jersey and Andros

in Guernsey.

The Cavalier parliament then passed the Clarendon Code and the Act of Uniformity, which caused dismay in Guernsey where the ministers and people clung desperately to the Presbyterian form of worship and discipline; their battle against the new dean, Jean de Sausmarez, was a bitter one. On the surface Anglicanism won the day but relics of the Presbyterian form of service remained. The islanders were, however, united by two factors. The new governor, Lord Hatton, was unpopular because of his arbitrary interference with justice and his dishonesty; he was removed and able men replaced him. Secondly, England was at war with the French and Dutch, so that the islands were threatened again. The governors did their best to prepare the islands' defences, and in Jersey Governor Morgan trained the militia to a high standard. However he clashed with the Jersey States over the Navigation Act which laid down that only English ships could carry goods to America, so causing much hardship to Jersey and Guernsey merchants. Further hardship was caused by attempts of English officials to interfere in the renewed smuggling trade between the islands and West Country ports. The knitting trade, too, was in difficulties over restrictions imposed by the French and only a limited quota of wool from England. When the quota of wool was increased in 1686 it enabled the industry to flourish for the next hundred years.

In a period of change, threat and struggle there came hints of James II's Popish plans; already the islanders were moved by the arrival of Huguenot families fleeing from the French persecution. James II sent over Catholic captains and Irish troops but the militia remained loyal, and the island was held for William of Orange. By prohibiting legal trade with France, he appeared to deal a blow to the islands' prosperity but the activities of smugglers were profitable, whether the Jersey and French seamen and traders met at the Ecrehos rocks or Guernseymen sent their goods to England.

Privateering

The second outlet for the islanders was privateering. This had gone on in a small way since the days of Elizabeth but now it was profitable and legal. After the naval victory of La Hogue, which gave the English and Dutch fleets command of the Channel, French sea-born trade was at the mercy of the privateers and by the end of the war some thirty Guernsey and eight Jersey privateers were in action.

After this war the islands settled down to a comparatively tranquil

and prosperous period. The island militias were kept up to scratch and were always ready to man the island defences in times of war. There was little interference from the English government and the island oligarchies generally ran the islands in an efficient manner. Not that there were no squabbles. In Guernsey there were complaints by the jurats against the overweaning power of the bailiff. In Jersey there was rivalry between the leading families and a popular party grew up, as in that island the jurats were elected by the parishes. This party got a majority in the Royal Court and the States and passed measures dealing with devaluation of the coinage and the farming-out of taxes. There was further trouble in 1769 over the price of corn; this was used as a basis for mortgages and when the price rose it hit at the little man. All this led to the appointment of Bentink as lieutenant-governor, with orders to initiate reforms. The most important of these was one by which the Royal Court lost its power to legislate, which was handed to the States.

Overseas Trade

Meanwhile the economies of the islands improved steadily. The Newfoundland fishing business continued prosperously now that French rivalry was removed and in Jersey the invention of the great plough for deep tilling of the soil improved the production of parsnips. This increase of income led to a higher standard of living so that the leading families tended to have a town house as well as a mansion in the country.

In Guernsey the merchant adventurers expanded their trade with foreign ports, at first St Malo and Southampton, but later to Spain, the West Indies and Newfoundland. They profited by the fact that St Peter Port was a free port and also climatically, in that the temperature was ideal for the storage of wines and spirits. This encouraged English smugglers to call in and carry away their cargoes to English ports.

Besides legitimate trade and supplying smugglers, they were ready too, to send out their ships to privateer when the chance came in a war. They more or less cleared the seas in Louis XIV's later years and in the War of the Spanish Succession there were about 115 Guernsey and 50 Jersey privateers in operation. In the Seven Years' War they were joined by privateers from Alderney, where the enterprising John Le Mesurier was governor. It was he who built the first breakwater at Braye harbour so that there was an anchorage for the privateers.

When war started again in 1778 against France and Spain the privateers went into action with great success. In this year £343,500

was brought in by twenty privateers, in 1779 £270,000 by six, and in 1782 £156,500 by five. It was reckoned that the total value of prizes in the war came to over £900,000.

The French were eager for revenge but their first attempt on Jersey, in 1779, was a failure. However, the threat induced the British government to see to the defences. Martello towers were built to guard against landings and Fort George was constructed to add to the defence of the harbour and roadstead. The French mounted a second attack in 1781 and managed to penetrate to the market place in St Helier, while holding the lieutenant-governor prisoner. He gave orders that the troops and militia should lay down their arms but Major Pierson disregarded his orders and counter-attacked. This led to the defeat of the French and the court martial of the lieutenant-governor.

Methodism

With the signing of the Treaty of Versailles the militia could relax and the fishermen and merchants go about their business. However, with the approach of the French Revolution, new ideas spread in the islands. In Jersey a popular leader, Jean Dumaresq, gradually won support for his case that the legislative powers of the island rested in the States and this was the start of a more democratic form of government. Another influence was the spread of the Methodist movement in the islands. Starting among the troops in Jersey, it was helped by the work of an ardent lay-preacher, R. C. Brackenbury and his young island assistant, de Quetteville. The movement spread to Guernsey and its influence was greatly increased by the arrival on a preaching tour of John Wesley himself in 1787. For the next few years there was considerable persecution but the members stayed firm and the first Methodist chapel was built in 1790. This movement affected the island militias, for the members refused to drill on Sundays; at last, after considerable pressure and support from the King's Council, they were allowed to drill on another day. This was of importance as the militias were relied upon for local defence and with the ferment of French revolutionary ideas it was as well to be on guard. Jersey, meanwhile, was affected by a large number of emigrés, who arrived to settle in St Helier and treble the population of the town.

At last Pitt was driven by the intransigence of the French Republic and horror at the execution of Louis XVI to refuse to recognise the Republic, which declared war in 1793. The French were determined to crush the islands and gathered a force of 20,000 men at St Malo for

invasion. This did not materialise as the British navy was on guard and French resistance movements started in Brittany and La Vendée.

The man who did most to thwart the French was a Jerseyman, Philippe d'Auvergne who, with a force of eight gunboats, kept a ceaseless watch on invasion ports. He also become the chief supplier of arms and money to the Chouans, the resistance movement in Brittany, and the organiser of reports from spies on the movements of French fleets.

Meanwhile, the privateers went on with their dangerous but profitable trade. It was calculated that the money from French and American prizes brought into Guernsey by 1800 topped the million pound mark. The merchants and seamen were also involved in large-scale open trade, paying a million and a half in customs dues, and there was, as before, the useful profit to be made as middleman in the smuggling business.

Island Defences

With the collapse of peace after the Treaty of Amiens, England and the islands faced the full force of the Napoleonic Empire. Napoleon fulminated against Jersey as a nest of brigands, forcing the two governors, Don and Doyle, to take further measures to improve the islands' defences, such as the building of Fort Regent and the improvement of the island's' road system. The garrisons were increased and the British squadron based on St Peter Port blockaded the French fleet in Brest.

The island merchants were hard hit by the enforcement of Napoleon's continental system, which closed all the ports to them, and by the extension of English customs departments to check illicit traffic. However the Peninsular War opened up Spanish and South American ports to them and a lucrative triangular trade grew up from Newfoundland to Spain, to Rio de Janeiro and home. Also St Peter Port became an important staging-post on the route to the Peninsula, so benefiting the island shopkeepers, merchants and farmers.

With the outbreak of war with the United States in 1812 the privateers found themselves with new and profitable targets, so that when peace was proclaimed amid the general rejoicing, there was the general realisation that the wars had brought great opportunities for the enterprising merchant and sea captain, steady markets for the farmers and regular employment for craftsmen and labourers.

The end of the wars brought the threat of depression to all the islands, but there were a number of factors which saved them from relapsing into rural backwaters. Firstly, they were still regarded as fortresses by

Fig 14   St Anne's Church, Alderney, from Les Butes. This is one of the best Victorian churches in the Channel Islands and the engraving was made soon after its completion in 1850

the English government and the garrisons were kept at a strength of one battalion plus artillery. This brought much-needed funds into the islands and served to leaven local society, particularly in the case of Alderney where a grandiose scheme to create a fortified naval base was put in hand.

Rights and Privileges

Secondly, the islanders stuck stubbornly by their ancient charters and privileges and resisted all attempts by Britain to interfere with or override these rights. The leading figure was Daniel Brock, bailiff of Guernsey, fighting to secure the islands' position as free ports, their exemption from customs dues on their produce and the right of their citizens to be tried in their own courts. However, political squabbles in Jersey and the fracas which followed from the domineering governorship of Sir William Napier led to the appointment of a royal commission on the position of the jurats. This was largely ignored, though Jersey did allow fourteen deputies to be elected to the States.

Thirdly, there was public spirit. This led to considerable development of St Helier and St Peter Port and extension of the harbours, the foundation or improvement of island schools and the setting up of new lighthouses.

Industries

Individual islanders were always ready to use their skills and geographical position to earn a living and in Jersey they developed the early potato trade, whose output had risen to 70,000 tons by 1890. Again the Newfoundland cod trade picked up as the merchants supplied the cod settlements, took the salted fish to South America and returned to Jersey with hides, wine and other goods. To supply the ships for their trade a considerable shipbuilding industry was created, though competition from iron- or steel-built ships eventually killed the shipyards. Another source of wealth, as communication by steam packet improved, was the tourist industry, rising to 30,000 by the eighties.

In Guernsey agriculture was more limited but improvement of the island cattle led to steady annual exports of about six hundred animals. Another new crop to be exported was grapes, grown under glass, and by 1874 the first 1,000 feet of semi-experimental tomatoes was planted. There was still overseas trading by merchant-adventurers, who sent out fast cutters on a triangular run to Spain for wine, then to South America for coffee, sugar and hides, and so to Antwerp and Hamburg for grain. Again, to supply and repair their ships, there was a shipbuilding industry which flourished for the first half of the century.

Locally-built ships too, were used in the carriage of very durable granite from St Sampson's area to London and south-east England for road surfacing, and by 1910 this trade had reached 458,000 tons. Herm and Alderney, too, had their share of this trade. A useful additional income in the years before the war came from the outdoor tomato crop in Jersey, and in Guernsey from the export of flowers and bulbs.

The First World War was an inconvenient interlude in Jersey's day to day existence, with about 6,500 men serving in the forces, but the Guernseymen suffered more severely as they formed their own unit, the Royal Guernsey Light Infantry, which suffered very heavy casualties in the battles of Cambrai and Lys.

After the war and a brief period of slump the Guernsey tomato industry boomed, using every modern technique and rising in output to 35,000 tons by 1939. The export of Guernsey cattle also thrived, as did the Jersey breed, with about 1,000 Jerseys being exported each year. In Jersey, too, the early potato crop proved a winner, averaging 10,000 tons annually.

The spread of the tomato industry in Guernsey and the booming Jersey tourist industry led to a proliferation of house building and

tended to spoil the natural scenic beauty of the islands. Yet in Guernsey a Natural Beauties Committee was set up to check this development, an example of the expansion of the civil service, which in both large islands provided the framework of a modern state. Committees were formed to control the 'nationalised' industries; in Jersey the airport, in Guernsey the airport, waterworks and electricity station.

The authorities remained very conscious of their ancient rights and liberties, so that when, in 1923, the English Treasury demanded an annual payment of £600,000 from the islands to the Exchequer, there was stubborn resistance. The trouble was ended in 1927 when the Treasury accepted once-for-all-gifts, a case which confirmed the constitutional independence of the islands and led to harmonious working with the Home Office.

The German Occupation

At the outbreak of the Second World War there was, at first, little change; in fact the islands were advertised as excellent for a wartime holiday. But with the end of the 'phoney' war and the German advance across Europe to Dunkirk the situation seemed serious and the island leaders waited for decisions as to their fate. By the middle of June 1940 the Admiralty advised that the islands were untenable and the British agreed to demilitarise them. The regular troops and the lieutenant-governors were withdrawn and there was considerable indecision whether to evacuate the islands or not. Originally it was decided to limit evacuation to children and men of fighting age, but in the end 10,000 were evacuated from Jersey and 17,000 from Guernsey. In Alderney, much closer to the enemy, after Judge French had put the problem to the people, the decision to evacuate was unanimous and the island was left deserted as the evacuees made their way, each with two suitcases, to Weymouth.

The threatening situation led to a reorganisation of government. In Guernsey, though the bailiff and States remained as the official government, a controlling committee of eight, presided over by Major Sherwill, was set up. Similarly, in Jersey the government was centralised and Bailiff Coutanche presided over a superior council.

Days of suspense followed until 28 June, when the Germans sent planes to raid St Peter Port and St Helier. News of this raid caused the BBC to publicise the demilitarisation of the islands whereupon the Germans decided upon invasion. On 30 June Luftwaffe aircraft landed on Guernsey airport and soon the dazed islanders found German orders

in the local paper, a curfew imposed and Germans moving by car and lorry around the island, while the islanders themselves were obliged to walk or ride bicycles. The next day the Jerseymen also surrendered to the German ultimatum and found themselves committed to the same situation—the central government to carry on provided that the Germans approved of the orders. The island authorities thus found themselves in the position of buffers between the Germans and the population, endeavouring not to provoke the Germans, yet at the same time keeping as much power in their own hands as possible. The Germans then put a small garrison on Sark where Dame Hathaway met the German commandant with fluent German and no intention of being brow-beaten.

The first phase of the occupation lasted until June 1941, the Germans behaving very correctly and endeavouring to pass off their presence as a copybook occupation. One of the difficulties for the island authorities was the landing of spies or commandos, as they feared that such actions would provoke the Germans and upset their own delicate balancing act. There were other problems too, the Nazi anti-Semitic laws, Press censorship, fraternisation by some local girls and women, and the billeting of troops. All this undermined morale, which was not helped by the Battle of Britain when German bombers and fighters roared over the islands. However, they were cheered up by RAF leaflets giving details of, the raids and carrying a message from King George VI.

After August 1940 the German military command was separated from the civilian government and the situation deteriorated. Fortunately the German commander-in-chief was von Schmettow, a fair-minded man who tried to see that the islands did not suffer full occupation treatment.

The islanders' main problem was food, both the growing of supplies for themselves and the prevention of its seizure by the Germans. Jersey had the advantage, as it was easy to switch to the growing of grain, while the best crop from the Guernsey glasshouses was sweet corn. Raymond Falla and John Joualt went on a buying mission to France and by clever dealing managed to make contacts and purchases. But stocks of all the main commodities became less and less, barter was a common practice, and ingenious substitutes were tried, such as tea from blackberry leaves.

At this time the German authorities grew stricter, angered by the escape of eight men and by the landing of a fact-finding mission of two English officers who were caught and sent to the Cherche Midi prison in Paris. There was sent, too, Ambrose Sherwill whose place as president of the controlling committee was taken by Sir John Leale, who in his

dealings with the Germans stuck strictly to the terms of the Hague Convention. Bailiff Coutanche followed the same policy in Jersey.

German Defences

After the German attack on Russia the situation in the islands changed dramatically. Hitler decided to construct the Atlantic Wall and in that immense scheme of fortification the islands were very important, as Hitler was certain that the English would attempt to recapture them. This policy was carried to incredible lengths, so that German officers who opposed Hitler's obsession referred to his 'island madness'. Thousands of troops, masses of artillery, shiploads of cement and large numbers of Todt workers were brought over, the effect of which was to pin down 36,000 men who would have been of more use elsewhere.

These defence systems had ugly and damaging effects on the islands, particularly in Alderney, which had a fire-control system like a great battleship. Huge tunnels and underground hospitals were constructed and for this work some 18,000 foreign workers were brought over. Many acts of surreptitious kindness were done for them, but in Alderney, with its camps and concentration camps, nothing could be done to relieve the terror and starvation.

With the conversion of the islands into important fortresses, there were natural consequences. Some of the more daring islanders tried with success to get information out. Secondly, as the Germans feared attack, they tightened up their control of the islands, attempting to confiscate all wireless sets and destroying any houses which overlooked gun emplacements. Then in September 1942 Hitler ordered that anyone born in England should be deported to internment camps in Germany. Some 1,200 people from Jersey and 800 from Guernsey were taken, causing much sorrow and distress.

Thirdly, there were commando raids on the Casquets and Sark which caused the Germans to double the guards and deport anyone who had ever held the King's commission. But for most islanders these years were ones of monotonous restrictions and scarce and dreary food, seriously affecting the people's health despite the ingenuity of chemists' attempts to ameliorate their condition.

There were, however, compensations, especially after the German defeat in North Africa when many of the occupying troops realised that the war was lost. The fiery disciplinarian General Muller was sent to the Russian front and copies of *Guns*, the Guernsey underground

newspaper, were circulated to cheer up the islanders. Unfortunately the editor, Charles Machon, was betrayed and died in prison. Other islanders caught possessing a wireless set, helping Todt workers, or committing minor acts of sabotage were sent to concentration camps.

D-Day and After

The third phase of the war for the islands started with the D-Day landings. This had been preceded by RAF attacks on the German radar installations and the islanders also heard wave after wave of planes going over on the night of 5 June 1944. Hitler, anticipating an attack on the islands, ordered them to be defended to the last, but General Jodl more realistically removed the Todt workers, as he expected the Allies would try to starve the islands out.

Buoyed up by the news of the Allied landings, the islanders hopefully expected early release, but all they got was a fanatical Nazi, Huffmeier, as naval commander and an increased shortage of rations, as Churchill insisted that the Germans were solely responsible for the food of the areas they occupied.

Eventually news of the islanders' plight got through to London and the bailiffs were authorised to contact the Red Cross. After many disappointments the Red Cross ship *Vega* reached Guernsey and the islanders looked with delight on the contents of their Red Cross parcels. Nevertheless, starvation had come very close and the islanders' rejoicings as they heard of the Allies' advances were tempered by fear of what might happen since their new commander-in-chief, Huffmeier, declared that he had only one aim—to hold out and use the islands as a bargaining counter.

Liberation

At last on 8 May the bailiff of Guernsey and Sir John Leale were summoned to German HQ to be told that the war was over. Even then Huffmeier quibbled and the surrender documents were only signed early in the morning of 9 May.

With the liberation there were many problems for the island authorities and the British forces to solve; German prisoners, food shortage, the concrete, mines and wire, and evacuees eager to return. However the debris was cleared up, the King and Queen came over, Whitehall officials arrived with a grant to redeem the worthless marks and a loan to help the States meet their debts.

There were demands for revenge on known collaborators, but this move was happily squashed and the islands quickly got down to the job of reconstruction. Seed potatoes were planted, tomato seedlings were pricked out, hotels were supplied and shops were restocked, and by 1947 the larger islands had regained their pre-war prosperity. Jersey sent away 24,000 tons of potatoes and nearly 29,000 tons of tomatoes in 1946, also 2,000 cattle per year. In Guernsey by 1947, seven million 12-lb chips of tomatoes were exported. The tourist industry also picked up, with 224,000 people visiting Jersey and 67,000 coming to Guernsey, rather to the islanders' surprise.

The reconstruction of Alderney was a very big task, since it had become a desolate island of barbed wire and concrete bunkers, derelict houses and waste farms. Heavily subsidised by the British government, parties of islanders returned and reclaimed the land on a communal basis. Guernsey cattle were brought over, market-gardening was started, and by 1947 the islanders had begun to stand on their own feet again.

Post-war Changes

Meanwhile a movement grew to bring the islands' constitutions up to date. A commission was set up under Viscount Samuel and in the main his advice was accepted. As regards the judiciary the jurats should be only judges of fact, leaving the experienced bailiffs to interpret the law. As regards the States, the jurats and rectors should no longer be members while the number of popularly elected deputies should be increased, in Jersey to twenty-eight and in Guernsey to thirty-three. The twelve Jersey constables were retained, as were ten of the Guernsey *Douzaine* representatives. To ensure continuity, twelve senators in Jersey and twelve *conseillers* in Guernsey were added. In Alderney the reforms were more far-reaching; a court was set-up with a chairman and six jurats, and the States of Alderney with a president and nine deputies. For finance Alderney came under Guernsey, a situation which is being queried at the present time.

In Jersey this brought some shrewd businessmen into power and the island economy boomed, with the number of visitors rising to over half a million in 1964, a figure which has since been surpassed. The finance for this came not only from island sources but also from outside investments. Finance houses and merchant banks settled in Jersey, as they did in Guernsey, owing to the favourable tax situation, and these invisible exports helped the islands' economies greatly. The Jersey farmers prospered, too, the tonnage of produce exported approaching

Plate 9 *A Guernsey field in early spring, newly planted with potatoes. The straight trunks and ascending branches of the hedgerow elms are a typical feature of the island landscape. In the background is St Martin's Church* (C. Toms)

Plate 10 *Picking early daffodils in a Guernsey field. When picked, the blooms are still in bud* (C. Toms)

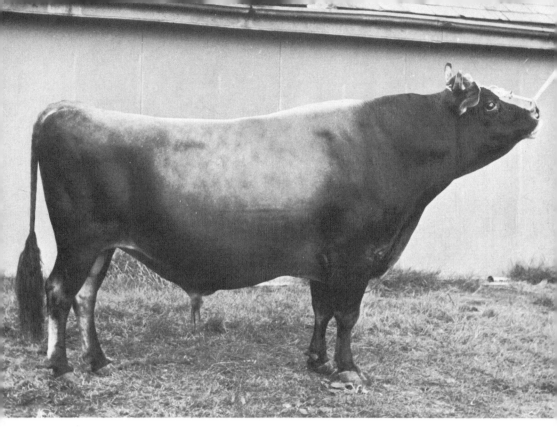

Plate 11 *A fine specimen of the Jersey breed of cattle. This champion bull is named 'Brilliant Victor'* (Le Brocq & Le Clercq)

Plate 12 *A prize Guernsey cow. The two breeds are distinctly different and are strictly segregated. In Alderney and Sark the cattle are invariably Guernseys* (Guernsey Press Co)

Plate 13 *The Seigneur's Mill, Fief Saumarez, St Martin's, Guernsey* (C. Toms)

Plate 14 *Picking tomatoes in a Guernsey greenhouse. Note the method of training the stems, and the trays which convey the fruit to overseas markets* (C. Toms)

80,000 tons in 1963, and there continued to be a steady export of island cattle.

In Guernsey the pace of modernisation and prosperity was not so rapid but there was a steady rise in tomato exports and a big expansion of flower exports. The tourist industry also flourished, rising to 180,000 in 1964.

There were, however, still problems—a housing shortage and a land shortage, which led to the imposition of a ban on house-building for outsiders, and also to the classification of houses as either 'open-market' or 'closed market' for islanders and licence holders only. The population rose to 52,000 and led to a considerable strain on the social services.

The Common Market

The islands were at first worried by Britain's negotiations for entry into the Common Market but Geoffrey Rippon's securing of associated status for the islands gave them the best of both worlds, half in and half out of the market.

All in all, at the end of the era, the islands continued to be busy and prosperous and ready to try out new ideas: for example, in Guernsey and Jersey the creation of leisure centres at Beau Sejour and Fort Regent, and in Guernsey the construction of three marinas which attract annually more and more visiting yachtsmen. The Guernsey tomato growers have also experimented successfully with the growing of the plants in peat modules.

Yet they still face many problems: inflation and the rising cost of state services, foreign competition, the threat of strikes, and the challenge to the islands' tourist industry of packaged holidays and cheap fares to Continental resorts. There is also the challenge of diversification, to attract light industry and to achieve more balanced economies than horticulture and agriculture, tourism and banking have produced to date. However the islands, with their sturdy independence, have survived many testing times in the past and will surely continue to prosper in the years ahead.

4

Fauna and Flora

Nigel Jee

Naturalists have long been intrigued by islands and the natural history of the Channel Islands is particularly interesting for a variety of reasons, the most obvious of which is their geographical position. Although historically part of the British Isles, geographically the Channel Islands are off-islands of Normandy so that it is not surprising that their fauna and flora should show more affinity with Normandy and Brittany than with the United Kingdom. Another important factor is the mild oceanic climate which the islands enjoy. In this respect they resemble the Isles of Scilly, but while Channel Island summers tend to be slightly warmer, sunnier and drier than the Isles of Scilly, winters in the Channel Islands are not quite so mild and frosts, though rare, are more frequent than in Scilly.

Their mild climate places the Channel Islands just within the range of a number of southern animals and plants which would otherwise fail to reach the British Isles. The ormer, the green lizard and the Jersey fern are examples, described in this chapter, of species whose distribution in western Europe just reaches as far north as the Channel Islands. In each case, since the organism is at the extreme limit of its range, its hold on life is precarious and careful conservation will be needed if it is to survive.

Each of the islands has a strong character of its own, with a different history of land management and with a characteristic assemblage of wild plants and animals. Also, within each of the larger islands there is a wide variety of habitats, a few of which are described in the following pages. There is no limestone and the soil is generally slightly acid, but the acidity varies from the calcareous shell-sand of the commons to the acid soils of the cliffs. The degree of shelter varies from the wooded inland valleys of Jersey to the treeless, windswept Lihou Island off the west coast of Guernsey. As one stands on the craggy cliffs of gneiss overlooking Venus' Pool at the tip of Lihou, the nearest land due west is Newfoundland. There is nothing between but 2,800 miles (4,500km) of Atlantic rollers.

Native Flora

Despite their small size and the density of their human population, the position and climate of the Channel Islands and their varied habitats have enabled them to accumulate an extremely rich fauna and flora. The richness of the flora is particularly striking. Among the native flowering plants are representatives of most of the European geographical groups. Large lords-and-ladies and hare's-tail grass are plants of the Mediterranean Basin. Jersey thrift and Guernsey centaury, so named because these islands are respectively the plants' only British stations, belong to a geographical group characteristic of south and west Europe. Others in this group are sand crocus, autumn squill, ivy broomrape and pennywort—the plant with round, fleshy leaves which is so common on cliffs and walls in all the islands. Portland spurge and sea radish are native in those parts of Europe which have an oceanic climate. Galingale and Jersey orchid belong to a large group characteristic of central and southern Europe, while oak and wild thyme are plants of the forests of central Europe. Only the plants of mountains and the Arctic regions are missing.

Alien Flora

Besides the native plants, many exotic species have been introduced by gardeners and some have become so well naturalised that they appear to be wild. Alexanders, a handsome umbellifer with bright, shiny green leaves is common in hedges, field corners and on the cliffs in all the islands and has every appearance of being a native plant. Yet it was introduced several centuries ago as a vegetable; the sheathing leaf-bases were eaten like celery.

Three-cornered garlic, commonly known in the islands as 'stinking onions', is abundant in hedges, which are resplendent in April with the massed white umbels. The flowers resemble bluebells but the petals are white with a green vein. This Mediterranean plant is so thoroughly at home in the islands that it is hard to believe that it was unknown (or at least unrecorded) here before 1847, when it was first noticed in hedges in Guernsey.

The delightful daisy that grows in exuberant cushions on old walls in Jersey and Guernsey is a native of Mexico, *Erigeron mucronatus*. It first became naturalised in St Peter Port during the nineteenth century and its parachute seeds have since carried it to many suitable walls in both islands.

The mild and comparatively frost-free winters mean that gardeners can grow many plants which could not be contemplated in most parts of the United Kingdom. One which visitors can hardly fail to notice is the 'cabbage palm', *Cordyline australis*, which imparts a semi-tropical if slightly scruffy air to public parks and private gardens. A native of New Zealand, it has been planted in all the islands and occasionally seeds itself. The tall, conical tree echium comes from the Canaries, while the sprawling 'mesembryanthemum', *Carpobrotus edulis*, with fleshy leaves and showy yellow or bright pink flowers, which covers many unsightly German remains round the coasts, is a native of South Africa.

All these examples of exotic plants are frost-tender. Mesembryanthemum in particular is cut back by the slightest frost, which perhaps is just as well for its dense mats smother everything else. During the exceptionally hard winter of 1962–3 cabbage palm, mesembryanthemum, eucalyptus and whole hedges of shrubby veronica and escallonia were either killed or cut back while the native plants, even those with a southern European distribution, were unharmed. In Jersey, annual rock-rose and large lords-and-ladies were unscathed, while Jersey thrift actually increased its flowering. A spectacular casualty was hare's-tail grass, which is known to have been introduced into Jersey. It was nearly wiped out but made a dramatic recovery in 1964. Some animals also suffered; the stonechat, for instance, is only now regaining its former numbers.

Insects

The animals, like the plants, are more continental than British and no doubt a study of their European distribution would reveal, as in the case of the plants, a number of overlapping geographical groups. It is impossible to mention more than a handful of the thousands of insects that have been recorded—nearly 2,700 in Jersey alone. One of the most beautiful insects of any kind is the great green bush cricket. It is built like a grasshopper but the body is about 2in (5cm) long and the wing-span nearly 4in (10cm). It is bright green and has long, slender antennae. This magnificent insect is quite common in meadows and long grass in the four main islands.

Far less beautiful is the heavily built mole cricket, with velvety thorax and broad, spade-like front legs adapted, like those of the mole, for burrowing. It is not often seen, for it is nocturnal and spends the day underground, but it still burrows in damp meadows, especially by the

sides of ditches, in Jersey and Guernsey. Among the various short-horned grasshoppers is the blue-winged grasshopper, confined in the British Isles to the Isles of Scilly and the Channel Islands. It is not uncommon on the Guernsey cliffs and in the west of Jersey. At rest, the insect is difficult to see against its background, until it spreads its wings to reveal bright blue hind wings, bordered with black.

Butterflies have decreased everywhere in recent years and the Channel Islands are no exception, but they are still plentiful in some years, particularly in Sark, Herm and Jethou. Speckled wood, wall brown, gatekeeper and meadow brown are still common in all the islands, and red admiral and small tortoiseshell fairly common as well. The dark green fritillary is a large and handsome butterfly with dark green and silver patches on its hind underwings. It may be seen in Sark or Herm and is particularly abundant on Jethou. The painted lady is a migrant from the Mediterranean Basin which arrives in the islands in most years and the peacock, formerly rare, is now actually increasing.

Amphibians and Reptiles

The amphibia, like the butterflies, are suffering a general decline because of a lack of suitable breeding grounds. The common frog, though no longer common, may still be found in all the main islands, and Jersey, Guernsey and Sark also have the 'nimble frog', *Rana dalmatina*, a continental species which does not occur in the United Kingdom. It is a slender frog, whose exceptionally long legs enable it to jump an extra long distance. In Jersey its breeding places are becoming so rare that its survival is in danger. Its position in Guernsey is not clear as it tends to be confused with the common frog. Jersey alone has the common toad and the palmate newt, while Jersey and Guernsey have the smooth newt.

The only snake, the grass snake, is confined to Jersey, but the slow worm, which is often mistaken for a snake, occurs in all the islands. There are two lizards, both continental species. The wall lizard, confined to the rocky parts of one extensive stretch of cliffs in Jersey, is marbled brown and greyish green, and is well camouflaged against the lichen-covered rocks. The other species, the green lizard, is a strikingly beautiful animal of a brilliant emerald green. It may be seen in warm weather sunbathing on a limited stretch of the Guernsey cliffs and it occurs in many parts of Jersey, but its territory does not overlap that of the wall lizard.

Mammals

The distribution of animals within the Channel Islands is complicated and sometimes extremely puzzling. This may be illustrated
by some of the small mammals. The mole, for instance, is abundant
in Jersey and Alderney but mercifully unknown in the other islands.
Shrews are common in all the islands, searching busily among the roots
of the vegetation in fields and hedgebanks for the invertebrates which
form their food. In Guernsey, Alderney and Herm they are all the
white-toothed shrew, which does not occur in the United Kingdom
but is common in the adjacent parts of France. It lacks the red-tipped
teeth of the common British shrew. Jersey and Sark have a different
species, the lesser white-toothed shrew, which in western Europe extends
only as far north as the Loire, except for Ushant, Jersey, Sark and the
Isles of Scilly. Besides this species, Jersey alone also has the common
red-toothed shrew.

Some of the small mammals have been isolated on the various islands
long enough to have evolved recognisible island races. The white-
toothed shrews of Guernsey and Herm are on the average slightly
smaller than their continental relatives; they have been described as a
distinct subspecies but the difference is hardly sufficient to merit this.

A better case can be made out for the voles of Jersey and Guernsey.
The Jersey vole is a distinctive form of the bank vole which is widespread in Britain and Europe. It is a reddish rodent with ears clearly
visible and a fairly long tail. Guernsey, on the other hand, has a short-
tailed vole whose nearest relative lives as far away as the Orkneys. It
is an attractive little blunt-nosed creature whose small ears are almost
hidden in greyish-brown fur. It lives gregariously in shallow burrows
just beneath the surface of the ground or in runs made through matted
grass stems. It is very like the common European vole, *Microtus arvalis*,
but, like the Orkney vole, it is larger and darker. The Guernsey vole
has been described as a species, *Microtus sarnius*, but it is probably
better to regard it as a subspecies of *M. arvalis*. Perhaps this species
was once widespread in the British Isles, but died out in competition
with other voles which arrived later but never reached Guernsey or
the Orkneys. There are no voles at all in Sark and apparently none in
either Herm or Alderney.

It is tempting to try to explain the distribution of these animals by
changes in the sea-level during and after the Ice Age. The sea between
Jersey and Normandy is quite shallow and Jersey would have been

joined to the continent more recently than the other islands. Thus the mole would have been able to reach Jersey by land—but how did it get to Alderney which is separated from Cap de la Hague by deeper water?

If the bank vole arrived in the region at this time it would have been able to walk to Jersey, while the older-established short-tailed vole remained safely isolated from competition in Guernsey. But changes in sea-level are not sufficient to explain the strange distribution of shrews. Jersey's two species do not seem to compete with each other, although their ranges certainly overlap. And why does Sark have the same shrew as Jersey rather than that of its nearer neighbours, Guernsey and Herm? The possibility of accidental or deliberate introduction by man cannot be ruled out. The lesser white-toothed shrew may have arrived in Sark as a stowaway—perhaps in a truss of hay when Sark was colonised from Jersey in the sixteenth century.

Birds

Birds are so mobile that one would hardly expect them to remain isolated for long enough to form island races. A few of the smaller residents, such as the robin and blue tit, may possibly have done so, but if they have the differences are extremely small.

The tree creeper, which may be seen in suitable places in all the islands working its way spirally up the trunk of a tree and leaning on its stiff tail while it searches for insects in the bark, is not the same as the British tree creeper. It is the short-toed continental species, which differs mainly in its song and in having brownish rather than silvery flanks.

Although a number of non-British animals and plants have been mentioned, it must not be thought that these are more important than the host of ordinary species which make up the communities in the various habitats. A few of these habitats are briefly described below.

The Sea Shore

The rocky shores of the Channel Islands are rich hunting grounds for the marine biologist for the tidal range is exceptionally great, especially towards the south of the archipelago. Very roughly, the vertical distance between high and low water at spring tides is 20ft

(6m) in Alderney, 30ft (9m) in Guernsey and 40ft (12m) in Jersey. At low tide an enormous area of sand and rock is exposed, with rock pools alive with prawns, hermit crabs, blennies and sea anemones.

Seaweeds

The dominant plants on the rocky shores are the large, brown sea-weeds. The species are the same as will be found on most rocky shores in western Europe and they form the same horizontal belts along the shore, from the hanging tufts of channelled wrack which are only covered by high spring tides to the flat fronds of oarweed which are only exposed to the air at the lowest tides. Seaweed, or *vraic* as it is known in the islands, formerly had an important place in the economy, for it was spread on the land as manure. Oarweeds, particularly, grow very rapidly and after a life of two or three years, they are cast up by the autumn gales to form deep drifts in the bays and gullies. The many fine stone slipways were built for horse-drawn carts which were taken onto the beach and loaded high with *vraic*, often collected from the waves with enormous wooden rakes.

Where beds of muddy gravel are exposed at low tide it is common to find them covered by a plant with green, grass-like leaves. This is *Zostera*, or eel-grass. It is not a seaweed but a flowering plant; the only one that lives in the sea. The leaves are long and strap-shaped, with spikes of inconspicuous flowers at their bases. The commonest species has leaves about $\frac{1}{4}$in (6mm) broad, and grows, for instance, in Grouville Bay and St Aubin's Bay in Jersey, at Perelle and Bordeaux in Guernsey and on the extensive areas of shell-sand which are exposed at low spring tides near Vermerette beacon to the west of Herm. It used to be far more widespread but in 1935 it suddenly died off, apparently from some disease, and it is still recovering.

Flocks of brent geese regularly spend the winter grazing the *Zostera* beds of Jersey and Herm, after breeding in the high Arctic. The Herm flock, which numbers about 100, grazes the beds off the west coast. In Jersey, brent geese winter in Grouville and St Aubin's Bays. The Jersey flock has increased greatly in recent years; in the winter of 1973–4 there were over 1,000 birds. Brent geese have been visiting the Channel Islands for some time, for their bones have been found in a Bronze Age deposit at St Ouen's Bay.

Crustaceans

Space does not permit us to deal with all the barnacles, shrimps, prawns and squat lobsters which live between the tides, but mention may be made of a few of the crabs. The common shore crab can be found in pools or hiding under seaweed on all the coasts. The shell is dark green, up to 4in (10cm) across, with five sharp teeth each side in front. Young edible crabs may also be found—those on the shore would be about the same size as the shore crab but the shell is brown and the front edge has ten rounded lobes each side, like the edge of a pie-crust. In deep water the edible crab reaches a large size and is caught in crab pots and by skin divers. In Guernsey it is called the *chancre*. In Jersey, although young specimens are common on the shore, adult edible crabs are sufficiently rare for them to be known as Guernsey crabs. A possible reason is that the crabs of Jersey have to walk further to reach deep water.

Two other crabs sold in the markets are the 'lady crab' or fiddler, and the spider crab. The 'lady crab', reddish-brown with dark blue lines on the legs, is a swimming crab, the last pair of legs being broad and flat, like oars. It can be found on the lower part of the shore; when disturbed it sits back on its tail and makes free use of its nippers. The spider crab has a brick-red shell covered with hard spines, and long, slender legs which may span 24in (61cm). By way of camouflage it often has sponges and pieces of weed growing on its back. It can occasionally be found on the shore but those for sale in the markets will have been collected from deeper water by skin divers or caught in crab pots. It is a complicated business to extract the meat, but it is worth it for it is delicious.

Molluscs

Numerous species of winkles, whelks, top-shells and limpets inhabit the shore but again we can mention only a few. An experiment on the growth-rate of limpets was begun in Guernsey in 1971,[1] Guernsey limpets appear to grow far more slowly than is indicated by work elsewhere; indeed, some actually grew smaller.

There are several species of periwinkle, each favouring a particular level on the shore. Perhaps the most noticeable is the flat periwinkle which swarms over the two large seaweeds, bladder wrack and knotted wrack, at the half-tide level. It is a strongly built little shell, smooth

and round with a rounded top. It is commonly yellow or orange but the colour varies greatly and it may be red, olive green or mottled. In spite of its striking colours, it manages to resemble the gas bladders of the plants on which it feeds. The 'common periwinkle' of English books is not particularly common in the Channel Islands.

The top shells are more strictly confined to zones than the periwinkles. Most of the Channel Island species, from thick top shell which lives high on the shore, to large top shell below the low-water level, will be found in English reference books. One which does not occur in Great Britain and has no English name is *Gibbula pennanti*. It is similar to flat top shell but has no umbilicus (the hole in the centre of the base). It occupies a zone from the middle of the shore to the low-water mark of neap tides. We have mentioned several animals and plants which extend no further north than the Channel Islands but have a wide distribution further south. *Gibbula pennanti* is most unusual in being a truly local species. It is entirely confined to the Channel Islands and the Atlantic coast of France and Spain.

The top shells are important constituents of Herm's famous Shell Beach. This consists almost entirely of shells and fragments of shells, many of them species of deeper water which do not live between the tide marks. Besides periwinkles, limpets and top shells by the million, there are tellins and Venus shells, tusk shells like miniature elephants' tusks, giant whelks and tiny cowries. The traditional story is that these shells have been carried across the Atlantic and washed up on the Shell Beach by the Gulf Stream. The truth is more prosaic; they have been cast up from deeper water around Herm by storms and the strong tidal currents which sweep past the island at high and low water.

Finally, mention must be made of the ormer; one of the objects, like milk cans and cabbage walking sticks, by which tourists remember the islands. The ormer is related to the limpet but the shell is tightly curled at one end. This makes it ear-shaped; ormer is a contraction of *oreille de mer*. There is a row of holes, of which five are usually open, the old ones being filled in as fast as new holes are formed at the growing edge of the shell. Through these holes are discharged genital products, waste and sea water that has passed over the gills. The flat, muscular foot is eaten as a delicacy. It tastes something like veal, but it needs to be beaten and thoroughly cooked to make it tender enough to eat. On this foot the animal can move over the rocks at a surprising speed.

The ormer is a Mediterranean animal which extends up the Atlantic coast of Europe as far as the Channel Islands. The main population is in deeper water but at spring tides those that have come inshore are

exposed at low water. It is during the lowest of these tides in the winter that ormering has traditionally taken place. In recent years, and particularly since the advent of skin diving, there has been a sharp decline in the ormer population and steps have been taken in both bailiwicks to conserve the animal. At the time of writing, in Jersey ormers may be taken by shore gathering at low tide but not by divers. In Guernsey a complete three-year ban on ormering ended in November 1976.

Any species which is at the extreme edge of its geographical range is in a delicate position and the ormer, because of its method of fertilisation, is particularly vulnerable. Since eggs and sperms are discharged into the water and the sperms have to find the eggs in the vast volume of the sea, a reasonable number of eggs will be fertilised only if there is a good population of adults producing millions of eggs and sperms. For this reason, if the population is allowed to fall below a certain level, it will not replenish itself.

Sand Dunes and Commons

Apart from Sark, which is almost entirely surrounded by cliffs, all the main islands have extensive areas of dune vegetation. A walk from the beach onto one of these sandy areas will give an idea of how the sand has been colonised by plants.

Mobile Dunes

As one walks up a sandy beach towards the land, the first vegetation will be a few scattered plants growing among the dead seaweed thrown up by the tide. Typical of these drift-line plants are sea beet, sea sandwort and various species of orache. Luxurious cabbagy clumps of sea kale can occasionally be found on the drift-line and on shingle banks. Formerly rare, it sems to be increasing round Jersey, on the west coast of Guernsey and in Alderney.

Continuing inland from the drift-line one would formerly have climbed over a series of mobile dunes with tussocks of marram grass growing among the otherwise unprotected sand. Such dunes are becoming increasingly rare in the islands. This is partly due to the demand for building sand, but mainly because sea walls have been built all round the coasts to prevent erosion by the sea. In Jersey there is now a sea wall all round the sandy parts of the coast except for a small stretch of Grouville Bay. In Guernsey a few mobile dunes survive at Port Soif

and Grandes Rocques, reinforced by rubble which has been dumped as a defence against the sea; the dunes at L'Erée have been removed to make a car park. Only in Alderney and Herm do mobile dunes of any significance remain. In Herm they form a rim right round the northern part of the island. They are breached by an occasional storm, but in general they successfully defend the low-lying fixed dunes of Herm Common. In Alderney, Saye Bay and the western half of Braye Bay are still backed by mobile dunes where sea spurge, sea holly, fennel and sea bindweed grow among the tussocks of marram.

Fixed Dunes

Further inland the sand is entirely covered by vegetation. The most extensive areas of fixed dunes are in the west of Jersey and the north of Guernsey and Herm. South of Jersey airport is an impressive area of dunes, Les Quennevais, rising to 259ft (79m) and continuous with a low-lying sandy area which extends the whole length of St Ouen's Bay. This is the home of Jersey thrift—the only place in the British Isles where it grows. It is a larger plant than the common thrift and has broader leaves with a characteristically tangled appearance. While common thrift begins to flower in April, Jersey thrift is not out until June. It used to cover large areas of western Jersey, but being at the extreme northern tip of its range it is sensitive to changes in the environment and today it is abundant only on the western side of the Quennevais and in St Ouen's Bay.

L'Ancresse Common, in the north of Guernsey, is a rolling expanse of dune turf used as a golf course, while Herm Common is a sandy plain, low-lying except for two hillocks, Le Grand and Le Petit Monceau.

In most of these areas the sand contains fragments of shell and lime-loving plants such as rue-leaved saxifrage and burnet rose flourish, especially on the more recently fixed dunes. On the older dunes the lime tends to be leached from the surface and the soil becomes acid. This is the case at St Ouen, where the dune soil is basic near the sea but acid island.[2] At L'Ancresse there is a similar graduation from west to east, the soil becoming acid towards Fort Le Marchant. On Herm Common the sand is particularly rich in shell fragments and the lime-indicating salad burnet and burnet rose grow, and yet in the middle of the common there is a tiny *Sphagnum* bog.

The vegetation of the fixed dunes depends very much on the amount of grazing, particularly by rabbits which were introduced for meat and fur, and for sport, in about the twelfth century. At first they were

Fig 15 Flowers of the coast (A–F): A, autumn squill, *Scilla autumnalis*, x$\frac{1}{2}$; B, hare's-tail grass, *Lagurus ovatus*, x1; C, burnet rose, *Rosa pimpinellifolia*, x$\frac{1}{2}$; D, sea radish, *Raphanus maritimus*, x$\frac{1}{2}$; E, dwarf pansy, *Viola kitaibeliana*, x1; F, sand crocus, *Romulea columnae*, x1 (*Patience Ryan*)

closely guarded in warrens or *garennes* but they soon escaped and, being adaptable creatures, are now to be found on the cliffs, in cultivated land and even on the beach. In particular, the rabbit is abundant on the sandy commons where its close grazing enables small plants, which would otherwise be crowded out by coarse grasses, to flourish. The rabbit's ecological importance was seen in Jersey in the late 1950s when there was an outbreak of myxomatosis. Mrs. F. Le Sueur describes how on the cliffs, for instance, there was at first a profuse flowering of plants which had for the first time been allowed to grow to their full size, but soon coarse grasses such as cock's-foot began to crowd out the more interesting plants.[3]

The rabbits are now back in force and where they keep the dune turf closely cropped the flora is astonishingly rich. If one were to go down on hands and knees and examine a square yard of such turf it would probably contain from twenty to twenty-five species of flowering plant, as well as mosses and lichens. Very often the commonest is buck's-horn plantain, the small plantain with side lobes to its leaves. In spring there is early forget-me-not and a minute pansy, *Viola kitaibeliana*, which grows in Jersey, Guernsey, Herm and the Isles of Scilly, but not on the British mainland. The flowers are cream, tinged with purple, and the whole plant is often less than an inch high. Later there is autumn squill, which in spite of its name flowers in the height of the summer, and wild thyme.

The rose with large, cream flowers and exceedingly prickly stems is burnet rose. It spreads by suckers and forms dense mats which vary in height according to the degree of grazing. It can be found over the whole of the St Ouen's area, on Herm Common and the western end of L'Ancresse Common, and it also grows in Sark.

Another attractive plant which grows in short dune turf is hare's-tail grass. It is a soft, hairy annual and the flowering stem has a single, oval, woolly head which looks like a rabbit's tail. It is so abundant in parts of Jersey and Guernsey that it is difficult to imagine that it has not always been there, yet it is known to have been introduced into Jersey in the late 1870s. Starting from a tiny patch at St Ouen, it spread over the whole of St Ouen's Bay and beyond, and is still spreading. The seed almost certainly came from Guernsey, where it grows on dunes in the north and west. It may be native there but it has been suggested that it may have been introduced accidentally from Gascony in the early middle ages when there was a flourishing trade between Gascony and Guernsey.[4] Grand Havre was the main anchorage in those days and the hare's-tail heads still dance on the dunes nearby.

Fig 16 Hedgerow and meadow flowers (G–L): G, large lords-and-ladies, *Arum italicum*, x$\frac{1}{2}$; H, Jersey fern, *Anogramma leptophylla*, x1; I, wall pennywort, *Umbilicus rupestris*, x$\frac{1}{2}$; J, three-cornered garlic, *Allium triquetrum*, x$\frac{1}{2}$; K, Jersey orchid, *Orchis laxiflora*, x$\frac{1}{2}$; L, Alexanders, *Smyrnium olusatrum*, x$\frac{1}{2}$ (I, Susan Jee; G, H, J, K, L, Patience Ryan)

Snails abound on the shell sand, for there is plenty of material with which to build their own shells. Pointed, banded and brown-lipped snails are common, but perhaps the most interesting is the sandhill snail, *Theba pisana*, which can sometimes be seen swarming over tall plants such as sea radish, fennel and marram; as well as feeding on them it climbs them in summer to escape from the hot ground. The shell is flattish and cream-coloured, with a variable pattern of spiral black or brown lines and short oblique streaks. In Jersey, which is probably the most northerly place where the snail exists as a native, colonies may be seen at Grouville Bay and St Clement's Bay.[5] If hare's-tail grass was introduced from Guernsey to Jersey, the sandhill snail had a few years previously travelled in the opposite direction, for in 1860 it was introduced into Guernsey. An attempt to establish it on the east coast failed but a colony at Vazon Bay prospered and has spread north to Port Soif and Portinfer. In Alderney there is a colony, presumably also introduced, at Platte Saline, feeding on the sea kale which is spreading there.

The Cliffs

All the islands have considerable stretches of unspoilt cliffs; besides providing magnificent scenery they form an unofficial nature reserve and the steeper parts support the only truly natural vegetation, unaffected by man's activities, in the islands. In Jersey the cliffs stretch the entire length of the north coast, with smaller stretches on the headlands of the south-west. Parts of the lofty north-facing cliffs are unusual in harbouring shade-loving and even woodland plants such as dog's mercury and Lent lily; royal fern, once frequent in most of the islands, survived the Victorian fern craze in the most inaccessible parts of these cliffs.

In Guernsey, the cliffs extend along the south coast from Pleinmont to St Martin's Point, then north as far as Fort George. The wildest parts are towards Pleinmont on the south coast, while the sheltered east-facing cliffs to the north and south of Fermain Bay have a character very much their own. Bracken, wood sage, blackthorn, ash and oak grow right down to the high-water mark. The view from the 'Pine Forest', looking through the trees across the Russel to Herm and Sark, is particularly fine.

The south coast of Herm has cliffs very similar to those of Guernsey, and like Guernsey there is a good cliff path. Sark is entirely cliff-girt and in Alderney the cliffs extend from Essex Castle, round the south

Plate 17 *La Seigneurie, Sark, home of the Seigneur. The present building dates largely from the eighteenth century, though the tower dates from the nineteenth. The building is set in gracious gardens, the entrance to which forms the frame for this picture* (C. Toms)

Plate 18 *La Maison de Haut, St Peter-in-the-Wood, a typical Guernsey farmhouse. The so-called Norman arch is a feature of island domestic architecture, like the granite chimney stacks and the stone masonry of this building dating from about 1650* (C. Toms)

Plate 19 *Bon Air, St Martin's, Guernsey, built about 1820 by Daniel de Lisle Brock, Bailiff of Guernsey, 1821–42. It stands in one of the island's most extensive grounds* (C. Toms)

coast and north again as far as Clonque. The scenery round Telegraph Bay is particularly magnificent and from the headland to the west of this is a view of Les Etacs, surrounded in the breeding season by a cloud of gannets.

The gannet is a large sea bird, about the size of a goose, white except for the black tips to the long, slender wings. When fishing it dives headlong with half-closed wings, closing them just before it enters the sea and making an impressive splash. The Alderney gannets took up residence during the Second World War, before which small parties were sometimes seen fishing off Alderney, though the nearest breeding colony was on Grassholm, 195 miles (314km) away. When the people of Alderney returned after the German occupation they found a large colony on Ortac, an isolated stack between Alderney and the Casquets, and a smaller one on Les Etacs, or the 'Garden Rocks', just off the south-west corner of Alderney. By 1966 there were 2,000 pairs on Ortac and Les Etacs, covering practically every inch of rock. After breeding, the gannets disperse until the following season and young birds ringed in Alderney have been recovered from places as far apart as the North Sea and the coast of West Africa.

To see the cliffs at their best they should be visited in May or early June, when there are drifts of sea campion, thrift and ox-eye daisies, banks of gorse in full bloom and sheets of bluebells in the more sheltered places. At the foot of the cliffs the only plants that can grow on the spray-washed rock faces are lichens, but a fern, sea spleenwort, grows in crevices together with a few flowering plants, such as samphire, thrift and sea plantain. This last is the food plant of the Glanville fritillary, a small marbled butterfly which reaches as far north as the Isle of Wight. It breeds on the lower slopes of the Guernsey cliffs and also in one part of Jersey. It may be seen on the wing in May and June.

Higher up the cliff the vegetation is more varied. Among the cushions of thrift and sea campion are plants which also grow inland—ivy, bramble, pennywort and gorse. The *Sedum*, so common on the drier parts of the cliffs is English stonecrop, a cushion perennial with small egg-shaped leaves. The star-like flowers are white, tinged with pink. Inland, it grows on old walls and roofs. Growing between the stonecrop cushions there may be Portland spurge, autumn squill and perhaps sand crocus. Like autumn squill, this is a bulbous plant with narrow wiry leaves. But while autumn squill has a stem bearing several purple flowers, sand crocus has solitary star-like flowers. When closed they are green and difficult to find but in the April sun they open to reveal the very pale purple petals, yellow at the base and with purple veins.

Sand crocus is common on parts of the cliffs and dunes in all the Channel Islands.

A delight of some of the Jersey headlands is annual rock-rose. The petals, which open and fall the same day, are pale yellow with a red spot at the base. Apart from a small colony on the Alderney cliffs, it grows in none of the other islands.

Contrasting with the deep gold of the gorse is the pale yellow of broom. In exposed parts of the cliffs there is a prostrate variety of the common broom which presses itself closely to the rocks over which it grows. It is frequent at the Pleinmont end of the Guernsey cliffs, on the south-west cliffs of Alderney and in parts of Jersey—for instance, the cliffs near La Corbière.

The gorse-covered cliff-tops provide a habitat, all too rare in the British Isles today, for the stonechat. The cock bird with his black head, white neck and rusty-red breast is still a familiar sight as he sits on a gorse bush making a noise like two pebbles chinking together. The stonechat was almost wiped out by the severe winter of 1962–3 but it recovered and is frequent again in all the islands, though still only a few pairs breed in Sark.

A much rarer bird of gorsy cliff-tops is the Dartford warbler. It is a very small bird, darker than other warblers, with an extremely long tail which is flicked erect from time to time. It breeds in Jersey and Alderney, and since 1961 on the south cliffs of Guernsey.

Hedgerows

Jersey and Guernsey were once well wooded; indeed, apart from the sandy areas they were probably entirely forested. Today, Jersey is the only island with any considerable woodland, though it represents a small proportion of the area of the island. The various valleys carrying streams south into St Aubin's Bay are wooded, as are those on the north coast leading down to Grève de Lecq, Rozel and St Catherine's Bay. Dog's mercury and wood sorrel, woodland plants which are common in the British Isles and on the continent, are in the Channel Islands confined to Jersey and even there they are rare. Jersey is also the only island where the daffodil is truly wild. Many old cultivated varieties have become thoroughly naturalised in fields and hedges in all the islands, but in early spring some of the wooded valleys and cliffs of Jersey are carpeted with wild daffodils, or Lent lilies.

The scarcity of woodland makes hedgerows with trees assume an extra importance. Besides giving the islands a deceptively wooded

appearance, they enable those animals and plants which formerly lived in the woods to survive. By far the most abundant hedgerow tree is the elm. It was planted extensively, perhaps mainly in the eighteenth century, to shelter cider orchards and cattle. Two kinds of elm were commonly planted; very often a whole hedgerow is of one kind or the other. The first is an extremely upright tree with a straight trunk and steeply ascending branches, particularly towards the tips. It is usually called by nurserymen the 'Jersey elm', although it grows in all the islands and is particularly abundant in Guernsey, where it replenishes itself in the hedges by suckering.

The second elm has larger leaves and a much more floppy appearance. The trunk is gnarled and tortuous, and the branches droop. It seems to be a hybrid elm whose nearest parallel is in the neighbouring parts of Normandy.

The elm, particularly the Jersey form, is ideally suited to the Channel Islands. The small leaves are not easily damaged by the wind; they appear late in the year, missing the spring gales, and the tree retains its leaves late into the autumn when there is usually a spell of calm, fine weather. Most unfortunately the aggressive strain of Dutch elm disease, which has wiped out so many elms in the United Kingdom, struck Jersey in 1974 and many thousands of infected trees had to be felled. At the time of writing it appears that the prompt action taken by the States of Jersey has been successful and that the worst is over. The aggressive strain has not yet reached Guernsey, although a milder form of the disease, which is not fatal, has been prevalent in both islands for several years.

Ivy is abundant in the hedges, on walls, cliffs and quarries, or just sprawling over the ground under trees. The strange, purplish, leafless spikes of orchid-like flowers which grow among the ivy are ivy broomrape, a parasite on its roots.

The hedgebanks beneath the trees are the home of lords-and-ladies. The common species, both with and without spots, occurs and there is also a larger species, *Arum italicum*. This is a plant of southern Europe which also grows on the south coast of England, never far from the sea. The leaves are light green, without spots, and are well developed in November, while those of common lords-and-ladies do not appear until the new year.

Among the ferns are hart's-tongue, black and lanceolate spleenwort, male fern and, of course, bracken. The Jersey fern, most unusual in being an annual, is known on a dozen stretches of hedgebank in Jersey and one in Guernsey. Like so many southern species its growth is in the

winter; the delicately minute sterile fronds appear in November and December, followed by the fruiting fronds which ripen in April. Here, at its most northerly point in western Europe, it was badly affected by the severe winter of 1962–3. It has since recovered but is now in danger from heavy traffic and weedkillers.

Woodmice and shrews burrow in the hedgebanks and emerge at dusk, while barn owls patrol the hedges in search of them. The only resident owl, the barn owl, also feeds on voles from the meadows, small birds and beetles. There are thought to be thirty or forty pairs in Jersey, and there are certainly far fewer than this in the other islands. Until 1951 all the barn owls were of the light-breasted race but since then an increasing number of the continental dark-breasted race have turned up, and in Sark a mixed pair set up home in 1971.

Bats also patrol the hedges and lanes after dark. The pipistrelle is common in all the islands; the greater horseshoe and long-eared bats have been seen, rarely, in Jersey and Guernsey.

Meadows

The final example of a habitat is the low-lying meadows which are scattered in parts of Jersey and Guernsey. There are extensive areas around Vazon and L'Erée in Guernsey, where the drainage is too poor to permit mowing until late summer. In May and June orchids, lady's smock, bugle and ragged robin can flower unchecked, with yellow flag in the wetter corners. The dominant plant is often galingale, a tall sedge with a mass of flowering spikes radiating from the top of the three-cornered stem. It spreads by rhizomes and was formerly used for stuffing horse collars and saddles but now it is simply a weed. A more serious weed is hemlock water-dropwort, a large umbellifer whose swollen roots, which resemble parsnips, are deadly poisonous.

In May and June some of the meadows are transformed to sheets of purple by the Jersey orchid, *Orchis laxiflora*. The deep purple flowers, each with a short blunt spur, are well spaced out along the flowering spike which may stand 2ft (61cm) or more high. This handsome orchid grows as far north as Belgium but is confined in the British Isles to Jersey and Guernsey. In both islands it is suffering from the draining and development of the meadows and is now confined in Jersey to two main areas.

In the winter the soil is too wet to support the weight of the cattle and the meadows are left to the snipe and, when the weather is severe elsewhere, to large flocks of lapwing, fieldfare and redwing.

Study and Conservation of the Fauna and Flora

The senior 'learned society' is the Société Jersiaise, founded in 1873, which is concerned with the study of the history, archaeology, geology and natural history of Jersey. Papers and reports on these subjects are published in the *Annual Bulletin*. The society's headquarters are at 9 Pier Road, St Helier, where there is a comprehensive museum, library and art gallery. The society also owns many of the prehistoric remains of Jersey, including La Hougue Bie, where there are further specialised museums.

La Société Guernesiaise, founded in 1882, covers the bailiwick of Guernsey. Its office is at the Guille-Allès Library, St Peter Port. There are sections covering the various branches of natural history, history and archaeology, and papers are published annually in the *Report and Transactions*.

Much younger but extremely active is the Alderney Society, founded in 1966. It takes an interest in all aspects of local research, becomes politically active when it feels that Alderney's heritage is being threatened, and runs an excellent museum in the Old School, High Street. Finally, La Société Sercquiaise was founded, with similar aims, in 1975. The address of the honorary secretary is La Perronerie, Sark.

The early Channel Island naturalists were mainly concerned with classifying the animals and plants and many lists were published. These are still being enlarged but today the emphasis is more on ecology— the ways in which animals and plants depend upon each other and their environment. Only in the case of insects, where hundreds of species probably remain to be discovered, is the emphasis still on classification.

Amenity Societies

All the above societies are concerned with the natural heritage and have taken action to preserve it on various occasions. But the two bodies which are primarily concerned with the environment are the national trusts in the two main islands. Both are independent bodies. The National Trust for Jersey was founded in 1936 by a group of islanders who were concerned at the despoliation of the island by uncontrolled building. Its first property, Le Don Le Gallais, consists of wooded slopes in La Vallée des Vaux, immediately to the north of St Helier. Other properties followed by gift and purchase, until by 1973 the trust owned forty-six properties scattered throughout the island. The office is at the Museum, 9 Pier Road.

The National Trust of Guernsey, founded in 1960, has similar aims. Its first property was a wooded valley, Le Vau de Monel, at Pleinmont. Other properties are on the south cliffs, in the Talbot Valley and elsewhere. The trust also runs, in co-operation with La Société Guernesiaise, a folk museum at Saumarez Park and makes representations to the States from time to time on matters of amenity. The address of the honorary secretary is Les Mouilpieds, St Martin's.

Conservation

The greatest threat to the animal and plant life is undoubtedly the destruction or modification of the various habitats by building, drainage and pressure of traffic. The importance of hedgerows has already been mentioned. Some hedges are being removed to make the fields larger but a more serious threat is from chemical sprays which kill the protecting vegetation and allow the banks to crumble into the lanes. Jersey fern is particularly vulnerable to spraying and an encouraging sign is that the St Helier authorities have agreed to give it maximum protection. In Guernsey the authorities have also been co-operative, for instance by agreeing not to spray or mow certain areas of coastal grassland.

Perhaps the two most threatened habitats at present are wetland and dune grassland. The water table in the low-lying areas is being steadily lowered and few ponds or reed-beds remain. Many insects, all the amphibia and some birds depend for their survival on these few areas. Apart from the resident reed warblers, moorhens and mallard, a host of passage migrants visit the reed-beds in spring and autumn. The largest natural expanse of fresh water in the Channel Islands is La Mare au Seigneur (St Ouen's Pond) on the landward side of the Five Mile Road. Since 1950, through the kindness of the seigneur of St Ouen, this and the surrounding reed-beds have been run as a nature reserve and bird observatory by the Société Jersiaise. Not far away are two fields which were bought in 1972 by the National Trust for Jersey in order to preserve the Jersey orchid.

In Guernsey a nature reserve is run by the ornithological section of La Société Guernesiaise at St Sampson's Marais, on land owned by Major T. D. Ogier. A general lowering of the water table in the area made it necessary in 1973 to excavate a new pond and this work has been rewarded by an upsurge in breeding and migrant birds. La Société is also the beneficiary of the Silbe Nature Reserve, set up in the Quanteraine Valley, St Peter's, by Mrs K. E. M. Silten.

Dune and coastal grassland are being destroyed by the sheer pressure

of trampling and, more especially, cars. The turf is thin and the soil dry, and wherever cars are able to drive on the headlands and commons, bare sand or rock rapidly follow. On one or two occasions rare plants have been saved by transplanting them to similar sites where there is less pressure, but this is usually unsuccessful and is no substitute for preserving the whole community.

Finally, there has been a drastic reduction in the number of sea birds breeding on the off-islands. The speedboat has brought all the reefs and islets within easy reach of the main islands and disturbance during the breeding season has reduced puffins, razorbills, guillemots and common terns to a fraction of their former numbers.

Burhou, an uninhabited island two miles north-west of Alderney, is a natural bird sanctuary with large breeding colonies of puffins and storm petrels, and smaller numbers of razorbills, oystercatchers and shags. The puffins, which breed in underground burrows, used to number tens of thousands; now they may be numbered in hundreds. The storm petrel colony, breeding in holes in rocks and ruined walls, was estimated after the Second World War at 10,000 birds; in 1973 there were thought to be only sixty pairs. Great black-backed gulls may be partly to blame for the decline but there would be an excellent case for closing the island to visitors during the breeding season.

Acknowledgements
The author is most grateful for the help given him by Mrs Frances Le Sueur and Mr John Perry of Jersey, Mr Roger Brehaut and Dr R. H. Le Pelley of Guernsey and Mr Ken Wilson of Alderney.

Notes to this chapter are on pages 242–3.

5

Farming and Horticulture

Peter J. Girard

It is generally believed that the first European farmers were the Neolithic peoples who lived during the transition period when hunting tribes were gradually turning their attention to growing crops and keeping domesticated animals. In these islands it is highly probable that the 'slash and burn' technique was used and when they had eventually exhausted the soil's reserves the tribesmen moved on, leaving the natural vegetation to grow before returning possibly some ten to fifteen years later. This could well be checked by examining the results of borings made in the island's deep peat deposits.

In time, these primitive methods of 'farming' gave way to a more settled existence and it has been suggested that these clearings were often associated with megalithic structures. No doubt well positioned as regards defence, water supply and reasonable shelter, they may well have formed the basis of at least part of the parochial divisions of the islands, which are believed to have been superseded by the fief system introduced by the Normans. Although there is little doubt that by means of tithes and other forms of feudal dues and services, the subjects of feudal seigneurs were made to contribute extremely liberally to the comforts and well-being of their seigneurs, yet there is no evidence of ill-treatment of serfs.

In fact, as long as dues and tithes were paid and services rendered by tenants of the strips, they were assured of considerable security of tenure. Indeed, there was far less distinction of class among the Normans than among the English of that period.

The original fiefs amounted to large areas of land granted to noble lords and ecclesiastical institutions, but the seigneurs of such large fiefs could fall out of favour and have their fief grants revoked, or they could sub-divide their fiefs. But whatever happened, it was obviously in the interests of the seigneurs to encourage the inhabitants to clear waste land so that they could benefit from an increase in profit from these 'essarted' lands in the form of increased feudal dues. In this way the original open fields were supplemented by new clearings.

More and more land was cleared and by the fourteenth century it seems that the islands were well cultivated. Large areas of arable land were in corn, especially wheat (even as early as the thirteenth century) and this provided the seigneurs with another source of profit because they established corn mills in various places on their fiefs. Thus, in Guernsey the Fief St Michel and the Fief Le Compte owned half the island between them and built at least nine mills to which the tenants were forced to take their corn to be ground—to the benefit, of course, of the seigneur.

Other seigneurial privileges included that of keeping pigeon towers or, in the case of the smaller estates, pigeon holes below the eaves of their barns. Hundreds of pigeons could be kept in each tower or *colombier* and as these consumed large quantities of the tenants' grain they caused grave losses. In Jersey a number of fine examples of seigneurial *colombiers* can still be seen.

The hunting of conies (as wild rabbits were called) was also restricted to the high-ranking officials of the island and although there was a considerable amount of poaching, in spite of extremely severe penalties, this did not compensate the tenants for the extensive amount of damage done by the rabbits. In Guernsey, a complete *garrenne* (warren), or more correctly *guerande*, is still to be seen. In Jersey in 1701, in the parish of St Ouen, there was a revolt against seigneurial dues, but it would appear that most of these privileges and dues were cancelled in Jersey before they were modified in Guernsey.

In time the tenants extended the range of their crops to embrace parsnips, oats, barley, onions, leeks, garlic, broad beans, peas, flax, hemp and rye. At the same time the farm animals included cattle, sheep, pigs, geese and poultry. For a very considerable time oxen played an important part in Channel Island agriculture but the more prosperous tenants increasingly became the owners of horses. Parsnips, introduced at an early date, were extremely popular for the fattening of bullocks and pigs.

As in other parts of Europe, the time eventually came to enclose the land and in the Channel Islands the enclosure movement is thought to have started, as in England, in the second half of the fourteenth century. Where large stones were available these were used to form walls, but in most cases soil hedges were made on which gorse was grown and subsequently, when cider apple orchards were abundant, the shelter of an elm or other tall hedgerow was sometimes essential to prevent the wind rocking the apple trees and not only producing early fruit fall but also eventually killing the trees.

The sixteenth and first half of the seventeenth century were periods of very active hedge building and, unfortunately for the cottagers, the parish commons and waste lands were not spared. In Guernsey, Queen Elizabeth's commissioners were reported to have bought most of them for themselves at a very low rate and in the mid-seventeenth century some of the tenants ran with spades to nearly all places where the commons had once existed and broke down the enclosures. The commissioners of the Commonwealth then recommended that the commons should be restored to the people's use and that under the supervision of officers of every parish they should be let out for a yearly rental to tenants who could improve them either by enclosure or otherwise, and that these rents should be used for the benefit of the poor. The matter of compensation to those who had already bought the common land and enclosed it was left unresolved and the commissioners' decision, which was probably never carried out, failed to result in the restoration of the commons, a matter which long continued to remain as a bone of contention between the island authorities, particularly the parochial authorities, and the Privy Council.

From ancient times in Guernsey the right of *banon* had been exercised after the gathering of the harvest so that animals could wander freely all over the stubble. Enclosures obviously restricted *banon* and though it was ended by the eighteenth century there is little doubt that animals continued to be grazed in grassy lanes and for some time little control seems to have been exercised over pigs. The enclosure of most fields probably ended in the middle of the seventeenth century, but marginal lands continued to be enclosed until about 200 years ago.

Smaller Islands and Feudal System

With regard to the smaller islands, there are in Alderney the remnants of what appears to have been a classic example of the ancient 'open field' system which was at one time probably characteristic of the whole of the Channel Islands. Curiously enough the feudal system was never really established in Alderney, which never had a seigneur.

The arable land was concentrated in one area and the individual holdings were separated only by narrow ridges of earth. All the land outside the arable area was held in common as pasture and the dwellings were concentrated in one area. It was not until 1831 that the common land of Alderney was shared out among fifty-two families and so passed into private ownership.

The fertile plateau of Sark offered an ideal environment for this

Fig 17 Former implements of Channel Islands husbandry (from Jacob's Annals). *Top row. Left to right*: 1, weeder; 2, garden fork; 3, hand meadow weeder; *Bottom row. Left to right*: 4, dock spade; 5, forked dock spade; 6, dray (used chiefly for conveying barrels)

system but the evidence is sparse, although we do know that the island was incorporated into the Norman fief system, with fishing and agriculture as the principal means of livelihood. But in the fourteenth century, due largely to French raids, the island remained uninhabited and was abandoned to rabbits, pirates and the occasional French occupation forces. It was not unti¹ the second half of the sixteenth century that Sark was resettled and divided into forty holdings, each of whose owners was required to provide one man armed with a musket to defend the island in case of need.

The fields of Sark are, on the whole, larger than those of Guernsey and subsistence agriculture was practised until the tourist traffic brought so much money to the island that agriculture could, to some extent, be partially neglected. In the case of Herm, the land has passed through very many ownerships, but when stable regimes have been established, as at present, it has proved itself capable of supporting a prosperous and thriving dairy industry.

Seaweed Gathering

In the Channel Islands it does not appear to have been a general practice to allow land to lie fallow. It certainly varied in fertility according to the type of soil involved but extremely large quantitites of seaweed, or *vraic*, was used; not only drift weed but also weed cut off the rocks. Some of this seaweed was used in a fresh condition, while quantities

Fig 18 Edmund Blampied's study of a Jersey farmcart returning after a hard day's work in the fields. The boxcart, the stunted winter trees and the roof of the farmhouse are still typical of the island scene when the visitors have left. Blampied was one of Jersey's most distinguished artists and his speciality was farming scenes in his native island

were dried in the *sechages* or drying grounds and later burnt to provide a valuable powdery manure, particularly rich in potash, magnesium etc. The gathering of the seaweed was at one time regarded as an opportunity for family participation—which meant hard work alleviated by fun and food on the beach—but eventually the demand for it became so great that the collection had to be controlled by law.

La Grande Querue

As parsnips appeared to thrive better in deep soil the more prosperous farmers, some 200 years ago, procured very large ploughs with a massive framework of wood which were able to plough to a much greater depth than the smaller simple ploughs previously used. Few farmers had enough draught animals to pull this plough and so *La Grande Querue* became an occasion for communal effort between neighbouring farmers. It involved hard work during which throats were well moistened with cider, while the evenings were celebrated with feasting and jollification. Oxen were used nearest the actual wheels and as many as eight horses were harnessed in front of them. As the fields were of limited length, the oxen had to be relied on to make tremendous efforts towards the headlands where men with spades finished off the work, while old men with wooden mallets smashed up the clods.

Sheep and Wool

The knitting industry apparently assumed great importance in the sixteenth century, although it certainly existed in the fifteenth century. 'Guernseys' and 'Jerseys' (*Le corset d'oeuvre*) became known all over the world and knitted stockings from the islands were worn by the greatest in the land. In fact, the knitting business became so remunerative that it tended to occupy the labours of men as well as women, so that in some areas agriculture was neglected.

The first sheep to be kept in Jersey (said to be peculiar to Jersey) are described as an inferior breed having four or more horns. The wool produced was inclined to be coarse and scanty, particularly from cliff sheep which grazed on the rougher pastures of the island, so that it was actually found essential to import wool into all the islands. The period of the French wars, 1776–1815, saw the decline of the knitting industry and thus sheep farming received a severe blow. However, sheep could still be found grazing on L'Ancresse Common in Guernsey well into the present century.

Tobacco

In the early seventeenth century tobacco was an important product of the Channel Islands—certainly of Guernsey. It was of such good quality that it became a dangerous competitor to the infant plantations of North America and the Privy Council took such a serious view of it that they prohibited any further cultivation of the crop in England or in any of the islands.

Flax and Hemp

Crops of flax and hemp flourished in Jersey and Guernsey in the middle ages and onwards and in Jersey alone in the seventeenth century each farm cultivated ten or so perches of flax to make clothes. Doubtless this practice was also carried out in Guernsey. Flax was still being cultivated in Jersey in the nineteenth century to provide thread for the shoemakers, and the culture of hemp, to produce rope from its fibres, continued there until the beginning of the same century.

Chicory

An inspection of old census records indicates that in 1848, 103 acres (or 41.8 hectares), of chicory were grown in a single parish in Guernsey and processed in local factories equipped with drying ovens. The dried material was then sent to London and it is recorded that on one journey the steamer *William Miskin* carried 542 bags of processed chicory probably to be used in the manufacture of coffee products.

Cider

From the middle of the sixteenth century until at least the first world war, apple growing and cider-making played a most important part in the lives of the inhabitants of the two largest islands. During the seventeenth century corn growing was, to a considerable extent, replaced by apple cultivation, so much so that in Jersey, in 1673, the States passed an Act which forbade the planting of orchards except in replacement of old ones. Nowadays little remains of the apple orchards, which were once to be seen within the grounds of every farm and every large house.

We know that, by 1670, Jersey was already exporting large quantities of cider to England and by 1815 it was computed that approximately one-quarter of the arable land of Jersey was occupied by apple trees. Taking the five years 1809 to 1813, an average of 1,800 hogsheads were exported to England and an average of 24,000 hogsheads were produced annually, (one hogshead equals 54 gallons or 245.5 litres). Cider production in Jersey rose steadily until about 1855, after which there was a steady fall until 1870, when the export of cider practically ceased and the island saw the birth of the famous Jersey early potato industry. The middle of the nineteenth century also marked the period of maximum export of apples from Jersey, 180,000 bushels being exported in 1856.

In Guernsey, cider-making was also carried on during the same period but the industry does not appear to have been at any time as intensive as that in Jersey. Apples were also exported as well as other fruits, including the famous Guernsey Chaumontel pears. As in Jersey, there came a time when no new orchards were planted and more and more land was taken over for the growing of early potatoes and broccoli for export to England. Later, much land was used for the building of greenhouses in which to grow vines.

Cauliflowers in Guernsey

Cauliflowers are today a most important crop in Jersey (especially the winter cauliflowers—broccoli) but this industry is of post-war origin, whereas Guernsey grew considerable areas of broccoli at least as far back as the 1860s. Some farmers specialised in the production of broccoli seed, and broccoli growing continued on a fairly large scale until well into the twentieth century when it rapidly declined largely because the Guernsey type could not compete with the much superior variety produced in the French district of Roscoff.

The French growers, not unnaturally, were reluctant to part with their seed but eventually some was obtained and, as the result of clever breeding work and selection, new and valuable types were introduced in England. The zest of Cornish growers for the new types contributed very much to the success of the venture, but no such enthusiasm was shown in Guernsey and the industry was allowed to die out, although as early as 1883 19,048 packages had been exported to England.

Using the latest new strains, Jersey has since built up an industry which was worth over one million pounds in the season 1973/74, and is able to supply the demand for good quality vegetables in the United Kingdom at a time when frost has stopped the supply from local sources.

General Development in Agriculture in Guernsey

Changes in agriculture tend to be slow in adoption and although the first mowing machine and harvester had been introduced into Guernsey by 1866 it was still common about fifty years ago to find corn crops being cut by hand and tied with ropes of galingale sedge (*Cyperus longus ssp longus*). In Guernsey, in 1849, farmers were being urged to grow the 'new' root crops which were, one supposes, beetroots and carrots, and by 1867 the bailiwick of Guernsey was growing the following crops:

	Guernsey		Alderney		Sark		Herm	
	Acres	*Hecs*	*Acres*	*Hecs*	*Acres*	*Hecs*	*Acres*	*Hecs*
Wheat	759.75	307.5	107.25	43.4	101.50	41	—	—
Barley	448.75	181.7	2.25	0.9	77.50	31.38	35	14.2
Oats	379.50	153.7	32.25	13.0	24.75	19.0	13	5.3
Potatoes	667	270.1	107	43.3	11.75	4.75	3.50	1.4
Parsnips	930	376.65	—	—	92.50	37.46	—	—
Carrots	181.75	73.6	32.75	13.26	6.75	2.7	—	—
Beetroots	194.25	78.67	33.75	13.67	—	—	16	6.48

(NB: 1 acre equals 0.405 hectares)

The established rotation was generally as follows : parsnips—wheat —barley—clover—wheat, but, of course, cash crops obviously upset this rotation and by 1925 little grain was being grown in Guernsey. The farms remained small and numerous, the average number of cows kept on each farm being only about half-a-dozen.

The Guernsey census of 1953 showed that only 5,124 acres (2,075 hectares) remained to dairy farming. However, most farmers had a few greenhouses and devoted some acres to the bulb and flower industry, but the cattle population in Guernsey dropped from 6,976 animals in 1866 to 5,255 in 1931, thence to 4,058 in 1953, but has risen rather over this figure at the present day.

Turnips, swedes and maize are mentioned as important animal foods in 1925, and parsnips were still being grown in 1921, as well as mangolds and carrots (cattle type). Clover, grass and hay crops were, of course, of primary importance and farm horses had not entirely been replaced by tractors even up to the period 1945 to 1950. Root crops were still hand-weeded and singled by men who worked on hands and knees, expertly wielding the traditional Guernsey 'weeder'.

The number of farmers in Guernsey in 1953 was 349, giving an average area of 14.9 acres (approx .6 hectares) per farm. Some of the small fields were scattered away from the farm and the census further disclosed that 82 per cent of the farmers had less than ten cows. While at the present time tethering is dying out, in 1953 the majority of cattle were still tethered, although electric fences were already being used by the more progressive farmers.

Crops of fodder beet had been introduced, as well as kale, and silage was becoming popular. The seed mixtures used for pastures were of the modern type and liquid manure, the effluent from byres, was still being used extensively on the pastures, as it still is today. Seaweed was also still in extensive use as a manure but the present-day cost of collecting and carting has now almost stopped its use.

Traditionally certain farmers used to have their own milk rounds but these were later supplanted by two large dairies which, in turn, were replaced just prior to the second world war by the States dairy. A subsidy was paid to the dairy industry, and has been ever since in a number of ways, but a serious problem is the tendency to over-produce in spring and autumn. Although this surplus milk is used to produce the lovely yellow Guernsey butter and rich cream, these cannot be sold at a figure commensurate with that obtained for the subsidised milk and this loss is deducted from the farmers' profit margin.

At the present time of high running costs, the number of farmers on

Guernsey has been greatly reduced, while the number of animals in each herd has vastly increased. The progressive farmers use every possible device to cut labour costs and to modernise production and large farmers have latterly tended to become tenants of land, possessed by land owners. Despite the size of the dairy herds, there are occasional times of milk scarcity and supplies have then to be imported from Jersey or from England at considerable cost in transport charges.

Pigs and Fat Cattle

For many generations large numbers of pigs were kept and reared in Jersey and Guernsey and pig-sties are still to be found among former farm buildings and at the rear of innumerable small cottages. The pig-benches and the bacon curing racks have now largely disappeared but in past times of low wages and low standards of living pig-keeping was a valuable source of food and a welcome aid to the household economy. Similarly the fattening of a steer for the Christmas market brought welcome cash to be spent in the festive season, and though in Jersey the 'porker' appears to have been the most popular Christmas fare, beef was also eaten.

Development of Agriculture in Jersey

Apart from a large export from Jersey of both fresh and salted butter in the early 1830s, much that has been written about Guernsey farming also applies to Jersey—the slow adoption of mechanisation and conversion to crops requiring a minimum of hand labour, followed by interruption of the established rotation of crops in favour of cash crops such as potatoes, tomatoes etc. The traditional rotation given for Jersey by Le Cornu was as follows:

parsnips or other roots
followed the next
year by
potatoes   or   corn
followed by corn   followed by roots

followed by clover and grasses for two or three years or even longer ley.

But farmers then, as now, no doubt tended to follow their own inclinations, though today the need for co-operation in marketing is being felt more and more and the States of Jersey are encouraging

the movement. At the same time the States, as in Guernsey, are sub-sidising the agricultural industry but to a lesser extent than in the majority of European countries.

In Jersey and Guernsey much the same trends are developing and farms are becoming fewer, larger and more modern. As in Guernsey, the Jersey States are becoming more and more involved in the industry, subsidising, advising, educating, determining the price of milk produced and providing production bonuses. In Jersey, however, the central dairy and the export of bull semen are in the hands of outside organisa-tions working in close liaison with the Department of Agriculture, while both are States-run in Guernsey.

Development of Agriculture in Alderney and Sark

In Alderney, the agricultural industry has so declined that there now remain only about half-a-dozen farmers. However, they are now about to be given the benefit of many of the facilities open to Guernsey's farmers, such as fertiliser subsidy, soil analysis, artificial insemination, and they already have a central States dairy. In Sark, as in Alderney, the industry appears to be almost wholly aimed at supplying the inhabitants and their visitors with their daily needs.

Jersey Potatoes

The first potatoes are said to have been grown in Jersey between 1772 and 1775 and by the end of the century the leading agriculturists on the island had brought them into general cultivation. By 1807 some 600 tons (1 ton=.98420 tonne) had been exported from Jersey and, by 1811, the quantity exported had doubled. Farmyard manure was used in the cultivation as seaweed was considered unsuitable, and so profitable did the crop become that potatoes (earlies and lates) soon became the leading crop of Jersey.

In 1845 the first signs of the dreaded 'potato disease' were seen and in the following year, at the end of June, rotting tubers and stalks were visible everywhere. In subsequent years the damage was not so serious but yields were much reduced and prices rose because of scarcity. Then, taking advantage of Jersey's general slope to the south and its early 'slopes', the potato growers wisely concentrated on early potatoes for export to England, Portugal and the Mediterranean. These earlies largely avoided the worst affects of the disease which was eventually controlled. Old varieties were discarded when better ones

were introduced and liberal use was made of guano to supplement the
other manures in use. In 1868, 496 tons of guano were imported into
Jersey.

The usual marketing practice was for the growers either to send their
produce direct to mainland salesmen or to sell to local merchants, tele-
graphic communication enabling them to know hourly the state of the
London markets. In 1870, one-twelfth of Jersey was devoted to potatoes
and 7,890 tons were exported, apart from what was consumed locally or
kept as seed for the following year. The increased fertility of the land,
following the potato crop, was also an important factor in the island's
agriculture. The following figures of those early potato exports are
indicative of the rapid growth of the industry :

Year	Tons	Year	Tons	
1807	600	1842	18,560	
1825	5,836	1845	3,822—(First year of 'potato
1828	8,364	1864	6,705	disease')
		1891	66,840	

By 1891 the industry had fully established itself as a valuable source
of local revenue and during the pre-war years about one-third of the
island—9,000 acres (3,645 hectares)—was planted annually to potatoes
and the value of the 88,186 tons exported in 1935 was nearly one million
pounds. By 1974, however, the weight of potatoes exported had been
reduced to 27,338 tons, which were grown on only 6,728 acres (2,724.8
hectares). This is a drastic reduction of figures recorded in the thirties
but in 1974 £3.6 million were obtained for this tonnage and early
potatoes still remain a most valuable Jersey export. Actually part of the
reason for the reduction in area and yield is directly attributable to the
ravages of the potato root eelworm which was first recorded in Jersey
in 1938 and has spread alarmingly. Inevitably, traditional methods of
manual and horse labour are now rapidly giving way to mechanisation
and since 1883 practically the only variety grown on a large scale has
been the 'Jersey Royal' (local name) or 'International Kidney'.

Potatoes in Guernsey

After the French wars 'potato spirit' was produced for export, so
stimulating potato planting that the area under cultivation rose steadily.
This led to a greater island consumption and an export trade, which
greatly increased when, eventually, the distilleries ceased to prosper. A

parish census of the Castel shows that 136 acres (55 hectares) of the crop were grown in that parish alone in 1848.

In 1837 the Society of Agriculture (Guernsey) imported seed potatoes from England known as 'Yorkshire Reds', which met with great favour on the London market and sold at a price nearly double that paid for the ordinary blue potatoes of the islands. By 1886 1,474 tons were being exported, while in 1921 an export of 3,000 tons is recorded. However, competition from Jersey with its sun-facing slopes, as well as from the Canaries, reduced the export so much that in 1931 only 274 tons were exported. Thus a once important trade was lost.

Channel Island Cattle—Guernseys and Jerseys

No review of the agriculture of the Channel Islands would be complete without a reference to the world-famous Guernsey and Jersey cattle breeds. Both are renowned for their rich, golden, high-fat milk and for their complete freedom from the more serious cattle diseases, such as tuberculosis, vibriosis, brucellosis, husk, trichomoniasis etc.

The 'Guernsey' includes the cattle of Guernsey, Alderney, Sark and Herm and is larger, less refined, less uniform but reputedly more robust than its Jersey counterpart, which is a beautiful and graceful animal. Both breeds have been exported to most parts of the world and there are millions of animals of these breeds in commercial production.

The comparative genetical isolation of the island herds has undoubtedly led to the evolution of the two entirely different breeds, especially when we consider that this geographical isolation was reinforced by a Jersey statute of 1789 and a Guernsey equivalent of 1819 which prohibited the further introduction of French animals into the islands. These animals had been imported into the islands and then re-exported as Channel Island cattle. The formation of breed societies in both islands also played a vital part in the selection, formation and preservation of a distinct 'Jersey' or 'Guernsey' type. The establishment and maintenance of herd books in both islands was another most important step, as was the establishment of milk recording schemes and, more recently, of artificial insemination centres. Cattle shows are still held regularly and the Jersey Society has recently wisely decreed that no animal with hereditary defects should be eligible to be judged in the show ring.

In 1866 the official census of cattle in the islands gave the following result :

	Jersey	*Guernsey and Bailiwick*
Cows	5,815	3,030
Other Cattle	6,222	3,946
Sheep	517	1,214
Pigs	6,332	5,559

The official census of cattle recorded in the islands in 1974 gave the following figures:

	Jersey	*Guernsey*
Cows	4,621	2,733
Other female		
cattle	3,048	1,809

Exports of Cattle from Guernsey

Although some exports of Guernsey and Alderney cattle commenced in the eighteenth century, the export in commercial numbers really started about 1810 when sixty-seven animals were exported. Between 1822 and 1827 an average of 465 head were exported per year, while the figure had risen to 708 in 1834.

The first mention of a number of animals being bought by Americans was in 1865. Exports continued between 1887 and 1912, when an average of approximately 500 animals were exported each year. In 1914 no less than 800 of the 1,000 then exported went to the USA.

The first world war had an unfortunate effect on exports but in 1919 the exports were back to 842, of which 587 went to the USA. From this date exports varied from 435 to 949. The second world war, of course, shut off this trade until 1946 when the old export figures were restored, though actually cut down by the States to preserve the milk supply. From 1952 onwards exports fell until by 1958 they had dropped to forty-four and ceased altogether in 1975.

Exports of Cattle from Jersey

Cattle export was already being carried out before the end of the Napoleonic War and an average of 750 head was despatched from 1810 to 1813, rising to 1,440 from 1830 to 1832. In 1861 cattle exports had risen to about 1,500 head per annum and by the 1900s a steady 700 to 800 animals were being exported each year. From 1906 to 1916 the average number of animals exported from Jersey was 1,684.

Naturally there was a fall in 1917, 1918 and 1919 but from then onwards the average export figure was just over 1,000. The German occupation, of course, brought all exports to a stop but after the war, as in Guernsey, there was a considerable revival of demand. However, by 1955 and up to 1965, a decline in exports set in and the annual average figure fell to about 600. Unfortunately after 1965 the average figure dropped even more to approximately 300 per year, although the Jersey breed continues to arouse considerable interest throughout the world.

Guernsey Bulb and Flower Industry (Outdoor)

As far as can be ascertained the first consignment of flowers was sent to the London market in 1864 and in 1933 this had been built up into an export of 5,000 tons. The first bulbs were grown as clumps in gardens and subsequently used as propagating stock and it was from this small beginning in the year 1929 that 913 tons of bulbs were exported. Some new varieties were actually bred in Guernsey but all failed really to establish themselves as commercial flowers. Meanwhile, in the early part of the century and until an embargo was introduced, a prosperous export trade to the USA had been established and bulbs were also sent to England, Canada, Holland and even to the Argentine.

In 1905 it was estimated that 300 to 400 acres of bulbous crops were grown (120 to 160 hectares). Then, in 1912, bulb eelworm destroyed huge quantities of bulbs until the hot water treatment was introduced. The trade then recovered and immediately before the Second World War an average of about 450 tons of bulbs were being exported annually. During the German occupation some bulbs were saved by being grassed over. Later, many new varieties were bought and eventually bulb exports were re-established and a health certificate scheme established, but at present the amount exported is negligible.

The export of blooms, as distinct from bulbs, was not confined to narcissi but included gladioli, anemones, tulips, iris etc., though narcissi (including, of course, daffodils) formed the bulk of the exports, amounting in 1896 to 84,644 packages, which by 1905 had increased to 450,820 packages.

The First World War reduced flower exports and then came the losses from eelworm disease, but by 1933 exports had risen to 5,000 tons, a phenomenal figure which was followed by a decline, partly due to over-production. The effect of the occupation was devastating and in 1947 only 586 tons were exported. New and better varieties were

then introduced and for a time prices were satisfactory until a decline
in bulb exports and flower prices set in and the island's bulb and outdoor flower industry can now only be described as being generally at a
very low level.

Laws of Inheritance

The old inheritance laws of Jersey and of Guernsey appear to have
had a profound influence on maintaining the continuance of a
particular family ownership of farm land. In both islands the eldest
son was given special privileges. In Guernsey, for example, he took as
his eldership the house and enough land to include at least the main
farm buildings, in addition to which he had a right, in Guernsey, to
retain all the land within the ring fence. He could also claim some
of the unattached land as well if the 'enclos' did not provide him with
a third of the property, but to retain possession of all the land other
than that connected with his eldership he had to compensate his
brothers and sisters on the basis of a valuation carried out by the
douzaine of the parish involved. The details of sharing could be complicated but the objective was to give a more generous share to the
male rather than the female heirs.

In Guernsey, the compensation to brothers and sisters could be made
in cash, or 'rentes' could be created. The latter were of great value
where cash was limited, because it was possible to compensate co-heirs
by direct cash payment or by an allocation of so many quarters of
wheat rente, at first payable in kind but eventually resulting in an
annual return of approximately 5 per cent on the original capital
involved. The rentes could be redeemed through the Royal Court and
thus annulled, but the great value of the system as a whole was that
while the rentes were paid the farmer had absolute security of tenure.

For many generations this system kept the island farms intact,
although they could be bought and sold providing the new owners
bought out the rente owners or continued to pay them the rentes due
really by the land. In fact, real property could be bought in rentes,
thus avoiding cash repayments where money was scarce.

In Sark, the tenements could not be lawfully divided whatever
happened, and the present Jersey law of inheritance still preserves, in
a modified form, many of the benefits already described as existing in
the old Guernsey law, the original objectives having undoubtedly
been similar.

In Guernsey, however, where small but valuable greenhouse estates

made the law extremely unfair to heirs other than the eldest son, all children were given the right to share alike. The effect of the new Guernsey law on the ownership of the old estates and larger farms has been rather disastrous, because in a large number of cases the properties have had to be sold to achieve an equal sharing. Thus in many cases the farmhouses and buildings have been separated from the land and used purely for residential purposes, the land being taken over by the much reduced numbers of farmers, who have modernised their methods, farm buildings, equipment and cropping, given up tethering, greatly increased their herds, adopted silage making (especially using maize) and replaced hand milking with machine milking. Unfortunately, unlike farmers working under the rente system, most of Guernsey's tenant farmers have no security of tenure and their tenancies now have to face competition from the increasing demands of up to about 400 riding horses.

Agriculture and Horticulture during the Occupation

In the spring of 1940 the entry of German troops into the islands had an adverse effect upon Guernsey's glasshouse industry where tomatoes, not already exported, had to be sacrificed and the glasshouses had to play an important part in a regime of subsistence agriculture.

During the occupation the general administration of Guernsey (with constant interference from the Feldkommandantur 515) was left in the hands of the States which entrusted the day-to-day administration to a 'controlling committee' and a similar body called the 'superior council' was set up in Jersey. In Guernsey the Glasshouse Utilisation Board looked after horticulture, the Potato Board looked after outside cash crops like potatoes and root vegetables and the Guernsey Farm Product Board was responsible for dairying, animal husbandry etc. The nurseries, abandoned by evacuated owners, released considerable numbers of workmen who faced posible conscription for the labour groups of the occupying forces. To avoid this and to take control of cropping etc, the Glasshouse Utilisation Board took over all possible glasshouses and adjoining patches of land.

This action really constituted a form of nationalisation, but the wage structure gave great dissatisfaction as a single man, however hard he worked, received only 30s per week and a married man 45s. Had he received extra money from the Insurance Department as family allowance, some of this discontent might have been avoided. As oil for

the Water Department's pumping machinery was limited, some greenhouses were left uncultivated and to absorb the surplus labour thus
generated the remaining glasshouses were overstaffed.

The variety of crops grown successfully in the greenhouses was
really surprising. Outstanding results were obtained with indoor
potatoes and among other successful crops were: beans, cauliflowers,
cabbages, carrots, parsnips, onions, peas, maize cobs and lettuce. Sugar
beet was useful and extremely popular for making a sweet syrup.
Tomatoes were grown every year, some being used locally while others
were exported to France. For the first two years all that was produced
went, in the main, to feed the civilian population but the Germans
later ordered a sharing between themselves and the local population.
In 1944, at the instigation of the German authorities, many properties
were handed back to the owners, but whether more food subsequently
reached the depôts is doubtful.

From the beginning there could have been difficulty in obtaining
seed but this was overcome, partly by the Purchasing Commission's
operation in France but largely with the establishment of a rather
remarkable seed farm, where most of the seed crops were harvested in
greenhouses. Medicinal herbs especially datura, digitalis and hyos-
cyamus, were also grown at the seed farm and manufactured into drugs.

The problems confronting the dairy industry were far simpler in
Guernsey and Jersey. In both islands, local inspectors or advisors were
employed to supervise all agricultural activities so that the best could
be obtained from the facilities and land available. The production of
extra food in Jersey was easier than in Guernsey as there was much
more fertile agricultural land and much of Guernsey's land was
occupied by bulbs which the owners were reluctant to destroy, pre-
fering to sow the surface of the bulb fields with grass and clover,
producing hay and pasture. In peacetime, when over 2,000 cows were
kept, an average of 4,600 tons of concentrated cattle food and 1,200
tons of chaff, hay and straw were imported, but of course this material
was no longer available.

In Guernsey additional problems had to be faced when the Germans
commandeered some 1,080 acres (437.4 hectares) of farmland and
German horses were let loose to graze in the farmers' fields. To some
extent this must also have occurred in Jersey, but its effect was especially
felt in Guernsey.

In Jersey, wheat, oats and barley largely displaced the potato. The
old water mills were repaired and brought into use again and were
made to work by some of the surviving millers. From the harvest of

1941 onwards Jersey produced almost enough flour to supply the civilian population with a minimum weekly bread ration of about 4.25 lb (approx 2,000 grams) per head for all adults, in addition to a breakfast food and baby food.

The Jersey farmers were also able to supply a ration of one half-pint, or .284 litre, of whole milk for everyone over sixteen years of age, with a more generous ration for children, nursing mothers and invalids. In Guernsey, on the other hand, although children, invalids and so on were well looked after as regards whole milk, ordinary civilians were allowed only a half-pint of skimmed milk per day, though it must not be overlooked that some of the milk had to be reserved for the manu-facture of Guernsey butter. It must also be remembered that on much of the restricted amount of good fertile arable land available the Guernsey farmer had to grow potatoes and root vegetables for human and cattle consumption, and as much grain as possible. Gleaning by neighbours was an accepted practice. Although more arable and dairy products were available in Jersey than in Guernsey, the inhabitants of the latter had earlier potatoes from the greenhouses and more fresh vegetables throughout the year.

Deficiencies were, as far as possible, made up by the Purchasing Commission from France until the islands were subjected to a state of siege and some time elapsed after the liberation before conditions returned to normal. But when in due course the import of petrol, agricultural machinery, fertilisers, feeding stuffs and veterinary require-ments was resumed conditions improved rapidly.

A valiant effort was made to look after Alderney, which had been completely evacuated of its inhabitants and animals in 1940, although one farmer had later insisted on returning. Early in 1941 permission was obtained from the Germans for a party to be sent to Alderney for the cultivation of the island, the produce to be used for the benefit of civilians of Alderney and Guernsey alone.

Faced with the system of medieval strip cultivation, with boundary stones marking one strip from another, these had to be cleared out to enable efficient large-scale tractor ploughing to be carried out over the whole area—a measure which was to cause great confusion when the inhabitants returned. As a result, besides a considerable amount of vegetables, the following crops were harvested :

| Barley | — | over 37 tons | Oats | — | over 90 tons |
| Wheat | — | over 38 tons | Straw | — | over 200 tons |

Wheat was the only crop harvested in Alderney in 1942. Oats were grown but were used for the German horses, so that in November 1942 the agricultural connection with Alderney ceased altogether.

As far as Sark was concerned, the Guernsey Agricultural Department obtained permission to utilise the uncultivated land in Little Sark. Here the Agricultural Department planted a successful crop of potatoes but further cultivation was interrupted by the D-Day invasion of the continent. The remainder of Sark provided a form of subsistence farming which, combined with fishing, kept the population alive. Herm was used to rear steers, and sheep rearing was also attempted but failed because of mineral deficiencies in the soil.

Guernsey's Glasshouse Industry

Grapes

Guernsey's glasshouse industry originated in the gardens of the wealthy, who enclosed their properties with high walls to provide privacy and shelter. Observing how their choice wall fruits, including grapes, were often damaged by frost and wind, they provided lean-to glass shelters against the walls, which proved most successful.

By 1792 a Guernseyman had already provided himself with a heated glasshouse and by 1830 an historian wrote that there was no spot of ground in Europe where there were so many greenhouses as in Guernsey, where scarcely a gentleman was without one or more and where even tradesmen had their graperies. Actually, in the same year 3,474 lb (1,577 kg) of grapes were exported, and by 1841 one reads that glasshouses were being built even by persons 'little above the class of cottagers'. Unfortunately, the prosperity of the grape industry was not to last and although in 1915 2,500 tons of grapes were exported the value of the produce exported continued to decline until the culture of grapes was replaced by that of tomatoes.

Tomatoes

The first commercial crop of tomatoes grown in Guernsey is believed to have been produced in 1841 and tomatoes were so successful in restoring the fortunes of the glasshouse industry that a very large building programme was set into motion; the lean-to type of structure having for some time been abandoned in favour of the span type of glasshouse built of rather massive timbers on a base of granite, in complete contrast with the present light traps.

Tomato production gained impetus and production rose from 10,634 tons in 1913 to 35,028 tons in 1939. So great was this expansion that in 1957 the States considered it necessary to control the erection of new glass. At the present time, however, satisfactory modern glass only makes up 42 per cent of the total acreage, whilst reasonably satisfactory structures make up another 18 per cent and the obsolete glass makes up the remaining 40 per cent, but everything is being done to encourage the replacement of obsolete glasshouses.

In 1974, 48,886 tons of tomatoes were exported from 689 acres (279 hectares) of glass, 72 acres (29 hectares) of which were not heated. In these houses tomatoes are often grown in combination with freesias, which are usually regarded as a winter flowering crop, and in 1974 8.5 per cent of the total glasshouse area cropped was devoted to flowers and tomatoes in succession.

A statutory grading system for tomatoes, involving rigorous inspection, is now carried out in the commodious premises of the Tomato Marketing Board—both size and quality as well as degree of ripening being factors involved in the inspection. The packing into trays remains the responsibility of the grower or of the privately-run packing stations to which he may send his produce. Set up in 1952, the Board has proved most efficient and successful. It assumes responsibility for both shipping and marketing and before being shipped the trays of tomatoes are wired in three, palletised and delivered to the docks to be loaded into suitable vessels.

In 1955, the Horticultural Advisory Service was established in a small way but it was not until 1962 that an efficient and comprehensive experimental station, advisory service and laboratory were established. Educational facilities for young horticulturists are also being improved and developed.

Tomato growing methods have changed drastically over the years and peat culture in modules and general automation and programmed growing are now the usual methods adopted. The amount of steam sterilisation of the soil has been drastically reduced, although promising experiments are now being made in the possibility of re-cycling the peat compost and sterilising it by steam. The yield per foot of greenhouse has also greatly increased but modernisation has not kept pace with the demolition of old glass, so that there has been a significant reduction in the total area under glass.

The new greenhouse structures are usually built of steel/alloy with very wide panes of glass allowing maximum light transmission. The total area occupied by the glasshouse industry in 1975 was 937 acres

(379.5 hectares), and the nett value of the tomatoes exported in 1975 was 15¾ million pounds sterling, but growing costs are very high.

The traditional and at one time unique Guernsey system of spacing, planting and training the tomato plants has been copied by other tomato growers and there is no doubt that it is in early season culture that the Guernseyman excels. The number of small growers is still high, but very large new nurseries are now being erected.

In 1968, the States of Guernsey introduced the principle of financial assistance to growers for the development and improvement of their holdings. To this was later added the Rented Vinery scheme and a grant scheme, all aimed at replacing the 40 per cent of obsolete glass-houses still in existence by modern buildings. Such schemes are evidently essential for the future well-being of the industry, as the increased competition resulting from a complete tariff removal on imports from EEC countries, combined with the problem of soaring costs, will call for the utmost efficiency from all concerned in the industry.

Greenhouse Flowers and Plants in Guernsey

A considerable number of nurseries have changed over to the culture of flowers, combined with tomatoes, or have started growing flowers as an all-the-year-round crop. The flowers most often grown with tomatoes are : iris, chrysanthemums and freesias. Asparagus fern is also sometimes grown with tomatoes and sometimes grown alone. Flowers grown alone include carnations, chrysanthemums, roses, freesias, iris, ornamental plants, etc and in 1975 flowers only occupied 277.2 acres (112.3 hectares) of glasshouses and flowers and tomatoes 68.9 acres (27.9 hectares).

A new venture is the culture of peppers. Other vegetables are grown but mainly in coldhouses. In 1975 the export of plants and bushes brought £95,160 into the island.

Unlike tomatoes, there is no collective system of marketing flowers, which are consigned directly to salesmen in the wholesale markets by individual growers, or marketed through flower marketing firms which are prepared to grade and pack the flowers on behalf of the grower. Nowadays, virtually the entire output is conveyed to the wholesalers by air and some measure of the scale of the trade is afforded by the fact that in 1975 exports of flowers and plants were valued at 5¾ million pounds (less 20 per cent marketing costs).

Export of Vegetables from Jersey

Export statistics show that the total value of agricultural produce sent to the United Kingdom in 1974 increased in value by £420,154 over 1973 to £8,851,308. Fruit and vegetables appear to show the highest increase (£365,846) and include such items as cauliflowers, lettuce, parsley, strawberries and a number of other crops. In 1974 cauliflower exports alone were worth more than double those of 1973.

Jersey Flower Industry

Flower growing under glass is a comparatively new industry for Jersey and an expanding one. The principal flowers grown are iris, carnations, roses, freesias and chrysanthemums and one-third of the 121 acres (49 hectares) of glasshouses were, in 1974, devoted to flower crops. In 1974 these indoor flower crops were responsible for adding over £400,000 to the island's revenue. Although the main market is the United Kingdom, new outlets in France, Holland and Western Germany are being investigated. A statutory bulb inspection scheme has been of value and the possible sale of bulbs in continental countries is being considered, as well as that of cut flowers. The best market varieties are grown and, in fact, Jersey has a much healthier outdoor flower industry than Guernsey. Altogether it is estimated that flower exports are worth about one and a half million pounds a year.

Jersey Tomatoes

Jersey has only a comparatively small area of tomatoes under glass because the island's special advantages (ie slope to the south, light soils and southern latitude) make it possible to grow them very successfully in the open. Information as to the early days of outdoor tomato growing is very difficult to obtain, but it has been recorded that tomatoes were being grown in 1901 and that during 1911 nearly 6,000 tons were exported. After the first world war the area of this crop rapidly increased and by 1933 about 2,000 acres (810 hectares) were being planted and 30,000 tons exported, while in 1947 44,590 tons were exported from 2,868 acres (1161.5 hectares). So remunerative was the industry at this time that in the year 1948 a record return of £3,000,000 was achieved.

An outdoor crop like tomatoes is particularly subject to fluctuations in yield, owing to climatic conditions or because of the presence of pests

or diseases, and in 1950—a poor year—only 29,179 tons were obtained from 3,412 acres (1381.86 hectares). Approximately, 15,750 plants are grown to the acre, each produces about $1\frac{1}{2}$ to 2 lb (680 to 900 grams) of fruit. Apart from weather risks, the grower of early outdoor tomatoes has also to contend with diseases such as blight, didymella and verticillium wilt, as well as pests such as potato cyst eelworm, which is also a scourge of potatoes.

At first, the tomato in Jersey was grown almost exclusively as a second crop following the potato, but its commercial value increased to the point where it was worth while to transfer land from potato growing to first-crop tomato growing. Nowadays greater security is obtained by growing the tomatoes in greenhouses, and glasshouse production from about 77 acres (31 hectares) now accounts for about a quarter of the total tomato exports. In terms of cash value the indoor crop now produces about the same revenue as the outdoor one and between them they net a total revenue of over £2,000,000.

Notes to this chapter are on pages 243–4.

6

Architecture in Jersey

E. J. Leapingwell

Architecture, to define it in the narrow sense as being the work of architects or conscious designers, did not exist in Jersey, with very few exceptions, before the beginning of the nineteenth century, but in the sense that architecture is any form of building, then the story goes back to the dawn of time.

Very little indeed is known about the island or the people that lived in it before the coming of Christianity. The people who lived in Jersey in the earliest days were probably not permanent dwellers, but fishermen and summer herdsmen who made shelters for themselves of whatever materials were freely available, as is the case with all primitive people. Most of Jersey must originally have been woodland and over a large part of the island stone can be picked up from the ground, so that it is probable that the neolithic beehive hut at L'Oeuilliere, which consists of a stone-lined hole in the ground which was almost certainly covered with a thatched roof, is typical of the earliest houses.

Of building from the coming of Christianity until the Reformation, very little survives. The island was permanently settled, and from a very early date divided into twelve parishes. The inhabitants were fisherfolk who farmed for their own needs and they were, for these eight or nine centuries, contantly pillaged by sea rovers, Norsemen and marauding pirates from mainland France.

There have been sacred buildings on the site of each of the parish churches since before the year 1000, almost certainly since the parishes were created, but nothing of the earliest buildings stands and there is no means of knowing the dates of the chapels which form the earliest existing part of most of the churches. It is a surprising fact that the structure, with thick rubble walls corbelled inwards at the top to form a solid groined vault and steeply sloped on the outside to shed water, is a form of building used in Ireland from the sixth to the twelfth centuries AD and which ceased there with the English conquest. The type of building is therefore Celtic and it seems likely that it was brought to the island with Christianity and lingered there for three centuries after

Plate 20 *A bullock cart on the Guernsey coast road in the last century. It is laden with* vraic, *gathered from the nearby beach at low water*

Plate 21 *An obsolete form of transport: the boxcart, formerly much used in the islands for the haulage of coal, stone, seaweed and other heavy loads*

Plate 22 (top) *The Great Western Railway mail steamer* Reindeer *at St Helier, Jersey, early in the present century. She carried mails, passengers and cargo between Weymouth and the islands*

Plate 23 (centre) *A Guernsey tram car leaving St Sampson's for St Peter Port. Beyond it are sailing vessels discharging coal and on the left are fishing craft. Along the deserted road a boxcart travels, laden with stone*

Plate 24 (below) *A Jersey train at St Aubin's station. It had arrived along the coast from St Helier and would continue to the terminus at La Corbière*

it had been superseded in Ireland, the last of the buildings of this type having been completed immediately before the Reformation (St Lawrence Church north nave). During all these troubled centuries the churches were places of refuge from plundering pirates and it may be that this form of roofing continued to be used because it was fireproof.

Although no church in the island remains exactly as it was during the early years, they must all have been very similar to St Brelade's Fishermen's Chapel with small narrow windows, but the windows would have been without glass and the interiors plastered and probably frescoed— there are traces of such decoration at St Clement's Church. The churches were undoubtedly very dark because the windows were so small, although this must have been useful for defensive purposes. At one time or another, when defensive needs were less important, almost every church has had its original windows enlarged or replaced.

By the fifteenth century the population must have increased, because at this time the churches were enlarged or a larger one built beside the old, as at St Brelade. Until the Reformation, and in Jersey probably until the middle of the nineteenth century, the church building was the only large building in the country parishes and was used, apart from worship, not only for refuge but also for all forms of communal activity. Elections took place there, arms were stored there, and in troubled times corn and food stuffs were brought in for safe-keeping. In the early days such 'use meant that the altar was surrounded by the hustle and bustle of daily life, which would have offended the clergy, but when the churches were extended the early chapels became chancels and were set apart by rood screens.

As the population increased yet again many of the churches built a further extension to the north or south of the original building, and this

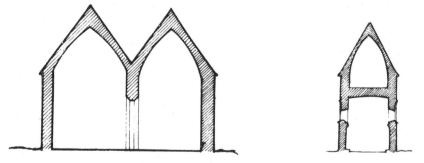

Fig 19   St John's Church, Jersey. Section through nave (Late Medieval)
Fig 20   Cormac's Chapel, Cashel, Ireland. Section through sanctuary and croft over
(1127–34)

may have been set apart for more purely secular purposes (an early print of St Lawrence Church shows the south nave still to have domestic windows, and such windows can plainly be seen at Grouville, where they have been blocked). It is possible that the curious double-aisled plan of so many Jersey churches arose because the Victorians, in church-going fervour, put in Gothic windows and converted the whole building to one use. In support of this theory, in St John's Church two buildings were added on the south side of the church, one next to the original chapel and another next to the nave. The one next to the chapel was originally a completely secular building used as a school and only had the Gothic-type windows added in the nineteenth century; the other, next to the nave, although much earlier and with windows apparently dating from the fifteenth century was used as an arsenal for the parish militia, at least until as recently as the Napoleonic wars.

Apart from the twelve parish churches there were several monasteries and priories, the most important of which was that of St Helier on the site of Elizabeth Castle; it is probable that the recently excavated remains on the Ile Agois are also of a monastic or eremitic settlement. There were, in addition, several chantry chapels but the only trace of these structures is in field names and carved stones incorporated in later buildings. The Elms at St Mary, now the property of the National Trust, has several such stones built into the farm walls.

There were, of course, larger places of refuge than the churches, where people could take their cattle and belongings if they had enough warning. Grosnez in St Ouen and Les Câteaux in Trinity were two of these: Les Câteaux was merely a large earthwork with a central keep, and Grosnez a walled bailey with fortified entrance and moat—both are now completely ruined. Mont Orgueil was already a considerable fortification at this time, but according to Major Rybot was not available to ordinary people as a sanctuary, being more of a military zone.[1] It seems likely that the houses of the period were made of timber and thatch, and that these were destroyed and repaired and destroyed again during the frequent raids. Very little building which can now be seen above ground dates from earlier than the sixteenth century.

From this period one very fine piece of consciously designed building does survive: the Hamptonne chapel of St Lawrence Church. The quality of the design and execution is so far above all other local work that one wonders who the designer and master mason could have been and where he came from; certainly from outside the island or there would be other of his work to be seen. The Hamptonne chapel can confidently be dated at 1542, which date is marked on the north-east

buttress. The chapel is simple, with three square inter-connected spaces, the roof of each having four ribs meeting at a beautifully carved central boss—the only parish church roof in Jersey so constructed. Not only are the bosses beautifully carved but the ribs spring from carved corbels. The two easterly spaces form the chapel proper and the westerly one forms part of the north transept. The chapel is connected to the chancel by pointed arches, again composed of moulded granite. The east window tracery is Flamboyant in style and therefore French in inspiration, whilst the two north windows are simple English Decorated, which in England would suggest a date 200 years earlier than that of the chapel. (I mention this to show how impossible it is to date buildings by style alone in Jersey.) Outside the chapel the most distinguished features are the gables formed over the north windows—most unusual anywhere but unique in the island. The pinnacled buttresses and the gargoyles are again finely carved and have survived well.

One finds it difficult to imagine the background of the design of this chapel which has used styles from over two centuries and two countries : a surprising feature, for in medieval times additions were usually made all of a piece and in the latest mode. Whoever the designer was, the result is extremely pleasing and it is certainly the finest piece of medieval architecture in the island.

By the beginning of the seventeenth century the island was no longer such a prey to marauders. In fact, during the whole period of the Civil Wars it was Jersey privateers who created havoc among the shipping up and down the French channel coast.

At the same time the islanders were carrying on their traditional dried conger trade with France, exporting cider to England, and knitting stockings on a large scale. The increased trade made for a modest prosperity and the increase in shipping meant that a greater variety of materials was brought into the island—for instance pantiles which in St Helier at any rate gradually replaced thatch as the principal roofing material. It is possible even now to see roughly the limits of the old town by standing on one of the hills round St Helier and noting the areas with the red pantiles, contrasting with the grey slate of later development.

As a result of the more settled conditions, some of the wealthier farmers and townsfolk were able to build much more solid and comfortable houses for themselves. In the early years of the seventeenth century the farms were frequently built around a courtyard and only approached through arched doorways, making them easy to defend. Perhaps because craftsmen's energies were no longer channelled into the carving of wayside crosses and other 'poperies' abhorrent to the

Reformation, the builders lavished attention on the adornment of their own houses. From this time date the more elaborate arched doorways and finely decorated stone fireplaces.

No farm of this period survives without very considerable alteration, with slate or pantile roof coverings in place of thatch and casements or sliding sashes in place of iron bars to window openings. Some still have the granite work unaltered; Greenhill at St Mary is one such and gives a good idea of the appearance of a prosperous farmhouse of the period. It also shows how Jersey's remoteness and transport difficulties dictated the appearance, for by 1674 even cottages in England would have had much larger windows and they would certainly have been glazed.

Towards the end of the seventeenth century France imposed a heavy tax on the importation of salt fish and this dealt a severe blow to both the conger and cod trades, resulting in much poverty and unemployment. Many Jerseymen left with Sir George de Carteret for New Jersey, and the island went through a period of economic depression until the cod trade revived again in the middle of the eighteenth century.

The first harbour in the island was built at St Aubin's at the beginning of the eighteenth century, but as all goods had to be carted across the beach at low tide the harbour was not very convenient. Eventually, after many delays, a small harbour was built at St Helier (near the present La Folie Inn), and came into use about 1755, but since there was no roadway where the Commercial Buildings now stand, cargoes still had to be carted across the beach at low tide and the harbour was so badly built that within thirty years it was considered to be positively dangerous. Nonetheless, having the harbour did increase trade and by the beginning of the Napoleonic wars prosperity was again increasing, with a flourishing smuggling trade into mainland France.

Although conditions were more settled during the whole of this two hundred year period it was nonetheless a time of economic stringency and unfortunately no public or private architectural works were commissioned. The only building of architectural significance dating from this period is the magnificent bulk of Mont Orgueil which, impressive though it is, was most certainly not a piece of conscious design but arose from the necessity to 'raise up a gun platform from which the Mont Saint Nicolas could be dominated'.[1]

During the last two decades of the eighteenth century, Jersey changed from being an island of poverty and subsistence farming to one of modest affluence, due to an upsurge of shipping and trade. The finest building of this period to survive until recent years is certainly the Debtors' Prison, demolished by the States of Jersey in 1975, although

the stones have been numbered and preserved. The architect for this beautifully proportioned and confidently detailed building, which was completed in 1812, is unfortunately not known. It consisted of an arcade of eleven classically proportioned granite arches with the joints strongly modelled, supporting a first floor of fine dressed ashlar granite with an entablature of Portland stone and with one window over each arch, and over every column a granite pilaster with Roman Doric capitals. Though very simple in design, the proportions were extremely pleasing and the workmanship superb. It is to be hoped that the States will find a new home for what I believe to be Jersey's most distinguished piece of architecture.

In 1815, at long last, a harbour which could be approached from dry land at any state of the tide was finally built. Shipping and trade increased enormously and this not only brought increased money with which to build houses but also greatly increased the variety of materials available. Ships taking salt cod down to the Argentine returned across the Atlantic with Honduras mahogany for fitting out the ships being built in the island and for making the fine furniture of the period and the doors and staircases for the newly-built houses. Up until this time every house was in what one might term the vernacular style : granite walls pierced with three or five openings on each floor and blank gables with fairly steeply pitched roofs. With the beginning of affluence came the desire for more elaborate styles, in some cases confined merely to a classical-type porch on an otherwise vernacular façade (the National Trust farm : La Vallette, is one example), and in other cases the whole house was designed in the classical style with pediments and parapets (Beechfield in Trinity, the home of the deputy bailiff, is a fine example of this period). Internally the rooms became lighter and much more elegant, with delicate timber staircases and continuous mahogany hand-rails supported on slender turned balusters. A very fine example can be seen at No 9 Pier Road, now the Museum but originally a merchant's house.

At this time local people appear to have considered that granite was a peasant material and quite often, when farms prospered, the old houses would be refaced with rendered and plastered frontages or pulled down completely and rebuilt in a semi-classical style. Examples of this type of house, often surrounded by outhouses of much earlier date, can be seen throughout the island. Sometimes the old houses were left in position for the use of the original owners whose children had moved into the new house, the most perfect example of this being Le Marinel at St John, the home of Mr J. P. Vaudin, where the old house was left

fully-furnished after the old people had died, and the house still had a great deal of the original furniture left in position until a few years ago.

To this period belong also the 'cod' houses (meaning houses built on profits from the cod trade, just as 'wool' churches in England were built on the profit from wool). These are distinguished from the grander farm-houses, generally speaking, by being built as country estates and not having any connection with farming. Melbourne House in St John, one of the finest examples, was for many years referred to as La Folie Carcaud, so-called because the owner, Carcaud, bankrupted himself in an effort to build a larger and grander house than La Grande Maison on the St John's main road—also a very fine house. The houses vary in style from the classical, of which the last two named are good examples, to the Gothic—Elysée and Dresden Hall at St Peter being fine examples of the latter. There are also some splendidly exuberant examples of smaller Victorian Gothic houses, both in St Helier and in the country. Unfortunately their very ornate bargeboards, balconies and wood-work make them expensive to maintain and they are fast being shorn of their adornments. As Jersey was so prosperous at this time there are very many examples and it is difficult to select any of special merit from that number, but Le Châlet at St Martin is one of the most com-plete, even the garden maintaining its original form to some extent. In St Helier, Le Châtelet in Victoria Street, although at present painted in rather unsympathetic colours, is also a fine example of the period.

Before the advent of the motorcar made it possible for people to work in St Helier and live in the country, advocates, professional people and shopkeepers built themselves spacious town houses with large gardens. All the fine terraces of Rouge Bouillon date from this time of prosperity, together with Almorah Crescent and Douro Terrace. More modest houses were built at Havre des Pas and here there were also built some very cheerful examples of Victorian and Edwardian seaside architecture : for instance the Ommaroo Hotel and Le Châlet opposite. Unfortunately their position, right on the seafront, has meant that the elaborate timber-work of many of these houses has suffered even more than those inland and much has been lost.

During this time public buildings, too, benefited from the general prosperity. Religious buildings proliferated : churches were built in St Helier and chapels both in the town and in the country, and these are almost the first buildings which can be described as true architecture, having been conceived and built as an entity rather than just growing as funds were available and extra room was required.

By far the most distinguished of all these religious buildings is St

Thomas' Roman Catholic Church, consecrated in 1893, the architect for which was a Frenchman—Alfred Franguel. The building suffers from its rather seedy setting but it has a nobility of proportion and a sureness and strength of detail which makes it one of Jersey's major pieces of architecture. The plan is traditional, with nave, aisles and chancel, and north and south transepts containing chapels. External quoins and columns and all carved stones are of grey Brittany granite infilled with pink granite from La Moye. The contrast between the two colours is not great and very pleasing. Internal columns and mouldings are of grey Brittany granite with brick vaults and infilling covered with plaster. Furnishings, including the altar, the confessionals, the organ and gallery are contemporary and in many cases were made in France and then brought to the island, as was the stained glass. I have been told that such was the prejudice against Roman Catholicism that almost all the materials and workmen to build this church came from France, since no Jersey Protestant would have anything to do with it.

So far as other public building is concerned, despite the prosperity very little of merit was built. The States' building itself was never conceived as a whole and is generally an undistinguished building, although a sympathetic coat of paint would enhance it beyond recognition. The hospital is undistinguished, with rather mean proportions. The railway terminal at the Weighbridge, though now sadly neglected and again in need of paint, has very interesting details but the whole does not cohere into a building of distinction.

The public market is, however, a very attractive building, not only from the outside but also internally. The building was completed in 1881 and the architect is believed to have been T. W. Helliwell of Brighthouse, Yorkshire. It was built on a corner site in the middle of St Helier and along the two street frontages it is divided from the streets by walls of elaborately dressed granite with cast-iron screens and gates. Internally, there is a large glass octagonal lantern and immediately under the lantern a large fountain with open stalls formally arranged around. The roof is supported by most elaborate and decorative cast-iron and timber trusses with spandrels incorporating the Jersey coat of arms and other decoration.

One more building of distinction dating from this period is Victoria College. The architect was Mr J. Hayward and the building was completed in 1852. Sited in a very commanding position overlooking the town, the frontage consists of seven bays with octagonal towers at either end and a central entrance door. The building has rather the air of a stage set, partly because the towers prevent one from seeing any of the

building behind, giving it a two-dimensional appearance. Nonetheless it is a handsome piece of work.

Two works at least were commissioned from architects of national repute, namely Trinity Manor (Sir Reginald Blomfield) and Steep Hill (Ernest Newton) and these, if not first-class examples of the work of their respective designers, are pleasing buildings.

After the First World War there was a very considerable change in the type of building in the island; shipping was cheap and the ships taking potatoes and tomatoes to England could bring back metal windows, asbestos tiles, and other materials previously quite strange to the island. Due to the Depression, little money was available for the better class of building and public works were at a minimum. Nonetheless, ordinary people demanded more privacy and ceased to live with two or three generations in the same house. It is to this inter-war period that we owe the building of a great many low-cost speculative housing schemes around the fringes of St Helier, and particularly on the erstwhile market gardens stretching from Samarès to Havre des Pas. Sun-worshipping and sea bathing became fashionable, resulting in the building of many houses and shacks around the coast, hitherto unspoilt. A few more distinguished houses were built, in particular the work of Arthur Grayson, the son of a local minister who was trained at the Architectural Association of London and set up his own practice in Jersey in the 1930s. He was responsible for many buildings, of which Temperley in St Lawrence (now called Château St Laurent) is a fairly typical example of semi-traditional style, and Les Lumières on Route Orange, built for Mr Ernest Huelin, is a good example of 1930s' architecture and was designed by the architect right down to the carpets and linen.

After the destruction and de-population of the German occupation (which produced some interesting building in the German fortifications) Jersey entered into probably the greatest period of prosperity it has ever known. A combination of a booming tourist industry and its position as a tax haven has meant that pressure of population has greatly endangered the beauty of the island. The coming of the motorcar makes it easily possible to live in the most remote parish and work daily in St Helier, and indeed the volume of traffic and the pressure to build houses all over the island has created some serious problems.

Immediately after the war the Natural Beauties Committee was set up by the States, with powers to prevent any building on agricultural land or in other places which might despoil the natural beauty of the island. At first this committee tried to employ a policy of common-

sense, assessing every application to build on its merits, but as the pressure increased it became clear that some form of island zoning plan was necessary and the States made the bold and wise decision to consult Sir William Holford, who put forward the name of William Barrett as being the man capable of preparing the necessary plan. Mr Barrett started work in 1960 and produced his recommendations in 1962. These were accepted by the States and incorporated in the Island Development Plan of 1963. Mr Barrett's two principal ideas were to form a green belt in the coastal areas, and inland areas of outstanding beauty where no building would be permitted, and to group other development around the parish centres or one or two other concentrated spots. The green belt has, on the whole, been scrupulously adhered to; some of the village developments have been implemented, as main services particularly sewers have been installed, but pressure for isolated building in the country is still enormous and not always resisted by the enacting committee, now re-named the Island Development Committee.

A note to this chapter is on page 244.

7

Architecture of
the Bailiwick of Guernsey

E. J. T. Lenfestey

Guernsey

As the largest and most densely populated island of the bailiwick, Guernsey has by far the largest number and the most diverse types of buildings of interest. Of these, the foremost types are the Guernsey farmhouse, representing the mainstream of domestic vernacular architecture and the Georgian and Regency houses of the town of St Peter Port, representing the highest expression of polite architecture in the bailiwick. Happily, numerous examples of both have survived unspoilt to the present day.

Early and Late Ecclesiastical Architecture

The oldest parts of the parish churches as they now stand, with the exception of Torteval Church, were built in the twelfth, thirteenth and fourteenth centuries. The parish church of St Peter Port, commonly called the Town Church, is the grandest in the Channel Islands. The north and south aisles, chancel, transepts, north porch and piers for the central tower were all added to the nave in the fourteenth century. The square tower dates from about 1500 and the octagonal spire is of the early eighteenth century. The interior underwent major restorations in 1822 and 1886.

St Sampson's Church, with its unique and very small saddleback tower, is the most primitive of all in its architecture, having not a single moulding or any other trace of craftsmanship. There is also little evidence of the skilled use of stone in the parish churches of the Castel, St Martin, Forest and St Andrew, in all of which the arches were built for strength rather than appearance. The parish churches of the Vale, St Peter-in-the-Wood and St Saviour (the largest of the 'country churches') are the only ones which approach the fine craftsmanship to be seen in the Town Church; the Vale Church being the work of monks. Its spire, like that

150

of St Martin's Church and the Forest Church, is an octagonal stump with spirelets in the splay of the octagon. St Apolline's Chapel (St Saviour's) is a medieval stone building of one cell, which has recently been restored.

Torteval Church, built in 1816 to replace an earlier building, is the work of John Wilson and is in marked contrast to the same architect's neo-classical church of St James-the-Less, built two years later. It is sturdily built of grey granite with stout buttresses and a tall, slender, circular spire rising from a short circular tower.

Holy Trinity Church (1789), in St Peter Port, is a bulky late Georgian building with a handsome façade topped by a small belfry. St John's Church (1838), by Robert Payne and also in St Peter Port, is a simple grey granite building with a short pinnacled tower and St Matthew's Church (1854), Cobo, a small and very pretty Victorian building of red Cobo granite. G. F. Bodley designed St Stephen's Church (1861) without adding to his reputation and Sir Arthur Bloomfield and partners were responsible for St Barnabas' Church (1874), now deconsecrated and abandoned.

The Roman Catholic church of St Joseph and St Mary (St Peter Port) was built in 1851 and is by Augustus Welby Pugin. Built of dark grey granite with white stone dressings, it has a nave with two aisles and a tall green-copper spire. The other Roman Catholic church in St Peter Port, Notre Dame du Rosaire, is an exceptionally fine example of contemporary architecture (1968) by A. Seguin of Paris, which has an unusual roof in the shape of an upturned boat inspired by the bark of St Peter.

Military Architecture: 1204 – 1944

From the time of the loss of Normandy until the middle of the nineteenth century the island was periodically fortified and re-fortified against invasion from nearby France. There were medieval fortifications at Jerbourg (St Martin's), and on the sites of the Vale Castle and Ivy Castle (or Château de Marais, St Sampson's), all of which have disappeared. The medieval castle of Castle Cornet, however, has survived, though not intact and with many additions. Commenced in 1206, by 1250 it boasted a chapel, hall, two baileys surrounded by curtain walls and at least eight towers; all crowned by a high circular keep, destroyed in 1672 when a magazine exploded. The barbican was built by French invaders during a period of occupation in the middle of the fourteenth century and in Tudor times the superb main gate was added, together

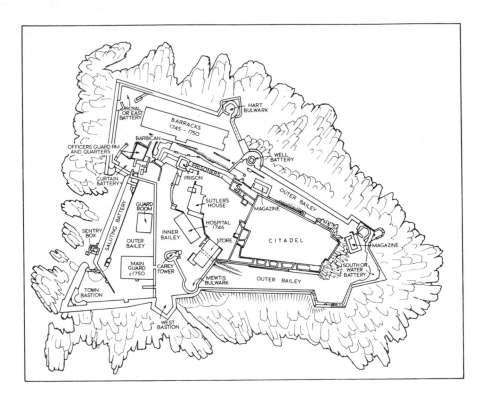

Fig 21 Castle Cornet, Guernsey. Additions continued to be made from early in the thirteenth century, when the castle was built, until late in the seventeenth century. (More modern buildings are not shown)

with formidable projecting bastions and more curtain walls encircling the medieval castle and turning it into a concentric stronghold. The southern bailey was then filled in to form a gun platform. New buildings were built in the eighteenth and nineteenth centuries and large concrete emplacements were added during the German occupation.

A large number of fortifications were built during the period of the American Revolutionary and Napoleonic wars. The projecting headlands of the low-lying north-west coast were crowned by small, square castellated forts and circular two-storey granite towers (called martello towers); watch-houses and batteries protected every possible landing place. The extensive works at Fort George, on the southern heights of St Peter Port, were largely built during that period. Comprising a central star-shaped citadel, four batteries, bastions and barracks, it served the garrison of English regiments which successively came to the island until 1939. Purchased by the States of Guernsey from the War Department in 1958, together with Fort Hommet (Castel), it was sold by them in 1961

to a development company. The citadel, barracks and guardhouse were then bulldozed out of existence to make way for a large residential estate.

Between 1940 and 1944 Guernsey was heavily fortified by the Germans, using captive labour under the Organisation Todt. Some fine examples of this extraordinary and awesome architecture are to be seen today in Guernsey above and below ground. A chain of defences of reinforced concrete was built round the island, including large coastal batteries imaginatively camouflaged to look like farmhouses. An enormous underground hospital was built at St Andrew's and circular observation towers of five storeys were constructed at L'Erée, Pleinmont and other places.

Rural Domestic Vernacular Architecture: The Guernsey Farmhouse

The plan and form of the prototype of the Guernsey farmhouse of the sixteenth and seventeenth centuries evolved from houses similar to the medieval houses which had become standard in England by the end of the twelfth century and which continued to be built for several centuries. These houses were generally dispersed in fields away from the ancient nucleated settlements around the parish churches, and were one-storey houses, open to the roof and consisting of two rooms, one larger than the other. Later an upstairs room (the solar) was added for the private use of the owner and his wife. This led to the development of the partial two-storey house, an example of which may still be seen in the uninhabited house at Les Pièces (Forest), where the arrangement of two ground floor rooms with a passage in between and a solar follows closely the medieval English and Elizabethan ground plan.

In the course of the sixteenth century the partial two-storey house developed into the older of the two main types of Guernsey farmhouses which continued to be built until the latter part of the nineteenth century. This was the two-storey, seven-window type, known as the 'small-parlour' house, with four windows upstairs and three downstairs; the front door having two windows on the side of the kitchen/living room and one window on the side of the parlour. The later of the two main types of Guernsey farmhouses, the nine-window or 'large-parlour' house (five windows upstairs and two on each side of the front door) did not appear until the latter part of the seventeenth century. A larger version of it made its appearance in the second quarter of the eighteenth century.

The round arched doorway is the most important feature of the older

farmhouses, the commonest form of arch having two rows of *voussoirs* on the same vertical plane. Another distinguishing and attractive feature of the older type of farmhouse is the semi-circular stone stair-tower or *tourelle* at the back of the house, containing a winding stone staircase. Inside some of the houses, near the front door, there are arched niches known as *bénitiers*, which are thought to have been church piscinae.

Most of the many surviving small-parlour houses were built in the eighteenth century, some of the finest examples being La Roque Balan (Vale), Les Bordages (uninhabited: St Saviour's), La Maison du Marais (Castel) and Les Poidevins (uninhabited: St Andrew's). La Maison de Haut (St Peter-in-the-Wood) is a link between the two types and fine examples of the large-parlour house may be seen at Le Bourg (Forest), Les Prevosts and Les Piques (both in St Saviour's), Le Ponchez (Castel) ad La Hougue Vaugrat (St Sampson's).

The Architecture of St Peter Port

The architecture of the town of St Peter Port is basically that of the late eighteenth and early nineteenth centuries. It was during this period that the town spread rapidly; until about 1780, it had extended to little more than the limits it had reached in the late middle ages, demarcated by official boundary stones, or *barrières*.

Elegant, stylish Georgian and Regency villas, some with spacious gardens, appeared to ornament Les Gravées, the Grange, Queen's Road and Hauteville. Elsewhere, whole streets of smaller houses of equal interest, free standing or in terraces, were built. From 1819 to 1829, no less than 400 houses were built at a cost of about £200,000.

The building of so many houses was attributable to a great extent to the massive fortunes made by the leading families from privateering under letters of marque from the Admiralty. By 1800, it was computed that money brought into the island by the sale of French and American prizes stood at nearly £1,000,000. The gentlemen privateers had large families and their large fortunes were used to build houses for their sons and daughters. Three of the sons of just one of them built respectively Georgian 'Rozel' (Mount Durand), castellated and Tudorish 'Summerland' (Mount Durand) and romantically Gothic Castle Carey, next to Les Côtils. The interior of the latter is the finest in the Channel Islands, having been fitted with Adam fireplaces, ceilings, dadoes, doorcases, doors and handles brought over from the Adelphi in London.

It was fortunate that Guernsey had at the peak of this period of change and expansion a designer of such a high order of competence

and imagination as John Wilson. He came to Guernsey in 1815 and left in 1831, his life before and after those years being a complete mystery. Fluent in Gothic as well as in classical architecture, he drew his ideas from both, sometimes adding 'Tudor' detailing as in the case of Elizabeth College, completed in 1829. More evidence of this is to be found at Castle Carey and Grange Lodge (The Grange). Wilson was very fond of using a bronze-coloured cement, referred to as 'Roman cement', instead of the prevailing white stucco.

Wilson's other buildings in the town include the Meat Market (1822) and the adjoining States' Arcade (1830), facing the French Halles and Assembly Rooms (built in 1780–82, and now part of the Guille-Allès Library). He was also responsible for the splendid, tall terraced buildings on both sides of the lower half of Fountain Street.

The court building (1792–1803, with later additions), the very impressive Constables' Office (1787), Boots (c 1780) and Moore's Hotel (c 1760) are large distinguished buildings of well-dressed granite in contrast with the white stucco and Roman cement of so many of their neighbours.

Of the Victorian additions to the town, John Newton's Fish Market (1879) is of outstanding merit and there are fine Edwardian buildings, like Amherst School (1900) and the States' Office (North Esplanade) (1911). There are also several very pleasant terraces of small vernacular houses in the precincts of St Sampson's harbour but, hemmed in and overshadowed by industrial buildings, they are sadly vulnerable to destruction.

Large Houses Outside St Peter Port

The oldest of the large houses outside the town which have survived virtually intact are Les Granges Manor (1685) and La Vrangue (both in St Peter Port), La Haye du Puits (Castel) and La Grande Maison (St Sampson's), all in the vernacular tradition and all of stone.

Sausmarez Manor (St Martin's) was built between 1714 and 1718 and its main façade of grey granite with red granite quoins is that of a modest five-bay, three-storey house of a type common in England from the late seventeenth century onwards. It has a central door up several steps, modillion eaves cornice, high roof with tall chimneys, a row of pedimented dormer windows and a gazebo. At one side and at the back are large Victorian additions (1873).

Saumarez Park (Castel) is a larger house dating back to the early eighteenth century but extensively altered and added to by the 4th Lord

de Saumarez in the 1870s. The façade of two storeys is of beautifully cut Cobo granite with grey granite dressings. The house, park and gardens were acquired by the States of Guernsey in 1937.

Smaller houses worthy of mention are St George (Castel), a late Georgian house of three bays and two storeys, the central bay being pedimented and having a flat-topped semi-circular porch with columns; Havilland Hall (St Peter Port), a neo-classical two-storey house of seven bays with a pedimented portico of four Roman Ionic columns in front of the three central bays, all covered with Roman cement; Le Vallon (St Martin's), a pebbled Gothic house; and the eighteenth-century parsonages of St Andrew, the Castel and St Peter-in-the-Wood, all in the vernacular tradition, together with the Regency parsonages of St Saviour and Torteval.

Harbours and Sea Defences

The harbour of St Peter Port has developed from the crude mole it was in the thirteenth century to the superb harbour it now is, enclosing a space of about eighty acres—a perfect example of a purely artificial harbour. The Old Harbour, dating back to 1580, has been turned into a yacht marina. Considerable extensions were made between 1853 and 1909, using massive stones, and the New Jetty was erected in 1928. The Albert Dock has also recently been converted into a yacht marina and a ramp has been added to enable cars to be driven directly from the car-ferries on to St Julien's Pier.

The harbour of St Sampson is sited in what was the eastern outlet of a narrow stretch of water separating the Clos du Valle from the mainland of Guernsey—the Braye du Valle, drained in 1812. The harbour suffered considerably with the decline in the granite export trade, but it is now active in connection with the importation of wood, coal and fuel oil.

Along parts of the coast of the island strong walls of bulky stone (some supporting handsome esplanades in the town) were built in the nineteenth and early twentieth centuries to withstand the onslaught of the waves.

Alderney

The town of St Anne's and the ring of Victorian fortifications around the island are the dominant, if not the only, architectural features of Alderney.

Plate 25 (top) *St Helier harbour, Jersey, in the last century. On the right is the paddle steamer* Aquilla *and on the left is the paddle tug* Rescue *of Guernsey* (Nautical Photo Agency)

Plate 26 (centre) *The ss* Courier *moored outside Creux harbour, Sark. Nearby is her rival, the motor vessel* Joybell 11. *Both plied between Guernsey and Sark between the wars and before La Maseline harbour was built* (Guernsey Press Co)

Plate 27 (below) *A de Havilland Rapide aircraft at Guernsey airport. This type of aeroplane was in much use on insular and cross-Channel services in the 1950s*

Plate 28 *La Corbière lighthouse is a Jersey landmark, as well as being a guide to mariners. It stands impressively on a lofty rock at the south-western corner of the island and at low water a causeway links it with the shore. It is then possible to see it at close quarters* (States of Jersey Tourism Committee)

Plate 29 *The late Dame of Sark, Dame Sibyl Hathaway, riding in a Sark carriage with a woman at the reins. Horsedrawn transport is still a common sight on that island*

Plate 30 *In 1966 an ancient custom, La Chevauchée de St Michel, was revived in Guernsey, when roads were inspected, a procession toured the island and there was dancing and merrymaking from morning to night. Here outside St Peter Port church, the Lieutenant-Governor proposes the Loyal Toast. Centre (left), is the Bailiff of Guernsey and near him is the Queen's ADC in the island. Islanders, some in costume, share in this colourful pageant*

Plate 31 *Channel Islands life as it was enjoyed a century ago. In the kitchen country folk sing the islands songs to a fiddler's accompaniment* (British Tourist Authority)

Plate 32 *Braye harbour is a picturesque part of Alderney. The rigging of the vessel on the right does not hide the charm of the old buildings of Braye Street and on the broad sands a yacht is high and dry. One of the buildings is a hotel and another housed John Wesley when he went to Alderney in 1787* (Guernsey Press Co)

St Anne's

Before it developed in the course of this century into the small, delightful holiday town and quiet haven of English rentiers which it very largely is today, St Anne's was more like a large village of farmhouses, redolent of those of lower Normandy and Brittany. Here the farmhouses were concentrated, unlike those of the other islands of the bailiwick and of Jersey which were dispersed far and wide.

St Anne's is still very rural in character, in spite of the addition of Georgian houses and the less attractive buildings of the post-war years. Most of the charming old vernacular houses were built between 1750 and 1850 of local stone with roofs of slates or pantiles. Few of them are of real architectural distinction but they form an essential and coherent feature of the most attractive hilly streetscape of the town.

The chief buildings are the imposing church by Sir Giles Gilbert Scott (1850), which is cruciform in plan, of purplish stone with Caen stone dressings and with a large pyramidal spire over-sailing the square tower above a cluster of subsidiary roofs; the Island Hall, formerly the home of the Le Mesuriers, hereditary governors of Alderney, built in the shape of a double-cube in 1763; Mouriaux House, another large double-cube house built by the Le Mesuriers in 1779, and the unpretentious and undistinguished Court House.

The Victorian Fortifications

The chain of thirteen superannuated forts encircling the island, many of them long neglected and falling into substantial disrepair, were built in the middle of the last century. With their high walls pierced for musketry, their moats, archways and extensive earthworks, they lend considerable grandeur and romanticism to the northern coastline of Alderney. Fort Albert is by far the largest of all the forts. Essex Castle is the most historic as being an enlargement of a fortress begun in 1549, and Fort Clonque is the most romantic, and is presently being superbly restored by the Landmark Trust.

Sark

Sark has barely any traces of its medieval buildings, the oldest dating back to the time of the colonisation of the island by Helier de Carteret in 1565. The new settlers from Jersey built single-storey houses with

local stone and imported Jersey granite. De Carteret, however, built a two-storey house for himself at Le Manoir, the original seigneurie. Many of these early houses still exist, with modifications and additions.

The spoils from privateering contributed to the erection in the first half of the eighteenth century of larger two-storey houses. Both the Jersey and Guernsey farmhouse types were built. More two-storey houses were built in the first half of the nineteenth century, following the period of economic depression during the latter part of the previous century. None of the Sark houses has an arched doorway and with few exceptions where two or three of them are grouped together, the houses are dispersed all over the island.

There are no large houses, apart from the seigneurie, home of the seigneurs of Sark since 1730. It is a superb Jersey-type house with Victorian additions, including a tall square stone tower. The church is a small undistinguished building of 1820.

Herm

The only buildings of architectural interest in Herm are the medieval parts of the chapel of St Tugual, a one-cell building of large irregular stones which was restored during the occupancy of Herm by Prince Blücher von Wahlstatt (1891–1914) and which is still in use as a chapel, and the manor house. The latter dates back to the eighteenth century and was extensively altered and added to by the prince with crenellations and machicolations.

8

Island Transport

Victor Coysh

Transport began in the islands, as elsewhere, when a man first rode a horse or harnessed it to some form of vehicle, and when he crossed water on a tree trunk or rude craft for the first time. Whether this was originally accomplished by visitors or settlers in prehistoric times cannot now be established. Today, transport, island-wise, is of two kinds : insular and non-insular, and both forms apply in some measure to each of the islands for it is obvious that while folk have always been obliged to travel from one part of their environment to another, there has been equal need for some of them to voyage further. Especially is this so with the smaller islands of the group which have always been dependent in some degree upon their larger neighbours, particularly from the nineteenth century onwards when insular self-sufficiency began to wane.

In more primitive times the islander resident in the country had small need to visit the town since his few wants could be met at home. Similarly, it was rare indeed for him to leave his parish, let alone his island, for he had neither the wish nor the means to do so. Yet transport, in some measure, was necessary if he wished to transfer a load of *vraic* from the beach to his farm, or if his corn was to be taken to the mill for grinding. Fishermen soon discovered that catches were usually more plentiful afloat than ashore and merchants found that overseas markets were a better method of disposing of their wares than the local one, and in this again transport was imperative.

For land conditions, horses, donkeys or oxen were used for haulage and the first two were employed for riding, too. Primitive sledges ultimately gave way to animal-drawn wheeled conveyances and these were in common use until after the Second World War, soon after which they became museum pieces, leaving motor vehicles to dominate island roads. Happily, this does not yet apply to Sark.

Jersey

Clearly in this island (like its neighbours), vehicles could not travel far without adequate roads, and until the beginning of the nineteenth

century they were, for the most part, totally inadequate. They were narrow, winding, with appalling surfaces and so badly maintained that until the lieutenant-governor, General Don, persuaded the States in 1810 to improve them for military needs the Jersey roads utterly deterred internal development. Indeed, until 1844 one could only reach St Helier from St Aubin at low tide, when the sands were available for use.

However, the ways were considered adequate for farming needs and along these lumbered the heavily-laden *vraic* carts, also used for other agricultural purposes. The original Jersey hay-cart has been described as the symbol of the island's mixed farming in the seventeenth, eighteenth and nineteenth centuries until it was succeeded by the four-wheeled van, used primarily for the transport of potatoes to the harbour for export. Nevertheless, *vraic* continued to be carried by the stalwart two-wheeled box-cart, or the open-ended long-cart, normally drawn by a team of horses.

Farm waggons were built locally, like the carriages of the well-to-do which became popular when the roads were fit to carry them and when wealth derived from privateering and other lucrative pursuits encouraged fortunate islanders to emulate a way of life enjoyed elsewhere. The advent of tourism in the last century increased coach-building, which also included char-à-bancs and, later, horse-drawn omnibuses and similar conveyances.

The influx of visitors prompted the shrewd Jerseymen to build two railway systems: from St Helier to St Aubin (later extended to La Corbière) in 1870 and from St Helier to Gorey in 1873. The former operated until 1936, when fire destroyed St Aubin's station, carriage sheds and much stock, while the latter continued until 1929. Both were succeeded by motor transport.

The Jersey Railway ran westwards from St Helier, with several stations en route, chief of which was St Aubin, four miles from the capital. The narrow-gauge train ran through a tunnel west of St Aubin, passed under two bridges and reached its terminus at one of Jersey's most attractive spots, La Corbière.

The Jersey Eastern Railway's St Helier station was at Don Street and several small stations were passed before the train reached its splendid destination: Gorey, at the foot of Mont Orgueil Castle. In the case of both systems, it is a matter of general regret that neither has survived to the present day when, as tourist attractions, both would probably have proved most popular.

Motor buses were responsible for the railways' demise, though they had operated long before the end of the trains. Jersey Railways & Tram-

ways introduced these buses in 1923 and they existed (as in Guernsey) even prior to this date, plying in opposition to the horse buses which had been in general use since the early years of this century. These vehicles, like the first motor buses, were usually island-built.

The bicycle has been popular since its inception a century or more ago. One might style it 'the poor man's horse' and even the introduction of the motorcycle, and later, the motor-scooter, did not greatly affect the appeal of the humble 'push bike'. Improved island roads made cycling a pleasure and the walker, before the days of universal motoring, enjoyed using them as well.

Like Guernsey, Jersey abounds in motor vehicles. Private cars, taxis and hire cars, commercial, industrial and farm vehicles as well as buses infest the island roads and the introduction of the 'roll on/roll off' system at the harbour has resulted in ferry-loads of visitors' cars augmenting the local motor population. Some of the roads can cope with this, others fail to do so and confrontations are frequent in the maze of lanes inland.

One road improvement in St Helier is the big tunnel running under Fort Regent. It bypasses the town centre satisfactorily, which is opportune since its principal streets have been turned into permanent pedestrian precincts to the comfort of shoppers and strolling tourists alike. Nevertheless, the increasing number of vehicles is causing constant concern and it may be that some sort of control—a system of priorities, perhaps—will soon become imperative.

The cultivation and export of Jersey potatoes clearly increased the vehicle population, for the conveyance of produce to the harbour and the return of empty barrels to the farms entailed much horse-drawn transport. So did the tourist industry, with the excursion cars and cabs used by visitors. The presence of the garrison and militia also increased the volume of road traffic to some degree.

Another Jersey industry involved with transport was shipbuilding. Seven yards were established at Gorey in the last century and there were others at Havre des Pas and St Aubin. Here were built sailing vessels of all types: some for the oyster fishery, others for deep-sea trade. By the middle of the century Jersey's merchant fleet numbered over 450, though not all of it was island-built. The vessels carried commodities such as coal, timber, machinery and other heavy cargoes to the island and, before steamers were common, took away Jersey's agricultural and horticultural produce. Some of them were used in the lucrative 'free trade' and conveyed much contraband to England. Perhaps some of Jersey's privateers were also locally built.

With the introduction of steamships, Jersey's tourist industry was born. In 1824 two rival firms started a weekly service apiece between Jersey and Southampton (by the paddle steamer *Ariadne*), Portsmouth (*Lord Beresford*) and in 1826, Plymouth (*Sir Francis Drake*). These carried passengers and cargo, like the government mail packets, the first of which were the Weymouth-based *Cockatoo*, *Dasher* and *Wildfire*. In 1831 the *Lord of the Isles* began running between Jersey and London. Similar links were established with French ports and, of course, Guernsey.

As time progressed the steamers became larger, more powerful (especially when propellers replaced paddles) and better equipped, resulting in more and more visitors to the island and a greater number of Jersey folk travelling to the United Kingdom, France and further afield. Pleasure steamers also operated excursions to French ports and the other islands and Jersey became popular among yachtsmen.

The establishment of a regular mail, passenger and goods service between England and Jersey wrought a marked change in island life. Travel became a reliable undertaking, no longer subject to weather vagaries as in the days of sail. Regular, fast and frequent sailings prompted the Jerseyman to take a leaf out of his visitors' book and become a tourist himself. This broadening of his outlook led him into the world of yachting (albeit on a small scale) and he delighted in sailing across to Granville or St Malo and perhaps even to Sark and Guernsey. He enjoyed the sailing races organised by the Royal Channel Islands Yacht Club and fishing expeditions.

With the enlargement of St Helier's harbour, bigger mail steamers called there. The last paddler to do so was the *Gael* of 1867 and the first screw steamer to arrive there was the *Griffin* of 1858, which plied chiefly between Jersey and France. Incidentally, Richard Mayne, in his book, *Mailships of the Channel Islands,* relates that she brought Victor Hugo and his family to Jersey in 1852, prior to his settlement in Guernsey some years later.

In 1857 the Weymouth & Channel Islands Steam Packet Co was formed and their two paddle steamers, the *Cygnus* and *Aquila*, maintained the service to the islands. In 1889 the *Aquila* was purchased by the Plymouth, Channel Islands & Brittany Steamship Co of Guernsey, which operated her between the islands and France and sometimes on excursions. She was sold in 1896.

The London & South Western Railway Co came into being in 1862 and its first vessel to call at Jersey was the *Normandy*. She was lost on passage between Southampton and the islands in 1870. Another of its

ships was the paddler *Brittany*, which operated across Channel from 1864 until 1900. The company also ran the screw steamers *St Malo* and *Caesarea* between Southampton and the islands and these were followed by several others, including the *Honfleur* (built in 1873 and still afloat in 1969 and perhaps later), *Guernsey*, *Diana*, *Ella*, *Hilda* (lost off St Malo in 1905) and *Laura*.

In 1889 the Great Western Railway Co purchased the fleet of the Weymouth & Channel Islands Steam Packet Co and became the rival of the LSWR. Outstanding among their fleet were the *Lynx*, *Antelope* and *Gazelle*, fast, handsome little ships which ultimately became cargo vessels when they were replaced by the larger *Ibex*, *Roebuck* and *Reindeer*. These enjoyed great popularity for many years, though the *Roebuck* was lost in 1915 while on war service.

The challenge of the *Lynx* and her sisters was met by the LSWR's *Dora* and the larger trio, *Frederica*, *Lydia* and *Stella*. The last of these sank after striking Les Casquets in 1899, with much loss of life. The LSWR also operated the *Victoria* between Jersey and St Malo. The *Alberta* and *Vera* were added to the LSWR's Southampton-based fleet and later came the fine *Sarnia* and *Caesarea*. The former was torpedoed in 1918 and the latter was sold to the Isle of Man Steam Packet Co in 1924.

All these vessels also called at Guernsey, with the exception of those on the Jersey–France service. Other ships belonging to the GWR or LSWR included the *Great Southern*, *Great Western*, *Princess Ena* and *Ardena*. Twin-funnelled Southampton boats were the *Hantonia*, *Lorina* and, later, the *Isle of Jersey*, *Isle of Guernsey* and *Isle of Sark*. The GWR operated the *St Helier*, *St Julien* and *St Patrick* for many years and after the Second World War another *St Patrick* arrived to replace her namesake, lost in the war. When all these ships had been discarded they were replaced by two, the *Sarnia* and *Caesarea*, operating for British Railways from Weymouth only. At the time of writing only the *Sarnia* is on the Channel Islands run, together with the car ferries *Earl Godwin* and *Caledonian Princess*.

Additional to these vessels were the smaller craft sailing between Jersey and France at about the end of the last century. They included the *Cotentin* (operating from Gorey), the paddlers *Cygne* and *Jersey* and the *St Brieuc*. Then followed the much larger *Vera* (a former Southampton packet), *Princess Ena* and *Brittany*, all plying between St Helier and St Malo.

Mention should be made of the cargo-carrying ships linking Jersey and Guernsey with England, some of which carried a few passengers.

One recalls the GWR's *Pembroke* and the more recent *Roebuck* and *Sambur*, under the same ownership. The LSWR's freighters included the *Cherbourg, Brittany* (later renamed *Aldershot*), *Ada, Bertha, Fratton, Ringwood, Haslemere, Whitstable, Moose, Elk and Winchester*, subsequently sailing under the British Railways' flag.

Various colliers, tankers, timber-carriers and other cargo boats also use St Helier and St Peter Port (as well as St Sampson's) from time to time and reference should certainly be made to the hydrofoils linking Jersey with St Malo, Guernsey, Sark and Alderney during most of the year. They provide the fastest service afloat and a simple and speedy link with the continent which brings more foreign visitors to the islands than ever before. Certain small French vessels also run to and from Jersey in the summer, some from Gorey.

It is claimed that Jersey's airport is the second busiest in the United Kingdom, pride of place going to London Airport—a far cry from the days when aircraft used the sands of St Aubin's bay—the tide permitting—for landing and take-off. This state of affairs persisted until 1937, when the present airport at St Peter was built.

In 1912 a seaplane from St Malo arrived at St Helier, the first aircraft to do so. By 1925 a flying-boat service was operating in Jersey (two years later than Guernsey) and a major step was taken in 1933 with the formation of Jersey Airways Ltd, whose de Havilland Rapide biplanes operated between the sands of West Park and Portsmouth. The service proved a success and 20,000 passengers used it in the first operational year. In 1934 a service between Jersey and London was introduced and a little later there were flights between the island and Southampton. By 1935 nearly 25,000 air passengers were being carried and in 1936 the figure exceeded 30,000.

After the German occupation numbers increased again and between 1947 and 1970 seventeen million air passengers were carried to and from an airport which, over the years, has been vastly improved from its original rather small dimensions. Runway extensions were necessary because of the use of bigger aircraft, the extension of services and the increase of private flying. More recently the advent of jet aircraft has presented a serious noise problem to those living in the airport's vicinity. Another problem, confronting its owners, the States of Jersey, is the need for still longer runways, a problem difficult of solution because the airport borders the sea on one hand and a busy thoroughfare and a built-up area on the other.

There is a sustained inclination on the part of the public to travel to and from the Channel Islands by air rather than by sea, despite the

mounting cost of air travel. This being so, it is imperative that airports should be capable of handling increasing numbers of travellers, by means of enlarged premises and adequate landing facilities for larger aircraft. How these requirements can be met in islands which clearly have their physical limitations are problems which must be solved within the next decade, if not sooner.

Guernsey

Obviously, much of what has so far been stated about insular and other forms of transport in Jersey also applies to Guernsey. The same mail and cargo vessels (with a few exceptions) visit both islands, for the most part both handle the same aircraft and the development of internal communications is, generally speaking, common to the two major islands of the group. They developed simultaneously and the making of roads and the vehicles which used them evolved on parallel lines. Yet there were some differences.

For example, the need to construct military roads in Guernsey during the Napoleonic wars was dictated not only because troops and guns might have to be rushed to some coastal zone threatened by invasion (as in Jersey), but because northern Guernsey was detached from the rest of it by an arm of the sea known as the Braye du Valle. It could be crossed on foot at low water and by boat at high tide. General Doyle, the lieutenant-governor, ordered the reclamation of this strait largely to prevent the Clos du Valle (north of the channel) from becoming a French base, with the water preventing the garrison from attacking the enemy.

When the filling-in was completed a military road was built, permitting troops to reach northern Guernsey speedily; a necessity since the Clos du Valle has a coast lending itself to enemy landings. That no such invasion befell Guernsey was possibly due to the excellence of its defences. The Braye reclamation, incidentally, added materially to the island's area.

The building of Doyle's military roads was fiercely resented by many islanders who feared that their properties would be encroached upon. Conservative, they detested radical changes and it took a good deal of tactful persuasion on Doyle's part before the States agreed to his proposals. Doubtless, in the interests of defence, he could have insisted on their adoption but he preferred to try the diplomatic approach first.

As in Jersey, winding narrow lanes are characteristic of the interior of Guernsey. The majority must be of some antiquity for they appear on William Gardner's map, drawn in 1787 for the Duke of Richmond,

Master-General of the Ordnance, and doubtless had existed long before then.

As well as serving as property boundaries, the roads and lanes provided access between the country parishes and St Peter Port, communication with the beaches (essential for fishermen and farmers) and for the movement of livestock. Probably pedestrians used them more than vehicles did. Coastal roads were constantly exposed to storm damage and consequent flooding until the nineteenth century when stout sea walls were built to keep the waves at bay and made travelling safe. Even so, hurtling stones and sheets of spray can often make a coastal journey hazardous on a stormy day and the strongest of walls is sometimes breached by heavy seas.

Like the Jerseyman, the Guernseyman of old was no great traveller. It was Victor Hugo who declared that Guernseymen were of two types: those who walked around their gardens and those who walked the world. This was stated in the nineteenth century and scarcely applies today, for the islanders are, for the most part, globe-trotters, often preferring a continental holiday to an English one, embarking on cruises, flying to the ends of the earth and, strangely enough, often quite ignorant of the other islands they can see on nearly every day of the year!

Visitors to the island often speculate on the meaning of 'Guernsey Railway Co Ltd', words seen on most of the buses, for no railway can they see. None, in fact, ever existed (save for the German trains of the occupation), but in 1879 a steam tramway was opened whose lines ran between St Peter Port and St Sampson's. The cars were drawn by diminutive locomotives but there was no conventional railway as in Jersey. The trams proved popular and seriously threatened the double-decked horse buses which had plied along the same route since 1837.

The tram terminus adjoined the Albert Statue, near the Town Church, and the St Sampson's terminus was at the Bridge. Basically, it was a single-line track with occasional loops for passing purposes. At first the rolling stock was kept in premises at Bulwer Avenue, St Sampson's, but a serious fire there in 1896 prompted the move to Hougue à la Perre, near the boundary between St Peter Port and St Sampson's.

By that time the horse buses had been taken over by the railway company and were ultimately disposed of. The tram service's popularity was enhanced by the introduction of electric cars, many of them double-decked. This was in 1892 and soon afterwards the steam trams were discarded. The Guernsey trams continued to run until 1934, when motor buses replaced them. The motor bus had actually been intro-

duced into Guernsey much earlier, in 1909, when the Guernsey Railway Co purchased London double-deckers and operated them on the L'Ancresse and L'Islet routes in conjunction with the trams.

Horse buses operated in the island from about 1900 until 1920; apart, that is, from those plying from St Peter Port to St Sampson's in earlier years. They were drawn by a pair of horses and ran between the town and St Martin's, the Forest and Cobo, with occasional buses to Pleinmont. In winter, passengers travelled under cover, otherwise the hoods were removed irrespective of possible weather vagaries. Often the vehicles were Guernsey-built, like the 'four-in-hands'—excursion cars carrying tourists in rows of seats reached from the sides by ladder. This was a most popular way of seeing Guernsey and their routes are closely followed by the island tours of today operated by motor coaches.

Coachbuilding was a fairly important industry in the nineteenth century. Waggonettes, brakes, 'chairs', landaus, gigs and governess cars were locally built and so were box-carts, vans, drays and other vehicles. Also manufactured were handtrucks and wheelbarrows. So well were the carriages built that several are still in running order and may be seen in Sark and when the members of the Guernsey Driving Society use them on the road or at shows.

Livery stables were in great demand before the days of the automobile. Relatively few islanders owned their own conveyances, since this entailed stabling and, perhaps, the employment of a groom. It was easier to hire a carriage when required, either with a driver or by driving it oneself. For the most part the vehicles and their horses were elegant and those used at weddings and funerals especially so.

Farmers in Guernsey, as elsewhere in the islands, used box-carts or the open-ended long-carts for the cartage of *vraic*, roots, hay and straw (using frames) and other loads, employing oxen as well as several horses in drawing the 'Big Plough', locally built and jointly owned by groups of farmers, who used it in parsnip cultivation. (See 'La Grande Querue', Chap 5, p 118.)

Horse-drawn vehicles made the roads filthy by horse dung and difficult because of the effect of hooves on soft surfaces and by dust or mud, according to the weather. Road surfaces were usually rough, to suit the horses, but they were hard on pedestrians' footwear as well as on cyclists' tyres. The volume of traffic in those days was, of course, but a fraction of today's and one could walk the roads and lanes of Guernsey with a freedom now unknown. That they were usually ill-lit seemed to worry few and if vehicles were unlighted it was of little consequence.

Roadsweepers helped to make foot travel easier and the use of water

carts in very dry weather laid the dust. In the early years of the present
century the rare automobile was chiefly responsible for clouds of dust.
When an uneven surface became really troublesome, it was made smooth
by the ponderous steam roller.

Out of the town, road-users had few street lamps for guidance and
these were lighted by gas. The lamplighter, with his long pole, was a
familiar sight. So, too, were ragged children, often bare-footed who,
especially in the country, begged for alms as the carriages passed by.
In pre-car times a drive around the island was a novelty and occupied
several hours, with pauses for refreshment of man and beast. Today, in
a car, such a journey can be accomplished in an hour or so and, to
most, is a commonplace experience.

The transport of grapes and tomatoes from vinery to ship was done
by horse-drawn vans and the haulage of stone from quarry to crusher
and from thence to St Sampson's harbour was by box-carts. These also
hauled house coal and growers' anthracite from the quays to their
destinations. Deliveries of milk, bread and other commodities were
normally by horse transport, sometimes by donkey cart.

Bicycles were popular in Guernsey in the past, but for the poor walking
was a necessity. Men walked miles to and from their work and many
others did so for pleasure. Troops on the march, headed by a band, were
a familiar sight and, as now, walking races were popular. Chief of these
today is the Church-to-church Race, held in the early autumn.

As elsewhere, the increasing use of motor transport in Guernsey
resulted in better road surfaces and more traffic. Horse-drawn vehicles
declined, although they were reasonably common until about 1950,
when it was still possible to hire a 'chair', a one-horse chaise surviving
in Sark to this day. Box-carts also continued in use on farms until about
that year, some of the draught animals employed being those left behind
by the Germans after the occupation.

In 1919 Guernsey Motors Ltd was formed and its Ford buses drove
the horse-drawn counterparts off the roads. Several smaller concerns—
some one-man affairs—ran buses, sometimes in competition with others
but often on routes previously unserviced. Enterprising coal merchants
even placed benches on their motor lorries and used them for excursions
in those care-free days of the 1920s when traffic regulations were far
removed from those of today.

During the German occupation it was a case of 'back to the horse',
for petrol was almost unobtainable, many islanders' cars had been
commandeered and bus services were practically non-existent. So horse-
drawn vehicles staged a come-back and fortunately there was no lack

of vehicles or animals. The Germans, too, used horses for transport and riding. In other respects travel was at a premium, bicycles were prized and rare, footwear was precious and, as time went on, health and strength had to be safeguarded from undue exertion. Overseas travel was almost impossible, save in very special circumstances, and then one could only go to the other islands, or possibly France.

Following liberation, restrictions were gradually lifted, and in a year or two transport had returned to normal. Cars and other motor vehicles increased, as elsewhere, and the cab and the cart faded into oblivion. Today they are to be seen in transport museums and sometimes on the road, cherished by their owners and admired by others as relics of a more gracious era. As in Jersey, car ferries bring hundreds of vehicles to Guernsey where they are landed on a ramp, and they make the roads even more congested than they were before 'roll on/roll off' was ever thought of.

Guernsey shipbuilding was important in the nineteenth century when, as in Jersey, sailing vessels of various types and sizes were constructed in large numbers. The period lasted from 1815 to 1895 and the yards were chiefly at St Peter Port and St Sampson's. They were on the seashore for the most part and traces survive of a slipway near Hougue à la Perre where, at low tide, the remains of its timber supports are still visible, though no ship has been launched there for over a century.

Like the Jersey ships, several of those built in Guernsey were for the deep-water trade and some never saw the island after their maiden voyage away from it. Such was the ship *Golden Spur,* the largest built in Guernsey. Her builder was Peter Ogier, who launched her from his St Sampson's yard in 1864. She traded between Britain and the Far East and was lost off Hongkong in 1879. Other fine Guernsey-built vessels were owned by W. Le Lacheur & Sons, and were chiefly engaged in the South American trade. Sometimes these and others returned to Guernsey for lengthening, repairs or maintenance. Some, such as those employed as colliers, did so frequently while others engaged in the Mediterranean fruit trade, called only occasionally *en voyage.*

Shipbuilding involved other industries, such as sail-making, rope manufacture and foundry work. It gave employment to many and when the sailing-ship era began to wane, when metal hulls replaced those of wood and steamers started to prevail, the industry died. True, repairs continued for some years but by the turn of the century Guernsey shipbuilding had become only a memory. The only steamship known to have been built on the island was the *Commerce*, which traded between Plymouth, the islands and France.

Boatbuilding has been carried on in Guernsey for very many years and it is still thriving. Craft of some size continue to be built at St Sampson's and there ship repairs and maintenance are carried out. The popularity of yachting and boating is so great that moorings at the harbours and around the coast are at a premium and the island's central position makes it an ideal base for cruising and for visiting its neighbours.

Although cross-Channel passenger and cargo vessels have almost invariably called at both Jersey and Guernsey, several smaller inter-island craft have been based on Guernsey alone, trading chiefly between there and Alderney or Sark and visiting Jersey only on occasion. There must have been sea links between all the islands for many centuries, though regular services seem to stem from early in the nineteenth century when sailing cutters were chiefly employed. With the coming of steam the regularity of communications obviously improved, but the cutters were still sailing between Guernsey and Sark during the First World War, admittedly assisted by auxiliary engines.

When John Jacob was writing his *Annals of Guernsey, Alderney and Sark* in 1823 he travelled to Alderney by cutter and if he visited Sark it must have been by the same means. So did Henry Inglis, author of *The Channel Islands* published in 1835, though he went to Alderney by open boat, 'of good dimensions, manned by sailors familiar with the navigation'. He stated that the usual conveyance was by an Alderney cutter of about forty tons burden, 'three of which trade between the islands'.

Travel between Guernsey and Alderney improved when the paddle steamer *Princess Royal* ran this service. She was owned by the con-tractors building the Alderney breakwater and was available for public use for a few years before her sale in 1853. Another paddle-steamer, the better-known *Queen of the Isles* succeeded her and was as familar a sight in all the islands as she was in St Malo, Cherbourg and other French ports. She was sold in 1872 and her owners, still the harbour contractors, did not replace her since their work was completed. How-ever, others supplied the *Princess*, a paddle steamer which was sold in 1875.

Thereafter the Alderney service was provided by two handsome screw steamers, both named *Courier*. The first arrived on the scene in 1876 and remained there until her sale in 1913. The second (a larger ship) came to Guernsey for the first time in 1883 and did not leave island waters (apart from the occupation years) until 1947, soon after which she was scrapped. During her long life the *Courier* sank twice, encountered

a U-Boat and travelled thousands of miles, often in heavy seas, chiefly between Guernsey and Alderney but also to and from Sark, Jersey and France. She was a wonderful sea boat and her name is still a legend in the islands.

The first steamer to operate a regular service between Guernsey and Sark was the paddler *Rescue*. She was primarily engaged on towing and was joined by *Rescue II* in 1878. Both ran excursions to the other islands in addition to towing sailing craft, like the screw steamer *Assistance* of 1886. Her consorts were the *Alert* and *Serk*, attractive little craft chiefly used on the Guernsey-Sark service. All three disappeared from the islands in about 1915.

In the last century the cutter *Fawn* was the regular trader between Guernsey and St Malo. In 1897 she was replaced by a steamer of the same name and was in turn succeeded in 1923 by the *New Fawn*, which also ran to Sark and Alderney on occasion. So did the last Channel Islands paddle steamer, the *Helper*, used locally between 1920 and 1926. Her replacement was the *Riduna*, employed on both the Alderney and Sark services in the 1920s. Another interesting group of ships was the 'Joybells', the first of which was a converted RNLI lifeboat. The second was a small motor vessel and the third, converted into a motor ship, was once a steam tug. They were in service locally in the 1930s, mainly between Guernsey and Sark.

During the occupation, communications between the islands were sketchy and uncertain. The local passenger ships had left and only an old vessel, the *Staffa*, remained. When she was wrecked in Braye harbour, a small motor vessel, the *White Heather*, ran between Guernsey and Sark while German craft maintained the Jersey and Alderney links. Few civilians were allowed to use these vessels and air travel, of course, was out of the question.

After the war, when inter-island services were resumed, at first one travelled to Alderney by a small naval vessel and motor launches plied to and from Sark. Eventually the steamer *Radford* was used on the Alderney run and to Sark went the MV *Sark Coast*, among others. A succession of small ships followed in her wake, including the 'Commodores' and, briefly, the *Courier*. In recent years the Condor hydrofoils have been running to Alderney and Sark in summer and the *Island Commodore* served Alderney for many years. Today, renamed *Ile de Serk*, she is on the Sark service, in addition to a fleet of fast launches. Apart from the hydrofoils, there is no passenger-ship route to Alderney and most passengers travel there by air.

Most Guernsey people saw aircraft for the first time during the First

World War when French naval seaplanes were based at St Peter Port. They escorted local ships, hunted U-Boats and, incidentally, provided much interest for the islanders. Civilian flying-boats came on the scene in 1923 on a service between Southampton and St Peter Port. It was started by the British Marine Air Navigation Co and was later taken over by Imperial Airways.

Amphibian aircraft—Supermarine 'Sea Eagles' with a single Rolls-Royce engine—were used and there was accommodation for a pilot and six passengers. In 1924 only seventy-three people used the service, although the flight took only one and a half hours and the service was reliable. Occasionally, the aircraft continued to Jersey and also flew to Alderney, where amphibians occasionally used the sands of Braye for landing purposes. In 1934 Guernsey Airways was formed and a month later Channel Islands Airways was established as a holding and directing company of Jersey & Guernsey Airways. While in Jersey St Aubin's sands was the 'airport', a small airfield was used at L'Erée, Guernsey, but the need for something better was apparent in both islands.

In 1936 the amphibian *Cloud of Iona* crashed on Les Minquiers rocks, near Jersey, after leaving Guernsey in very poor visibility and all aboard perished. Three years later Guernsey airport was opened at La Villiaze, Forest, and at once the number of air travellers increased. However, a few months later war broke out and the airport was temporarily closed to civilian flying although a limited service between Guernsey, Jersey, Shoreham and London was started in October 1939 and ended just before the occupation.

Civilian flying was resumed in 1945 with 36-seater Bristol Wayfarers, augmented by de Havilland Rapides and Dominies. As well as operating inter-island services, these aircraft flew to and from Croydon and Southampton. In 1947 British European Airways took over Channel Islands Airways, not without opposition. Ten years later Guernsey airport was greatly enlarged at a cost of over half a million pounds and concrete runways succeeded grass, thus eliminating flooding problems. Later the terminal buildings were improved and further improvements are currently in progress.

Several members of the royal family have used La Villiaze airport, as indeed they have used those of Jersey and Alderney. They include the late King George VI, Queen Elizabeth the Queen Mother, the present Queen and the Duke of Edinburgh, the late Duke of Gloucester, Princess Royal and Duchess of Kent, Princess Margaret and Princess Alexandra. Princess Anne has visited Guernsey in the royal yacht *Britannia*.

Happily, air disasters in Guernsey have so far been rare. The worst,

Plate 33 *On Jersey's north coast is Bonne Nuit bay, an attractive place flanked by tall, green cliffs. Here is a little harbour, formerly used by oyster boats and now popular among yachtsmen and swimmers, who use the steps as a diving stage when the tide serves* (States of Jersey Tourism Committee)

Plate 34 *The broad sands of St Ouen's bay, Jersey, make an excellent place for sand-racing and here one may watch cars and motor cycles travelling at speeds unknown on the island roads. This huge bay is popular with surfers too. An old fort stands in the middle and beyond is high ground, contrasting with the gentle hinterland of St Ouen's bay* (States of Jersey Tourism Committee)

Plate 35 *Fort Les Hommeaux Florains, one of the many Victorian defences built in Alderney when fortifications erected in Cherbourg caused consternation to the British Government. On the right of the picture, near the fishing boat, the ship* Liverpool *struck the rocks and sank in 1902. Today the fort is ruined*

Plate 36 *Yachts moored at St Aubin, Jersey's second port. Today the quayside is a car park and large vessels no longer call there* (States of Jersey Tourism Committee)

as yet, occurred in 1961, when a Bristol Freighter crashed near La Villiaze in poor visibility. Two members of the crew were killed, but the passengers escaped with a shaking. Today, vast numbers travel to and from Guernsey by air and several private aircraft are based at La Villiaze. Much produce, too, is exported from there and many imports come in. As in Jersey and Alderney, the bulk of overseas mails is airborne. Helicopters use the airport for the relief of Les Hanois lighthouse keepers and so busy can it be at the airport that the problem of its enlargement is constantly in the minds of thoughtful islanders.

Alderney

Roads are clearly marked on one of the earliest detailed maps of Alderney: that of the Chevalier de Beaurain in 1757, a French cartographer of note, and there can be little doubt that they existed well before then. St Anne must have been linked with the coast for centuries, since in medieval times *vraic* was hauled from the shore, probably at Braye and perhaps Longy, to fertilise the fields bordering St Anne's and, above all, the open field system on the Blaye. Again, the ancient fortress known as the Nunnery, and Essex Castle, built in the middle ages, must have had roads linking them with the town.

Victoria Street, once called Rue Grosnez, had an earlier name: Rue des Sablons, suggesting it was either a sandy track or possibly a road on which sand was carried from the beach. Another old road is Little Street, formerly Petite Rue and, still earlier, Rue des Vaches. Cattle descended it from the Blaye to drink at the fountain in Marais Square. The Longis road, too, is an ancient highway.

Roads obviously existed in St Anne's since its first settlement, though initially these may have been little better than spaces between farmhouses and other buildings. Later, when wheeled traffic became general, they would have been widened, surfaced and maintained, allowing passage to men and animals as well as vehicles. Military needs probably dictated access from the town to parts of the coast which were fortified, as well as to Telegraph Tower and the beacon on La Giffoine. The harbour, too, needed a means of reaching St Anne's and vice versa.

Yet traffic in Alderney could never have been heavy. The island is small, the majority of its inhabitants lived in the little town and most were content to remain there. Very few had business at the small port: only the farmers needing *vraic* and fishermen requiring access to the sea, not forgetting those engaged in smuggling. It was only in the last century that roads in Alderney were needed by many people, most of

whom were not islanders. The wave of fort-building and the construction of the breakwater in the 1840s and 1850s demanded thoroughfares capable of carrying cartloads of stone, rubble and other materials, even though much of it travelled by railway and barge. Because so vast a quantity of stone was needed for the building of the breakwater, Little Crabby harbour (the New Harbour of today) and adjacent forts, it was conveyed from quarries in the Mannez area by a light railway which ran along the shores of Braye Bay for much of its length. In 1847 it was opened and the first train to use it comprised a locomotive and no less than fourteen wagons, each laden with three and a half tons of stone.

On the completion of the breakwater the railway was retained to service it. Great amounts of stone were hauled from Mannez to be deposited on the mole's seaward flank for protection against the waves, and it was also used for repair work. The railway also carried stone for export by arrangement between the Admiralty and the granite merchants. When Queen Victoria visited the island in 1854 she rode in a railway carriage owned by the contractors and drawn by two horses. The less exalted travelled in a locomotive tender.

During the occupation the Germans used the railway in the construction of their fortifications and it is still occasionally employed today on breakwater work. Between 1940 and 1945 the Germans maintained the island roads and in some cases they altered and improved them, as they did in the larger islands. At the present time several of them are excellent, especially the Lower Road running eastwards of Braye, though some in the vicinity of the Blaye are rugged.

The town streets are picturesque to view but rather uneven to walk on. The charming paving stones of St Anne's are of Alderney extraction and may well date from the eighteenth century. Probably the setts were Alderney's first attempt at road-paving, since no evidence of the kind seems to exist at Braye or elsewhere. Until recently, traffic was so light that grass could be seen growing between the setts but today Alderney abounds in private and hire cars, lorries and some exceptionally large buses, as well as taxis, motorcycles and delivery vans.

Sea communications between Alderney and Guernsey have already been mentioned. Attempts have been made to run a direct service between the island and England but they have not proved successful, though there was a time when steamer excursions to the island were run from Weymouth and Bournemouth, as well as from Guernsey.

By far the greatest number of travellers to and from Alderney use the Islander and Trislander aircraft of Aurigny Air Services, founded in 1968 and using the Alderney lion as its emblem. The firm started with

one aircraft serving Alderney and Guernsey only. Today it has two Islanders and six Trislanders and its staff includes seventeen pilots. This is the only carrier serving three Channel Islands with a regular scheduled service, with connections to Southampton and Cherbourg, as well as operating private charter work and ambulance services in an emergency.

In 1968 the company carried a total of 45,989 passengers, a figure which rose to 104,795 in 1969 and 145,899 in 1970. By 1971 the total had reached 152,007 and has continued to mount annually. In 1972 it was 157,213, it was 181,433 in 1973, in the following year it was 189,900 and it reached 210,412 in 1975. In addition to carrying passengers, Aurigny aircraft also carry freight, mail and newspapers, not only in the summer but throughout the year.

Sark

The island's roads almost certainly date from Helier de Carteret's colonisation in 1565, though prior to this rough tracks probably linked one part of the island with another and one of these must have crossed La Coupée to take the traveller from Big Sark to Little Sark. Perhaps there was a path to L'Eperquerie from the settlement in the island's centre and there may have been a way to the western cliffs. De Carteret was responsible for the tunnel leading from Le Creux to the foot of the hill leading to La Collenette. 'Les Grands Chemins', the wide roads of today, were also his idea. Twenty-four feet wide, they run to all points of the compass, with their centre at La Collenette.

They serve the tenements in Little Sark, those in the vicinity of Beauregard, others in the north and near La Seigneurie and the mansion itself. As well, there are old lanes running from main roads to more remote properties, in addition to cliff paths, though, unhappily, these do not provide a continuous coastal walk such as can be enjoyed in the other islands of the Guernsey bailiwick.

Until a few years ago the tenants were responsible for road maintenance by way of personal labour, or by providing substitutes. The practice was known as La Corvée. Today, the usually good road surfaces are used by horse-drawn carriages, tractors and a multitude of bicycles, especially in summer, when visitors hire them. How they reach the island has already been dealt with in the Guernsey section.

While the main harbour is at La Maseline, the older and more beautiful port, Le Creux, is still used, especially by yachtsmen and fishermen. Until quite recently Havre Gosselin was an important land-

ing place when an easterly wind proved too strong for the eastern harbours. Boats conveyed passengers from the anchored ship to the landing, where a stiff climb awaited them. Today this very rarely happens, though fishermen and yachtsmen still use the steps and also make use of other Sark havens. The main moorings are at Les Laches, close to Creux harbour.

Horse-drawn cabs (some from Jersey and Guernsey, others from England) are characteristic of Sark, though horse-drawn farm vehicles are almost non-existent, since tractors have now replaced them. Tractors also draw the ambulance and fire appliance, for no other motor vehicles are permitted. At one time those who declined to walk up the hill from the harbour could ascend by carriage or, more cheaply, by perching on a tractor-drawn trailer. Today they can travel in comfort on a 'toastrack' bus towed by a tractor, though it goes no further than the Bel Air Hotel. They can return to the harbour by the same means.

After the Second World War an attempt was made to link Sark with Guernsey by a helicopter service. Members of Chief Pleas were offered sample flights but, while they enjoyed the novelty of viewing Sark from the air, they rejected the notion of an air service and even the ownership of private aircraft is frowned upon if the machine is kept in Sark. Yet Brecqhou's owner may use a helicopter.

Sark, so far, is the only Channel Island without an airport. Few regret this and the many who love the island for its distinctive charm, quietude and undoubted natural beauty hope that for many years to come access to and from Sark will be only by that ancient medium, the sea.

9

The Islands' Way of Life

Herbert Ralph Winterflood

The present-day inhabitants of the Channel Islands can most aptly be described as a 'mixed bunch', though in each of the main islands—Jersey, Guernsey, Alderney and Sark—there are those of Norman heritage who consider themselves to be the true islanders. There are also the families whose ancestors emigrated from the United Kingdom to set up home in the islands. These, too, have full residential qualifications and are now as much a part of the islands as the rugged cliffs which form a bastion against the sea.

Of recent years the islands have seen the arrival of a new type of resident—usually wealthy mainlanders who find the climate, pace of life and the tax arrangements more congenial than in the United Kingdom. These newcomers, many of whom have high intellectual and cultural abilities, have added a richness to the island communities and have been anxious to contribute to the general wellbeing of the inhabitants.

However, some friction has been generated by small sections of the island folk who have thought, perhaps mistakenly, that the newcomers were dabbling too much in island affairs. In many instances the true English settlers have had to shoulder the blame in place of the property speculators whose only interest has been to make a quick killing.

The authorities in the islands have seen the move by well established English people to settle there as a means of increasing revenue from taxation, and although strict controls are now exercised, land has been made available for the building of luxury homes. A classic example of this can be seen in Guernsey where, at Fort George, a high-standard residential estate has been built, most of the homes being occupied by wealthy settlers. Naturally, many islanders opposed the plan to sell this land to a developer but, apart from the fort demolition costs, it was thought by the island parliament to be the right thing to do. This has been one way in which Guernsey has broadened its economic basis.

Channel Islanders are proud and independent, seeing the need to be continually vigilant against those who might wish to change the

landscape, character or atmosphere of the islands. At the same time they recognise their dependence on the United Kingdom in matters of defence, fishery protection, the provision of sea and air travel, and the supply of foodstuffs and manufactured products. They also rely on Britain to supply the bulk of the many thousands of tourists who play such a vital part in boosting the economy, and to provide customers for the large quantities of potatoes, cauliflower, tomatoes and flowers which are grown locally and exported to all parts of the United Kingdom. The growers have also looked to the continent for suitable markets for their produce, but here there are difficulties and usually they have had to turn again to the English markets for a living.

Government Links

The Home Office provides the link between the island administrations and the British government and every effort is made to maintain an harmonious atmosphere. During the complex negotiations over the position of the Channel Islands as a result of Britain joining the European Economic Community, the value of this friendly association was well exemplified and though the islands' dependence on 'Big Brother' has been forced on them by reason of their geographical position, size and limited financial resources, they have accepted the position gracefully, and in turn the Home Office has not attempted to interfere with their internal policy matters. New laws introduced by the local parliaments go to the Privy Council for study and general approval and are normally returned duly 'rubber stamped' for local registration. This method, though slow in operation, does at least safeguard the populations against the introduction of undemocratic legislation and certainly direct government from Whitehall would be vigorously opposed in all the islands.

In Jersey, Guernsey, Alderney and Sark local parliaments attempt to govern in what they consider to be in the best interests of each community and, within reason, they follow the wishes of the majority.

Island States

In Jersey, the States comprise twelve senators, twelve parish constables and twenty-eight deputies, with the bailiff as president. The bailiff is appointed by the Crown and also presides over the Royal Court, which consists of twelve jurats. The lieutenant-governor, the dean, the attorney-general and the solicitor-general are all appointed by the Crown and

sit in the States. They are entitled to speak, but they have no vote.

A referendum taken in 1947 showed that 64 per cent of the population were in favour of a reform of the assembly and 36 per cent against. The following year the States passed its own reform law which made it a truly democratic body with regular elections by universal suffrage.

Guernsey

The States of Guernsey consists of twelve *conseillers,* thirty-three deputies of the people, ten representatives from the parishes and two Alderney representatives, again with the bailiff of the island as president. Elections are held every three years, so giving electors an opportunity to put into office those whom they consider will best follow the wishes of the majority.

The States of Election meets for two specific duties—to elect jurats to the Royal Court and *conseillers* to the States of Deliberation. This system has been questioned, but only recently the States re-affirmed its decision not to elect *conseillers* by universal suffrage.

Alderney

Alderney has a local parliament consisting of twelve representatives of the people with a president who, as in the larger islands, is the civil head of the community. However, the president, like the representatives of Alderney's parliament, is voted into office by the people.

Sark

Sark has its Chief Pleas, with its tenants, twelve deputies elected by the people, and the seigneur. Originally only the tenants of the fief could attend the assembly, a privilege accorded them as owners of the original island tenements granted by Seigneur Helier de Carteret in 1565. Even to this day the Seigneur of Sark has considerable power and influence over the affairs of the island, but the inclusion of the deputies in Chief Pleas has helped to create a more democratic atmosphere.

Parochial Administration

Both in Jersey and Guernsey a parish system is in operation which takes some of the burden of administration off the shoulders of the

representatives of the States. In Jersey the constable is civic head of his parish. He represents it in the States, presides over the parish assembly, and is head of the parish police. The position is an honorary one and there is a new election every three years. The Jersey parish assemblies are involved in much more administrative work than those in Guernsey.

In Guernsey, each parish has a *douzaine*, or committee, whose function it is to ensure that the duties conferred by law on the district are carried out. There is a rota system for elections in order to ensure continuity. Each parish has a senior and junior constable to ensure that the law is enforced, that taxes are collected and appropriate notices issued regarding parish meetings, road closures etc. They are also held responsible for the parish accounts.

It will be seen that there are no party politics within the governing organisations, but this does not prevent various shades of political opinion being expressed in the 'corridors of power'. In both Jersey and Guernsey politically-motivated groups have attempted to gain a foothold in the respective States assemblies, but so far the electorate has been reluctant to lend the necessary support to make such moves successful.

Trades Unions

There is, however, a growing body of opinion that the so-called working classes should be better represented, since at present the majority of States members are successful business people with ample time to spare for lengthy debates and committee work. To some extent this opinion is now making itself heard in the assemblies through the trades unions, which have become far more united within the last few years and have often put forward a common policy to be followed. The result has been that more statesmen now speak with the interests of the lower-paid members of the community very much in mind. At the same time this increased union activity has brought with it a number of strikes, some serious, but the deep-rooted independence of the islanders is also allied to the firm belief that unity is strength and there has been a gradual move towards a combined effort for the common good.

States committees visit each others' islands for joint meetings which are held at regular intervals between various chambers of commerce and hotel associations, and there is now a Channel Islands Air Advisory Council, incorporating a transport committee, which negotiates with airlines and shipping operators, Alderney is usually included in discussions, especially if that island is affected.

Alderney

Since the Second World War, Alderney has depended on Guernsey for assistance in many ways. Proposals approved by the Alderney States are placed before the Guernsey States for final approval and there have been occasions when decisions of the Alderney States have been questioned. Hence the need for two Alderney States representatives in the Guernsey House and though the urge for independence has frequently been voiced in this northern isle, economic considerations make it difficult for Alderney to sever her links with the larger island of Guernsey.

During the Second World War the island was evacuated by the civilian population, leaving the German forces free to do what they wished, and shelling by the Royal Navy added to the havoc they caused to island properties. Following the war, Guernsey took over some of the administration and the British government assisted financially in the rebuilding of damaged structures. Thereafter the island made a remarkable recovery and the population has grown with the arrival of settlers, mainly from the United Kingdom. Tourism has proved a good source of income, but light industry has not been so successful. Transport has always proved difficult, but the Alderney Shipping Co now has three ships, and Aurigny Air Services provides a daily series of flights to the neighbouring islands, with services also to France and Southampton. But so far as hospital and airport facilities, as well as police and postal administration are concerned, Guernsey is still relied upon to assist.

There have been moves to increase the population of Alderney, but there are limits to such a project and, as regards any future independence, present-day inflation and the higher cost of administrative and other labour has, if anything, increased the reliance of Alderney on the Guernsey governing body and the civil service.

Sark

The island of Sark has not been so worried by such financial matters. With no airport or hospital to maintain and only a small school to worry about, paid officials are few and the population exists without many of the facilities which most modern societies demand.

Mainly through tourism and a tax system whereby people pay by way of a personal appearance yardstick, Sark is able to pay its way and although it sometimes looks to the Crown officers in Guernsey for advice on legal matters, it manages to run its own affairs in a very independent

manner. It relies on Guernsey for its supplies of foodstuffs and manufactured goods, but these are transported from St Peter Port in its own
boat service.

Entertainment and Sport

Entertainment in the Channel Islands reaches its peak during the
summer months when many forms are available with visitors always
very much in mind.

Both in Guernsey and Jersey cabaret shows, combined with dances,
are staged in many of the hotels, most of the artists being imported
for the season, and local amateur productions, in the form of plays or
variety concerts, are also organised in a bid to keep the 'live' theatre
in being. The two largest islands have their own purpose-built cinemas
where all the latest films are screened, and even in Sark and Alderney
film shows are regularly organised.

Agricultural and horticultural shows are major features of the season
in the four main islands and though nearly all have been, or are faced
with financial problems, somehow they manage to survive, thanks
largely to the dogged determination of the organisers.

A full range of sporting events is held in the islands, both during the
summer months and in the winter. A limiting factor to these activities
is, however, the lack of adequate space. Guernsey, for instance, has only
one golf course at L'Ancresse Common and efforts to establish a second
course have met with strong opposition both from conservationists and
from farmers protesting against the use of good agricultural land for
such a sport.

There has been local opposition, too, to the flying of model aircraft,
which is now strictly controlled. It may only take place well away from
the airport, and in Guernsey it is restricted to a barren headland in the
north of the island. It had been allowed on L'Ancresse Common until
residents rose up in anger over the constant noise from the midget aero
engines.

Motorcar and motorcycle racing on the sands in Guernsey and Jersey
attracts a faithful following and motor hill climbs have also proved
extremely successful, attracting numerous entries from outside the islands.
In the main, local soccer matches now have a small following compared
with pre-war days, perhaps because professional football is so easily
watched on television. However, some enthusiasm is still shown for the
annual Muratti Vase competition, a three-cornered fight between
Alderney, Guernsey and Jersey. Alderney usually gets knocked out in

the first round, leaving Guernsey and Jersey teams to fight for the trophy.

Other such sports as tennis, badminton, table-tennis, darts, swimming, basketball and netball are all popular, inter-island challenges are keenly contested and competitors from England help to set yardsticks for the local people. As with open-air games, indoor sports suffer from the same problem of limited accommodation but the situation has recently shown some improvement in Jersey and Guernsey following the erection of leisure centres.

Religion

Christianity is still a vital factor in the lives of many islanders but, as in Britain, congregations in churches and chapels have declined in numbers and this has perhaps been more noticeable in the Established and Methodist churches. Breakaway evangelical movements now seem to have more appeal and in some instances have built up considerable followings.

Each parish has an Anglican church as its focal point, Methodist chapels are numerous, while Methodism itself has for long exercised a powerful influence on the islands' way of life. It is still not uncommon to hear such comments as: 'We won't get a casino—the Methodists in the States would never allow it.' And although the influence of Methodism and other kindred non-conformist movements is now weakening in the face of a more secular approach to life, these religious movements have at least been able to exercise some control over the rate at which change has been achieved.

Bookmakers are now permitted to operate under licence and all the islands join in a public lottery. Thus the door to a fuller life of secular pursuits has been opened gradually, giving time for every move to be carefully considered and its likely affect on the community studied. For, apart from the religious aspect, there has always been a desire among true islanders to preserve the charm and dignity of the land of their birth, and not to permit outside interests to sweep away that which their forefathers so zealously guarded.

The Media

The newspapers of the Channel Islands have also played their part in stemming the twentieth-century tide of development, permissiveness and speculation. Conservative in their re-action to change, the *Jersey*

Evening Post and the *Guernsey Evening Press*, although not strong campaigning papers in the truest sense, have at times expressed powerful opinions which have been heeded.

Their circulation is widespread and although there have been the customary complaints of a news media monopoly, newspaper owners and journalists do, in fact, strive hard to ensure that all shades of opinion are expressed. At the time of general elections, for example, all candidates for public office are given the opportunity to express their views freely in print.

Television

The BBC provides the islands with a VHF radio service and a television service, initially 405-line and now 625-line, in monochrome and colour. The Independent Broadcasting Authority also offers a black-and-white, and more recently, a colour television service. It operates through Channel Television, providing both network and local programmes, and though this small station has had to struggle against considerable financial difficulties, it has always made a brave showing. Despite its limited facilities, as compared with mainland companies, it has mounted some ambitious local affairs programmes and has contributed in no small way to drawing the island communities closer together.

Bringing a reliable colour television service to the islands was no mean engineering feat. Interference from other stations, bad weather conditions, and the distance which the signal had to travel from the main transmitter in the West Country—all had to be taken into account if an efficient service was to be maintained. Alderney was the obvious choice for the siting of the main reception equipment, with a microwave link to Jersey.

In Guernsey and Alderney secondary transmitters have been established for providing an efficient signal in difficult reception areas. Both the BBC and the IBA share the transmitter masts, but each organisation has undertaken to install its own transmitting equipment.

There are now States broadcasting committees in Jersey and Guernsey studying the need for local radio. Medium wavelengths have been allocated but opinion differs as to whether such a service is really needed. Views are also divided as to who should run the service—the BBC, Channel Television, the States, or a completely new commercial undertaking. At the time of writing no decision has been reached.

Welfare

The islands are rich in welfare and community organisations, both religious and secular. Some are branches of national or international movements, while others are completely local and independent. All provide an opportunity for undertaking service to the community, much of it being carried out away from the glare of publicity.

Both the aged and the sick benefit from the efforts of these voluntary workers, while other organisations cater for the specialised interests of those wishing to increase their basic knowledge in such fields as photography, film-making and local history. It is not uncommon for such groups to take a direct interest in the affairs of state and to make strong representations on points at issue, thus providing yet another means of pressure in the event of government ignoring public opinion.

In Alderney a people's meeting is held prior to States meetings and members of the assembly are left in no doubt as to the wishes of islanders on specific matters to be debated.

Shipping Disasters

Channel Islanders are people of the sea. Hundreds own small craft, while others are content to stand and gaze at the changing moods of the great expanse of water, or watch the ships go by. One vessel which did not pass by was the giant bulk ore carrier *Elwood Mead* which grounded on Les Grunes reef off the west coast of Guernsey. For sixty-one days from Christmas 1973, the islanders followed the resultant salvage drama by a Dutch firm. Every day the local newspaper gave up-to-the-minute accounts of the progress made and reported the despair of the salvage team as hurricane-force winds wrecked their preparations to lift the vessel clear on a carpet of air. There were cheers from the islanders when at last they saw the tugs free the ship from the jagged rocks. The *Elwood Mead* was towed to Rotterdam and has since entered service again, this time under the name of the *Good Leader*.

It was while the *Elwood Mead* was imprisoned on Les Grunes that a maritime event occurred which struck at the very heart strings of Channel islanders—the foundering of the Greek timber ship *Prosperity*, again off the west coast of Guernsey. With her engine out of action, the ship was helpless, and hurricane winds drove her ashore on a reef off Perelle Bay, from which she eventually slipped off and sank. All the crew, including a married woman, were lost, but sixteen bodies were retrieved from the

storm-lashed sea off Les Hanois lighthouse. Large quantities of timber washed ashore were gathered and stored under salvage regulations. Nine of the dead seamen were buried in Guernsey, one was cremated, and the rest taken back to their respective countries for burial.

Springing from this disaster was the formation of a Prosperity Memorial Committee, inspired initially by St Peter Port harbour signal-man Mr Jack Diamond. Later came the establishment of the Guernsey Merchant Navy Association, whose aim is to provide assistance to young people wishing to join the Merchant Navy and to help the relatives of those who have lost their lives at sea. A memorial in local granite has been erected at L'Eree headland in tribute to the crew of the *Prosperity* and to others who have perished in waters adjacent to the islands. Numerous local firms and individuals donated materials and labour to the project and every year Guernseymen pay homage to the sailors whose bodies were washed ashore during the German occupation. The men were from HMS *Charybdis*, which sank in the Bay of St Malo as the result of enemy action. Their graves at Foulon Cemetery are carefully tended, indicative of the great respect the islanders have for the Royal Navy.

From time immemorial the islands have served as a refuge for shipping in time of storm or war. The breakwater at Alderney's Braye harbour was originally built by the British government to provide a safe anchorage for the British fleet and today it provides quiet waters for visiting yachtsmen and trading vessels bringing supplies to the island.

Rescue Services

The islands provide an important rescue service and new fast lifeboats have been stationed at Jersey and Guernsey, ready to speed to ships or small craft in distress. In Guernsey, the St John Ambulance organisation provides a marine ambulance, *Flying Christine II*, for transporting sick or injured from the neighbouring islands to hospital in Guernsey. They also provide an inshore lifeboat service, a task which in Jersey is undertaken by the States fire service.

In Guernsey, the St John Ambulance employ a mobile radar unit which can be towed to headlands to pin-point ships or boats in distress and all the islands have a close link with Crossma, the French rescue co-ordination centre on the Cherbourg peninsula, where wide naval radar coverage is available. Close co-operation is also maintained with the British Coastguard service on the mainland.

Trinity House plays a vital rôle in maintaining certain lighthouses

and navigational buoys round the coasts of the islands, and their vessels are frequent visitors. At both Les Casquets and Les Hanois, helicopter pads have been built to facilitate the re-provisioning and relief of keepers, especially in bad weather conditions.

Museums

With the development of diving techniques, a number of ancient wrecks have been uncovered off the islands, cannon have been raised, and coins, muskets and pottery discovered. Some of these finds are now housed in a maritime museum, Fort Grey, at Rocquaine Bay. Other museums, with which the islands are well endowed, can be found in Alderney, Guernsey and Jersey. In Guernsey a purpose-built museum has recently been erected where the island's treasures are displayed to advantage. There are also a number of German occupation museums and underground hospitals, while Hauteville House in Guernsey, Victor Hugo's former residence, mentioned in an earlier chapter, is a mecca, especially for visitors from France.

Stamps and coins of local origin also help to preserve the individuality of the islands. New issues of Jersey and Guernsey stamps are made at regular intervals, all with a local flavour, and since the local authorities took over the postal service from the British Post Office the philatelic sections have become big business, with a world-wide demand for every stamp issue. The States of both Jersey and Guernsey have also taken over responsibility for telecommunication services to the United Kingdom and beyond. These have since been improved to include trunk dialling to selected parts of the world, both from Guernsey and Jersey.

Since all the Channel Islands have a story to tell, it is not surprising that many books have been written about them: historical publications, books on the fauna of the islands, on shellfish, and most important, the German occupation of the Channel Islands from 1940 to 1945. Several authors have told their own stories of those harrowing years, but the States of Jersey and Guernsey decided to engage an author to write the official history of the occupation, and it became a local best-seller overnight.

The Future

What of the future? Plans for development are constantly under active discussion and in both Guernsey and Jersey banking organisations have been consolidated and tourism expanded to tap still further the

continental markets. In Guernsey particularly, there has been a determined bid to modernise the glasshouse industry in order to achieve earlier and heavier crops of tomatoes and flowers. Light industry has been encouraged and has proved an ideal method of broadening the base of the economy, besides providing congenial employment for young people.

Through good housekeeping, the avoidance of over-ambitious projects and careful control over the expenditure of public money the two major islands have been able to withstand world recession and galloping inflation. Nevertheless, there are other internal matters which have been and still are creating problems for the larger islands.

Island Transport

In Jersey and Guernsey the car population has grown out of all recognition, and the increasing popularity of British Rail's car ferry service from Weymouth has further aggravated the situation. The provision of parking spaces for this influx of vehicles is a particular headache for the authorities and though the problem has been somewhat relieved in Jersey by the erection of multi-storey car parks in St Helier, none has yet been built in Guernsey, although planning permision has been given for one such car park. Even in Alderney, the effect of the motor car has been felt, with the need to introduce one-way systems in the town area.

Population growth has also proved extremely worrying and efforts have been made by means of stringent housing regulations to limit the numbers of people setting up home in the islands. Emergency, social and other public services have begun to feel the strain from the population growth rate and there is already urgent need for an expansion of hospital facilities, the police, fire and ambulance services and the civil service organisations.

The pace of life in the islands generally has noticeably quickened in recent years and even on the two smaller islands of Alderney and Sark measures have had to be introduced to guard against over-development. Some of these have been unpopular in certain quarters but to those who cherish their island home it is obvious that a firm measure of control is vital if the peace and beauty of these unique islands are to be preserved in the years ahead.

10

Visitors' Channel Islands—
the Big Four

Victor Coysh

The Channel Islands attract the visitor for a variety of reasons. Their special character is one and another, obviously, is their outstanding scenic features, coupled with a clement climate. There is scope for the historian, the seeker after natural history, the geologist and philologist, but the islands are not the magnet for specialists alone. Those with but an unscientific interest in studies such as these will find here a rich yield.

Moreover, the islands are equally attractive to those in search of pleasure only. Visitors may enjoy the quietude of a remote beach or the solitude of a distant headland, or if their tastes are quite the opposite and the goal is entertainment, this will be found in equal measure, for there is something for everyone. The accessibility of the islands by air and sea is yet another reason for their popularity, and to the visitor who arrives in his own craft, yacht marinas and spacious harbours await him.

Jersey

This, the largest of the islands, has an area of forty-five square miles (11,655 hectares) and is the most southerly of the group, lying twenty-eight miles (44.8km) from Guernsey (port to port). The 1971 census gave the population as 72,300. The island slopes from north to south, providing a favourable aspect, climate-wise, though its proximity to the continent can, in winter, make it colder than Guernsey. Its finest coastline is in the north, where the cliffs are majestic. On the east lie the large inlets of St Catherine and Grouville, while westward much of the coast is filled by the great bay of St Ouen. On the south coast are the ports of St Helier and St Aubin, with St Brelade's and St Aubin's Bays furnishing a beautiful contrast to these settlements.

Jersey's valleys are among its prime tourist attractions. There are several, but the most visited are those running from the south coast inland. St Peter's valley extends from near the airport to St Aubin's Bay and its stream formerly turned more than one mill. Waterworks, or St Lawrence's Valley, is the most famous and its chain of reservoirs

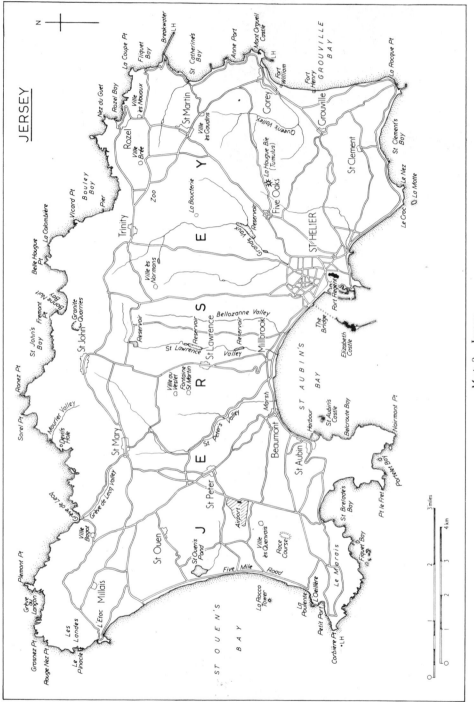

JERSEY

N

Grosnez Pt
Rouge Nez Pt
La Pinacle
Les Landes
L'Etac
Grève du Lançon
Plémont Pt
Grosnez Pt

ST OUEN'S BAY

Five Mile Road

La Pulente
La Moye
Petit Port
Portelet Bay
Corbière Pt LH
L'Oeillère
Pt le Fret

St Brelade's Bay
Ouaisné Bay
Belcroute Bay
St Aubin's Castle
Harbour
St Aubin

ST AUBIN'S BAY

Noirmont Pt

Elizabeth Castle
The Bridge
Fort Regent

ST HELIER

Millbrook
St Lawrence Valley
Bellozanne Valley
Reservoir
Reservoir
Marsh
Beaumont
St Peter's Valley
St Peter
Airport
Ville ès Queuvais
Race Course
La Rocco Tower

St Ouen
St Ouen's Pond
J

St Mary
Mourier Valley
Devil's Hole
Sorel Pt
Ronez Pt
St John's Bay
Fremont Pt
Bonne Nuit Bay
St John
Granite Quarries
St John

Ville au Véslet
Fontaine St Martin
St Lawrence
R
Reservoir
Grands Vaux
Reservoir

Trinity
E
Ville ès Normans
La Boucterie
Zoo
S
Five Oaks
Grands Vaux
La Hougue Bie (Tumulus)
Queens Valley

St Mary
St Peter
E
J

Belle Hougue Pt
La Colombière
Vicard Pt
Bouley Bay
Pier

Rozel
Ville ès Brée
Nez du Guet
Rozel Bay
La Coupe Pt
Ville ès Nouaux
Fliquet Bay
Breakwater LH
St Catherine's Bay
Anne Port
St Martin
Ville ès Goadins
Y

Mont Orgueil Castle
LH
Fort William
Fort Henry
Gorey
Grouville

GROUVILLE BAY
La Rocque Pt

St Clement
St Clement's Bay
Le Nez
La Motte
Le Croc

0   1   2   3 miles
0   1   2   3   4 km

Map 2   Jersey

enhances its beauty. Running down from St John, the brook reaches the sea at First Tower. Bellozanne valley, unhappily, has been marred by industry, unlike Vallé des Vaux and Grands Vaux, north of St Helier. Remains of water mills add interest to the scene and the pedestrian may profitably use their paths on his journeys into the pastoral delights of the hinterland.

Jersey's glorious countryside is enhanced by its numerous stately manor houses, chief of which is St Ouen's, set in fine grounds hard by the venerable parish church. Not far off are the manors of Vinchelez de Bas and de Haut. In the eastern sector are the great houses of Trinity, Rozel and Samarès manors. Many smaller manorial residences survive.

Castles

Unquestionably, the most spectacular building in Jersey is Gorey Castle (often styled Mont Orgueil Castle), standing high above the little port and dominating the east coast. This splendid place is open to visitors and its history (and that of Jersey) is well illustrated by its museum-pieces and realistic-looking waxworks. Elizabeth Castle stands beside St Helier's harbour, an island fortress accessible at low water by causeway and at high tide by ferry. Both these fortifications figured in Jersey's important rôle in the Civil War, during the French wars and in the German occupation. Small wonder that so many visit them.

Of the two, the medieval character of Gorey Castle is probably the reason for its greater popularity and there is no doubting its majesty, nor its fascination when seen under floodlighting. Its story is older than that of Elizabeth Castle, but this is not to say that the newer fortification is at all inferior. It was named after Elizabeth I by Sir Walter Raleigh, governor of Jersey, and is basically a sixteenth-century fortress, with later additions including German work. One of its best buildings is the Governor's House, where realistic tableaux are on view. Nearby is a spacious parade ground, flanked by an art gallery and refreshment place. The ramparts are worth exploring and so is the castle's neighbour, the rocky hermitage of St Helier, perched high above the breakwater. Elizabeth Castle lacks a chapel today, unlike Gorey Castle and both are now the property of the States of Jersey.

Around Jersey's coastline are lesser forts, martello towers and extremely prominent, massive German defences, harsh concrete buildings which the passing years are gradually mellowing. The German occupation museums afford a deep insight into the manner in which Jersey was defended and, of possibly greater interest, how the islanders fared in

that unhappy period. More attractive, probably, is the impressive ancient monument of La Hougue Bie, near Gorey. Here is one of the finest prehistoric structures in western Europe, as well as two medieval chapels, a folk museum and much else.

St Helier

The town of St Helier has much to offer the visitor. Its harbour is spacious, though at low tide when it is dry it is less attractive, but the waterfront has character. Overlooking the town is Fort Regent, once the site of an unusually fine dolmen, later an important defence work, now Jersey's principal place of amusement. A leisure centre, its military character has been retained to a great extent and within its great walls are a first-class swimming pool, adventure playground, facilities for 'hazard golf', table tennis, squash and a solarium, among other attractions. One may reach it by cable car from the town. When completed it will have a conference centre, a piazza with shops and cafeteria and the whole will provide entertainment for visitors and residents alike, particularly in inclement weather.

Well worth seeing is the Royal Square, beside which are the Royal Court building and States Chamber. The modern churches of the town are equally interesting. The Royal Parade gardens have a distinctive charm and the environs of Havre des Pas are inviting. The vicinity of Westmount is popular among tourists, both for the entertainments available and the fine view of St Aubin's Bay from that end of the town. Incidentally, shops in town and country offer tobacco, intoxicants and perfumes at prices far lower than those of the United Kingdom and HM Customs' allowances in this respect are generous. Such advantages apply in all the islands, in none of which is VAT applicable.

It is erroneous to suppose that St Helier is purely a pleasure resort. It is, in fact, an important business centre, Jersey's only town of consequence and the hub of its political, administrative and social universe. The shops are excellent, pedestrian precincts make it a joy to walk in and its public buildings are dignified and well sited. Admittedly, there is little of great antiquity to be seen, but buildings of the eighteenth century onwards abound and, while extremely modern architecture is to be observed, it is not unduly obtrusive. The rich and sturdy Jersey granite is everywhere, whether it be in sea wall, slipway or edifice, and this element is common in both town and countryside.

In Pier Road is the museum of La Société Jersiaise, a fine spacious building which also serves as the society's headquarters. Built in 1815,

it was given to the States in 1893 and it may be used by the society while it exists. Its contents are numerous, valuable and of the greatest interest. Especially so is the replica of an old Jersey kitchen and bedroom, and well worth examining is the Barreau Art Gallery, full of local pictures. The National Trust for Jersey also uses the museum as its headquarters.

One of the sights of St Helier is the market in Halkett Place. Its fine granite buildings, of Victorian vintage, house a collection of shops and stalls selling meat, vegetables, flowers and fruit. This is the New Market. In Beresford Street stands the Old Market, selling produce, and nearby is the Fish Market. These premises are not only useful in rainy weather: they are one of the town's major attractions at all times.

St Matthew's Church, Millbrook, the so-called 'Glass Church', originally Victorian, was rebuilt as a memorial to Lord Trent (formerly Jesse Boot) in 1934. Its glass, by René Lalique, has become a prime attraction and is admired by a host of visitors. Over the altar is a glass cross, supported by pillars, also of glass, while windows and side screens are of the same material. The designs on glass are beautiful, particularly in the Lady Chapel where four glass angels stand behind the altar. This and the communion rails are transparent, like the font. The building itself is of various kinds of stone. The first Lord Trent is buried on the cliffs near St Brelade's Church.

The parish church stands near the Royal Square, and should certainly be viewed. Hereabouts, in 1781, was fought the Battle of Jersey, when the French were defeated. Not far away stands Victoria College, Jersey's public school. In this direction lies the attractive Howard Davis Park and, at the opposite end of the town, is the People's Park, overlooking the sands of St Aubin's Bay. Northward is Springfield, the sports centre, and another place of interest to the visitor is the Weighbridge, Jersey's main bus station.

At Augrès manor, near Trinity Church, is the Jersey zoo, a major attraction. The old house and grounds provide the setting for a particularly fine collection of rare creatures, collected by Gerald Durrell. All the parish churches well repay a visit and as much applies to the Fishermen's Chapel, beside St Brelade's Church. It overlooks the bay and near it runs the ancient sanctuary path which, once upon a time, could be used with impunity by criminals seeking refuge in the church and making their way to the shore and liberty.

Nearby is the Winston Churchill Memorial Park, whose dedication stone bears these words: 'The Right Honorable Winston Spencer Churchill, K.G., O.M., C.H. "And our dear Channel Islands are also

to be freed today" '. The words recall their liberation in May 1945, an event still commemorated by a public holiday every year.

St Aubin

Jersey's second town, St Aubin has a good deal of charm and its position on the great sweep of foreshore is magnificent. Its little harbour has no commercial significance today and from its granite arms one may survey the picturesque St Aubin's fort, accessible on foot at low water. It was built in 1542. St Aubin's High Street is delightful and there are some fine old houses to be seen in this cheerful little place. It has, naturally, a maritime flavour and makes a capital introduction to the attractive shores and country close by. There was a time when one could reach St Aubin by train. Today it is served by bus, but traces of the railway survive.

Other Attractions

Jersey is not only spectacular : its industries are also of great appeal. The sight of its cattle in the small meadows is as attractive as the prospect of acres of land under cultivation, whether it be potatoes in the fields, tomatoes in the sunny valleys or flowers under glass. Fishing craft offshore, the busy life of St Helier's harbour, the airport's intense activity and the vitality of the town and its environs all provide a welcome contrast to the riches of Jersey's historic heritage and scenic attractions. There is no lack of entertainment, too, and at night this is very apparent.

Jersey's bus service, island tours and numerous hire cars make exploration easy, while the rider and pedestrian are both well served. An especially fine walk is along the former railway track from St Aubin to La Corbière, a wild headland in the south-west, where a lighthouse flashes a warning to ships passing a few hundred yards away. Beyond La Corbière are the broad sands of St Ouen, famous for surfing. Northward stands the ancient Grosnez Castle, on a lofty cliff, and not far off is Le Pinacle, a mighty stack of rock, 200ft (60m) high, below which is a prehistoric settlement. The remains of another are nearby, at La Cotte à la Chèvre, where there is a remarkable cavern.

La Cotte de St Brelade is a fine aperture at l'Ouaisné. Others are at Grève au Lancon, Plémont, and along the north coast, some of which are hard to reach. Also in this region is L'Islet, in Bouley Bay, and Ile Agois in Crabbé Bay, islets offering scope to the climber. La Motte

(Green Island) has prehistoric associations and is easily reached from the coast at St Clement. Ile au Guerdain, in Portelet Bay, once held the tomb of Philip Janvrin, who died of the plague in 1721. Later he was re-interred elsewhere and in 1808 the present tower was built on the islet.

An unusual cave is the so-called Devil's Hole in St Mary's parish. Other coastal features of note are the enormous rock masses, natural arches, the Needle Rock at Grève au Lancon, rock pools and vantage points from which to watch the sea's action, particularly impressive on stormy days. To stand on a headland at night and watch the lights of buildings and passing ships is a rewarding experience. In good visibility one may, in daylight, observe the neighbouring islands and the French coast. A trip around Jersey by boat is to be recommended.

Grève de Lecq, in the north, is visited for its beauty, bathing and available refreshments. Here is a martello tower and a fine old water mill, now serving as an inn. This small village and former port enjoy a delightful setting and equally agreeable is the journey across the island to reach it. This is only one of Jersey's many sandy bays, all of them of prime interest to naturalists, geologists and those content to bathe in the clear sea or bask in the sun. The inlets along the high north coast are of special appeal and a favourite is sandy Grève au Lancon. The diminutive harbours at Bonne Nuit, Bouley and Rozel Bays are most agreeable, while Gorey, its castle apart, has much character as a port and holiday resort.

The breakwater at St Catherine's Bay makes a splendid promenade and the shore road from there to Gorey forms a first-class stretch of walking terrain. Jersey's south-east corner, seen at a low spring tide, is extraordinary, for the mass of rocks and sand extends for a mile or more.

Towards the end of the summer, a most colourful attraction is staged : the Battle of Flowers. A great procession of decorated floats proceeds along the St Helier waterfront, watched by thousands. Millions of real flowers adorn highly original presentations and the colour, music, beauty and sheer fun of this world-famous annual spectacle must be seen to be believed. It is the highlight and climax of the tourist season. Another great event is the Bouley Bay hill climb. Show jumping and horse racing are there to be enjoyed, and regattas and cattle shows are additional features of island life. There is also sand racing at St Ouen's Bay.

Like Guernsey, Jersey has its own postal system and issues its own paper money and coinage. The stamps, issued periodically, beautifully depict island scenes and aspects of insular life or history, and the notes are equally attractive. These peculiarities, however, are invalid beyond their particular islands. The museums display former coins and rare

tokens and one is reminded of the days when, in both bailiwicks, French silver was legal currency. The arms of the bailiwicks are those of England: three leopards *passant regardant*. Those of Guernsey bear a sprig as crest, thus distinguishing them from Jersey's armorial bearings, to be seen on coins, notes, stamps and public buildings.

Of all the islands, probably Jersey most retains a French flavour, possibly because it is so close to France. Jersey-French, the ancient tongue, survives, especially in the country parishes, more strongly than the dialects of the other Channel Isles, though it must be admitted that in Jersey many English street names have replaced their former French titles. It is good to know that the National Trust for Jersey has saved several worthwhile properties from unwelcome changes. In its care are the impressive Noirmont Point, overlooking St Aubin's Bay, the headland of Col de la Rocque, in St Mary's parish (one of the island's best viewpoints) and the attractive Morel Farm, in the parish of St Lawrence.

Reference has been made to the degree of contrast to be savoured in Jersey and this is well exemplified by an evening of gaiety either in St Helier or perhaps at some country hotel or bar, to be followed the next day by a drive through the maze of lanes in the island's interior to some remote headland away to the north. Here the sound of the sea and the cry of a gull may be the only distractions from the great silence such a solitude can offer. True, it may soon be broken by the roar of a passing aircraft, but peace is swiftly restored. Yet within minutes one may be back among the happy holidaymakers on a beach where it is impossible to feel lonely.

Guernsey

With an area of about 24 square miles (6,216 hectares), Guernsey is thus considerably smaller than Jersey. Its capital, St Peter Port, is most attractive and its spacious harbour is flanked by Castle Cornet. Beyond lies the ancient town, clinging to its hillside, and on either hand are green regions, admirably contrasting with the weathered granite of the buildings. Observed from the sea, and especially in the early morning, St Peter Port looks enchanting, with the newly-risen sun illuminating its many windows.

Within its massive arms are quays where visitors land and tomatoes depart, among other exports. Nearer the town are two yacht marinas, tightly packed with local and visiting pleasure craft, and from the Old Harbour leave launches bound for Herm, heavily laden with tourists in the season. It is exciting to watch a hydrofoil sweeping out of harbour,

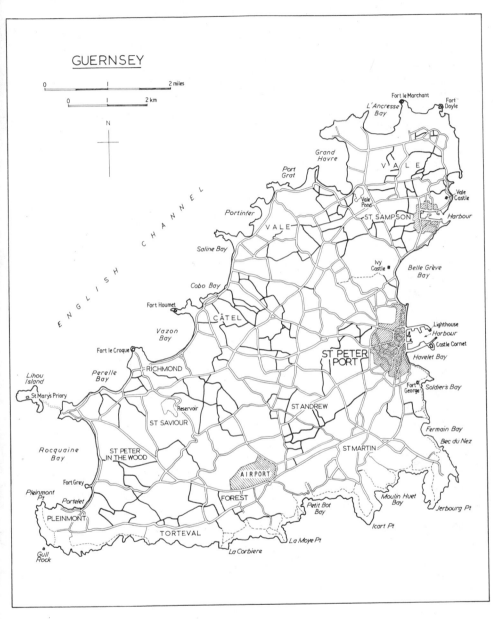

GUERNSEY

0   1   2 miles

0   1   2 km

N

E N G L I S H   C H A N N E L

Fort le Marchant

L'Ancresse Bay

Fort Doyle

Grand Havre

V A L E

Port Grat

Vale Pond

Vale Castle

Portinfer

VALE

ST SAMPSON

Harbour

Saline Bay

Ivy Castle

Belle Grève Bay

Cobo Bay

Fort Houmet

CÂTEL

Vazon Bay

Lighthouse

Harbour

Castle Cornet

Fort le Croque

ST PETER PORT

Havelet Bay

Lihou Island

Perelle Bay

RICHMOND

St Mary's Priory

Reservoir

ST SAVIOUR

ST ANDREW

Fort George

Soldier's Bay

Rocquaine Bay

ST PETER IN THE WOOD

ST MARTIN

Fermain Bay

Bec du Nez

Fort Grey

AIRPORT

Pleinmont Pt

Portelet

FOREST

Moulin Huet Bay

Jerbourg Pt

PLEINMONT

TORTEVAL

Petit Bot Bay

Icart Pt

Gull Rock

La Corbiere

La Moye Pt

Map 3   Guernsey

bound, perhaps, for St Malo, and stirring to witness the arrival of the Weymouth car ferry or, maybe, a laden cargo vessel, outward bound.

Small wonder, therefore, that visitors spend so much time in and about the harbour. Many of them head for Castle Cornet, a medieval fortress of special appeal, for while its battlements are of the greatest interest (to say nothing of the magnificent view from the summit), the castle houses several museums. On view are maritime exhibits, an attractive collection of pictures, German occupation relics, many reminders of the castle's former grandeur and a fascinating RAF exhibition, whose No 201 Squadron is associated with Guernsey.

Near the castle is wooded La Vallette where there are fine swimming pools, numerous seats and a very well-stocked aquarium set within a tunnel above which is Clarence battery, one of Fort George's defences. From there one may glimpse some of Guernsey's matchless cliffs, the town and port and the neighbouring islands.

Guernsey's Capital

St Peter Port is a mixture of old and new, resulting in a contrast, seldom disagreeable, thanks in large measure to the vigilance of the States Island Development Committee. Some of the streets retain their granite setts (within living memory most of them were cobbled) and, because it is built on a cliff, the lower part is linked with the upper by long flights of steps, from which yet more sweeping views may be enjoyed.

Church and Markets

Overlooking the harbour is the Town Church, agreed by most Channel Islanders as the finest place of worship in the group. It stands at the foot of High Street, its spire emerging from the surrounding buildings and forming one of the most impressive features of the quayside. One could spend an hour within, absorbing its ancient atmosphere, viewing the rich colours, impressive masonry, interesting windows (mostly modern, since the older ones were destroyed during the German occupation), and its memories of the past brought to life by numerous memorials and the colours of the Royal Guernsey Militia.

Adjoining the church are the markets, whose stone so admirably blends with it. In summer the markets are thronged with visitors, especially where shellfish are sold, and as much applies to the arcaded flower market (the French Halles), bordering Market Square. Les

Arcades, beneath the colonnade, accommodate some delightful little shops and overlooking the scene is the impressive Guille-Allès Library, open to visitors.

St Peter Port is a place to stroll in, thanks to many of its streets being pedestrian precincts. Wander through narrow Mill Street and Mansell Street, with their small, attractive shops. Peer into High Street's windows or take your ease in the Commercial Arcade, reserved for pedestrians since it was built in the last century. See Trinity Square, with its Victorian atmosphere and notice Cornet Street on your way to Hauteville House.

Victor Hugo's Home

In this hillside building lived France's illustrious poet and writer for fifteen years. Open to visitors, this singular residence must be seen. Resembling a museum in some respects, it was still his abode and something of Hugo's spirit broods there still. From his roof-top study the prospect is vast.

From the top of High Street it is good to proceed down the quaint Pollet, descend North Pier Steps to the quay or climb the hill past the Post Office, where local stamps are available, to the Royal Court House, stately, elegant in its granite dress and well worth visiting. Here one may attend a States meeting or a Court session and learn how Guernsey is governed and how justice is done. Here, too, ancient charters are on display at the Greffe.

Parks and Gardens

Further up the hill are St James's Church (disused and ear-marked as a concert hall), Elizabeth College (a public school founded in 1563) and, not far away, the peaceful and charming Candie Gardens. In the lower section are many rare plants and in the upper part a statue of Victor Hugo. Also there is one of Queen Victoria and between them an island museum and art gallery is to be built. One cannot fail to notice Victoria Tower (commemorating her visit in 1846) and one may obtain the key from the Town Arsenal opposite (it is now the fire station) and, after a climb, enjoy yet one more prospect equal to that seen from an aircraft.

Close to the tower is the Priaulx Library, worth noticing, and from there it is an easy walk to Cambridge Park, green and pleasant. Continue eastward past the nineteenth-century Castle Carey to Les

Côtils belvedere and sit awhile to enjoy what is to be seen from this viewpoint.

Not far off is Beauséjour leisure centre, set in fine grounds. Recently completed, it comprises a swimming pool and another for children, a small boating pool, squash courts, a bowling green, facilities for football, softball and an extensive landscaped car park. The main sports hall is also available for other activities. It is divisible into sections and is available for conferences. A smaller hall is used for indoor bowls and another is available for theatrical presentations, dances etc. Bars, lounges and a restaurant are further amenities available.

Between Elizabeth College and Victoria Tower is the Odeon cinema and another, the Gaumont, is in St Julian's Avenue. The Little Theatre is rather hidden away up a flight of steps off Market Street. There are spectacular floor presentations at some of the hotels. The friendly pubs of town and countryside offer warm hospitality, though they are closed on Sundays.

St Sampson's

Guernsey's second town lies about three miles (4.8 km) north of St Peter Port and at the Bridge there is a thriving shopping centre. Probably the prime attraction is the venerable parish church, near the South Side, with its rugged exterior and endearing interior. The colours of the bygone militia hang there, as they do in many a parish church, all of which are very well worth seeing.

The port is usually active, with vessels discharging oil, coal, timber, cement and other essential commodities. Boat-building is practised on the South Side and opposite, near the electricity station, is a busy shipyard. St Sampson's is the usual venue for the North Regatta, a prime summer attraction.

Near the New Road shops is Delancey Park, on a grassy hill, where bowls, tennis, football and cricket are played. From there one looks down on the harbour, protected on the south by a martello tower and battery at Mont Crevelt and on the north by the ancient Vale Castle. Both these former defences were included in the German system of fortifications and each should be seen, though the castle has only its old walls and lofty situation to offer nowadays.

Bordeaux and L'Ancresse

Especially attractive is Bordeaux, less than a mile north of St Sampson's, where, at high water, fishing craft ride at their moorings. There is good diving and swimming off the pier and slipway when the tide is suitable and there is a sandy beach, too. Further along the coast are Les Houmets, engaging islets reached at low tide (and the tide must be reckoned with) and well worth exploring, if only because of their quietude. The centre islet, Houmet Paradis, is the most interesting. Northwards lies Beaucette yacht marina, whose masts mark its where-abouts.

On L'Ancresse Common are several dolmens, the coast is ringed by forts, martello towers, disused batteries and German defences and there are also quarries, small fields and grazing livestock. Here one may enjoy golf, occasional race meetings and a magnificent beach. Sometimes there is shooting at the range by Fort Le Marchant.

Between L'Ancresse and Grandes Rocques, on the north-west coast, are small bays, some of them sandy, attractive to anglers and those in quest of relative solitude. Grandes Rocques is more popular, and with good reason for the red granite outcrops are colourful and impressive, the sands are broad and the bathing is good.

The West Coast

Cobo enjoys the same advantages and at both bays (as at most other resorts) are places of refreshment. High above Cobo stands Le Guet, an old watch-house now almost masked by trees. It is worth climbing the hill to regard the stretch of coastline and to gaze across the sea towards America! Fort Houmet, on its attractive peninsula, lies below and north of Vazon, on whose spacious sands one may sometimes witness car and cycle racing. Very often fine surfing is to be had there.

Along this coast are many defences, built to withstand Napoleon's invaders and, later, British intruders, for the Germans heavily defended this vulnerable shore-line. It is also open to attack by heavy seas and massive walls are there to combat them. The reefs of rock seen at low tide add character to the scene.

L'Erée overlooks Lihou island and at a low spring tide there is sufficient time to cross the paved causeway and pay it a visit. There are the ruins of St Mary's priory to see, a fine modern house to observe, a glorious rock pool in which to bathe and the chance to walk around

a green isle innocent of traffic. The rocky environs, including Lihoumel, are remarkable, but do not linger too long, since the rising tide must never be overlooked.

On the L'Erée headland stands Fort Saumarez, with its German tower and nearby is the dolmen of Le Creux ès Faies, well concealed within its tumulus. L'Erèe's sands are enjoyed by many and equally patronised is the great beach of Rocquaine. Here stands Fort Grey, now a well-appointed maritime museum.

The South Coast

For many visitors, this is the best of Guernsey. The stretch of cliffs extending from St Peter Port to Torteval is rugged, exquisitely beautiful and excellent for walking, thanks to the cliff paths. Do not stray from them, though, for the heights can be dangerous. First of its inlets is Soldiers' Bay, below Fort George and, further on, popular Fermain Bay, backed by a wooded valley and, among other approaches, reached by launch from St Peter Port.

At Jerbourg there is Marble Bay (Pied des Murs) below the diminutive Pine Forest. Telegraph Bay (Vaux Bêtes) lies at the foot of St Martin's Point, where there is a small lighthouse, and at Jerbourg Point the rocky chain of the Peastacks (Les Tas de Pois d'Amont) must be the grandest in the islands. Not far off are the splendid sands of Petit Port, lying below steep cliffs down which runs a long flight of steps. The climb is strenuous but worth the effort.

It is easier to reach Moulin Huet Bay by way of its gentle valley or water lane. Near is Saints Bay, again simple to visit, though apart from Petit Bôt some walking from bus or car is inevitable at all these bays. Icart Point is a magnificent headland above the secluded cove of Le Jaonnet, a particularly appealing bay and far less visited than its neighbour, Petit Bôt. This is approached by two beautiful valleys. Further west is Le Gouffre, a savage gulf adjoining the tiny fishing haven of La Moye, a good place for the angler and diver.

From this point to Pleinmont, the cliffs are mainly for the walker, though there is some access to headlands by car. Bays are scarce, but the heights are superb. La Corbière has a grandeur shared by the cliffs above Le Creux Mahie, a big cave rather difficult to reach. Westward lie the glories of Les Tielles, cliffs especially lovely when spring flowers adorn them. Beyond is lonely Mont Herault watch-house and then come the Pleinmont cliffs, where television masts and German towers lend a modern touch to the noble scene. From the heights a path

descends to Les Pézeriés and Portelet fishing harbour, two agreeable places where an aged fort, disused batteries and a distant prospect of Les Hanois lighthouse make this region one of the best in Guernsey.

Inland

There is much to see in the island's interior, which a coach tour reveals. Enjoying great popularity is the Little Chapel at Les Vauxbelets, close to St Andrew's Church, a tiny shrine made of shells, broken china and other odds and ends. Not far away is the German underground hospital, while by the Forest Church is the Occupation Museum. In this region, too, is the Guernsey zoo, near the airport.

Saumarez Park, venue for the Battle of Flowers, is inland from Cobo and here the National Trust of Guernsey has a very good folk museum. The mansion, impressive, is open to visitors. From there it is simple to reach the King's Mills and Talbot Valley, sylvan regions where woodlands and streams are the meadows' neighbours and where many a fine old farm adorns the picture. Here one may glimpse what Guernsey was like a century ago. Another reminder of yesterday is stately Sausmarez Manor, in St Martin's, which may be visited.

It is most pleasant to stroll through the lanes of St Pierre du Bois, St Saviour's and Torteval and to walk from the high ground down to the west coast. Pastoral attractions abound in the shape of mellow walls, old wells and mounting blocks, picturesque arches, delightful gardens and sometimes reminders of Guernsey's feudal past. How good it is to see St Saviour's reservoir flanked by trees and haunted by bird life!

Restful, too, is the nature reserve of La Société Guernesiaise near the church of St Pierre du Bois and there is charm in such ancient settlements as La Bellieuse, beside St Martin's Church, Le Variouf, not far from the Forest Church, and Les Buttes, St Saviour's. The environs of Torteval Church are also attractive. Indeed, inland Guernsey has a character from which the presence of greenhouses and other buildings cannot seriously detract.

The National Trust of Guernsey owns several properties, all of which are open to visitors without charge. Many are stretches of cliffland and the first to be acquired and perhaps the most impressive is at Le Vaux de Monel, a property running from near the television masts on Pleinmont headland down to the coast road. Another in this vicinity is La Varde rock and adjacent land and, further north along the west coast, is Le Catioroc, pleasant terrain between the dolmen just off the coast road and the former watch-house inland.

The islet of Houmet Paradis, north of Bordeaux, is under Trust
control and, away to the south, it owns a well-sited field on the Jerbourg
cliffs, not far from the monument. The majority of its properties have
been presented, but a few have been purchased. In Talbot Valley is an
attractive cottage and some pleasant land nearby. This is the first
building to be acquired by the Trust, which is also responsible for the
Langlois collection of farm implements at the Folk Museum, Saumarez
Park.

Alderney

Alderney, slightly larger than Sark, has an area of about six square
miles (1,554 hectares) and is the most northerly of the group. It is also
the least known and many regard this as a virtue, since it is never
crowded. This lack of popularity among the masses probably dates from
the time when one reached it by sea only and then only via Guernsey,
involving a double passage to and from England, whereas today the
position has changed and, in addition to a twice-weekly hydrofoil service
in summer, access can be gained by air from Southampton, Guernsey,
Jersey and Cherbourg. Its airport dates from 1935.

Visitors rejoice in Alderney's atmosphere as much as in its scenic
splendour. It is a most amiable place and the cordial welcome extended
is not simply because tourism is its main industry: hospitality has been
Alderney's characteristic for generations. Added to this is the sense of
freedom, the absence of formality, the bracing air and, of course, the
glory of the coast and the undoubted charm of 'serene St Anne', as
Swinburne poetically described it. A further merit is the ease and speed
with which one may travel to and from the island, unless adverse
weather dictates otherwise.

As one drives from the airport to St Anne it is easy to grasp the lie
of the land, with the lofty cliffs, arable country and town in the western
sector and a plain lying eastward. Much new building has sprung up
since the German occupation (signs of which are not wanting), but the
actual town retains its old charm and fascinating atmosphere. Its paved
streets recapture yesterday and the buildings, for the most part, do
likewise.

St Anne

St Anne's most outstanding edifices include the parish church, dating
from 1850 and considered to be the best designed of the islands' modern

Plate 37 *Fort Tourgis, Alderney, standing on high ground on the north coast. Its cannon commanded the Swinge and the approaches to Braye harbour. The fort is one of a chain of nineteenth-century defences which were used by the Germans during the Second World War, when they occupied the island. One of their bunkers is visible just above the beach on the left of the picture* (C. Toms)

Plate 38 *Pedigree Guernsey cattle grazing in a Herm meadow. On the left is part of Jethou and near the right margin is the conical islet of Crevichon. A corner of Guernsey rises above it. This is one of the most charming parts of the Channel Islands* (British Travel Association)

Plate 39 *Guernsey has three yacht marinas, two of which are seen in this aerial photograph of St Peter Port. Here hundreds of local and visiting craft are berthed in summer. Behind them, and on the hillside, rises old St Peter Port, whose main harbour accommodates larger and more business-like shipping*

Plate 40 *From Essex Castle, Alderney, one obtains a fine view of Longy bay, with its silver-white sands and reefs of rock. The castle has an Elizabethan origin, though much of it is Victorian and the Germans also added to it. Away over Longy Common is Mannez lighthouse and German observation tower*

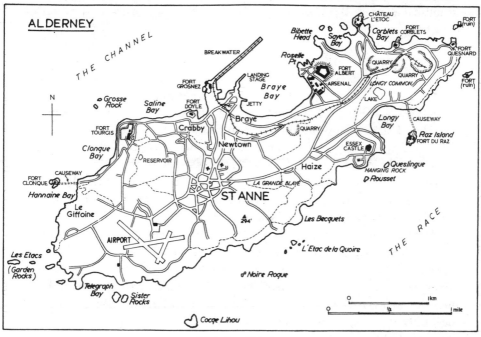

Map 4 Alderney

churches. Of mellow Alderney stone, it is spacious and has a good peal of bells. Its size recalls the time when it was used by the garrison (as well as islanders), when the island was a fortress. Opposite is the Court House, not without merit, especially within, and nearby is Royal Connaught Square, reminiscent of a French *place*, where stands the stately Island Hall, once Government House, housing the excellent Alderney Library and a large room for public meetings.

In the paved square are the vicarage and an attractive hotel. Others are located at Le Huret and Marais Square, interesting parts of the little town, whose narrow lanes are worth exploring. The High Street, despite its name, is not the main thoroughfare, though it is interesting, since the building styles are so contrasting. Here one finds the Jubilee Home, with its modern annexe, dwellings, shops and some of Alderney's friendly pubs.

Victoria Street is the chief shopping centre and here one may buy a great variety of goods. Part of it is a pedestrian precinct. There are more pubs, restaurants, shops interspersed with private houses, a pleasant little war memorial garden and some offshoots worth seeing. At the foot of the street is a road leading to two major hotels and the recreation ground known as Les Butes. From here is a sweeping prospect of the

English Channel, the Casquets lighthouse, Burhou, Braye and much of Alderney.

The Coast

It is easy to stroll down to Braye by serpentine path and watch the shipping, yachting and angling activity, the quiet boat maintenance at the New Harbour and possibly men at work on the massive breakwater. This makes a capital promenade in calm weather, though heavy seas pour over it in stormy conditions. Much shorter is the Old Pier, close to delightful Braye Street, with its pubs and old houses. Just above the school is Newtown, full of character, with yet another hostelry below the heights topped by a television mast.

One may hire a cycle or even a horse, or travel by bus around much of the island, though the pedestrian probably sees it best of all. The bus starts from Marais Square and calls at Braye before travelling eastward along the sandy shores of Braye Bay, past massive Fort Albert and the fine sands of Saye. At Corblets is more sand and good surfing can often be enjoyed there. Several forts will be seen and of special interest is Mannez lighthouse, open to visitors.

The bus continues along the shore to Longy, a broad, sandy bay, protected by a German anti-tank wall, more forts and the ancient 'Nunnery'. Above the beach is the golf course and the bus passes it on one hand and Longy common on the other on its return to the town. It is a good idea to climb up to Essex Castle and walk along a first-class path running west. Only thus can one savour the full glory of the cliffs.

Most of the bays hereabout are rather difficult of access, but they can be well seen from the headlands and from the many seats on the cliffs. It is possible to scramble down to Cachelière pier, now derelict, where stone was once shipped. On the right are the green acres of the Blaye and then comes the airport. Seaward, a great view is enjoyed over the Race and the French coast and before long Telegraph Tower will be seen on the heights.

Alderney's finest coastal feature lies below: Telegraph Bay. Its high, steep cliffs are majestic, the headland of Tête de Judemarre is one of grandeur and the sands exposed at low water make the long climb down steps and path worthwhile. At high tide the bay cannot be reached, since the sea reaches the foot of the path and care must always be taken in this respect. One could spend hours there, swimming, exploring the caves, basking below the sheltering cliffs, examining the interesting beach and gazing with awe at the lofty rocks, La Nache and

La Fourquie, at the far end of Telegraph Bay, so called because the cable to Guernsey was brought ashore there.

Walking onwards, the cliffs retain their beauty and dignity. There is a wide view from Tête de Judemarre and on a clear day the other islands are easily seen. Inland is Trois Vaux, a three-pronged valley, while seaward are the Garden Rocks, or Les Etacs. From the headland of La Giffoine one can look down at these stacks, the home of a host of gannets. It is breathtaking to watch them dive and if a boat can be secured at Braye, a visit to the gannetry is not to be missed.

On Le Giffoine are the remains of a heavy German battery. Here the path forsakes the cliffs and the main road must be used until a zigzag path downhill is reached. It leads to Clonque and the end of the cliffs. A fine fort, reached by causeway, an interesting foreshore and little Hannaine Bay are there to be enjoyed. Clonque is easily reached by road from St Anne or Braye and this coastal route is glorious.

It passes under the shadow of Fort Tourgis, on the hillside, and soon the golden sands of Platte Saline are reached. Here one may bathe in the clearest of seas, but the tide's strength must be watched. Crabby Bay comes next, where there are more forts and signs of the German occupation. The hospital is nearby and after passing the electricity station one is back at the New Harbour. There one should notice the Alderney Sailing Club's premises, the harbourmaster's office and Fort Grosnez, once the breakwater's guardian.

Entertainments

Reference has been made to golf—the clubhouse is on the Longy road —and tennis is also available. One of the hotels has a swimming pool and, nearby, on Butes, cricket and football are sometimes played. Another soccer ground is below Fort Albert. During Alderney Week Butes is a busy spot. The Week is the summer's highlight, during which there are a cavalcade, fancy dress competitions, torchlight procession, a great bonfire and other forms of amusement. It is Alderney's answer to the Battles of Flowers of the larger islands.

In addition to St Anne's Church, places of worship are the modern Roman Catholic church in Braye road (worth seeing), the Methodists' Butes church and the Salvation Army's citadel in High Street. The fine school at Newtown replaces one at Le Huret, now the really excellent museum of the Alderney Society and one of the most fascinating buildings in the island. It stands beside the clock tower, all that survives of Alderney's first parish church.

Eating out, so popular in the islands, is something greatly encouraged in Alderney, where good restaurants abound, not only in St Anne but at Braye and Longy. Occasional stage shows and concerts at the Island Hall add to the pleasure of visitors, who may also witness occasional film performances and will be cordially welcomed at all places of refreshment. Many enjoy watching the activity at the airport or meeting the hydrofoil at Braye. Even if this does not happen, there is always something to see there.

From there one may embark on a marine tour of Alderney or, possibly better still, a trip to Burhou. Rich in bird life, its shores alone are worth inspecting. It is quiet there—apart from the bird cries—and if solitude is to be prolonged, its hut may be rented from the Alderney States.

A Court sitting is to be recommended and, probably more interesting, a session of the States, both of which are held at the Court House. There is, in fact, so much to see and do in Alderney and, equally, there is so strong a temptation to accomplish the minimum, that the island as a holiday centre is truly admirable.

Sark

To style Sark as unique may be a commonplace but it is the truth. An island under feudal rule at the present time is in itself remarkable, but if, in addition, there is natural beauty of the highest order, the result is altogether unusual. What is equally extraordinary is that it retains its elusive magic, its ancient spell, its quiet charm, despite the popularity it enjoys. Long may this continue!

Approximately four and a half square miles (1,165 hectares) in area, Sark is edged by shores which are almost entirely lofty; only in the north do they decline in height somewhat. Otherwise there is an average height of about 250ft (75m) and the grandeur of the cliffs is unsurpassed in the islands. Their appearance is enhanced by the massive rocks offshore, by Sark's attendant islets, including Brecqhou, off the west coast and, in the south, l'Etac. Westward, nine miles (14.5km) is Guernsey and six miles (9.5km) from Sark are Herm and Jethou.

The island's two harbours, Le Creux and La Maseline, lie beside each other on the east. The former, and more attractive, is the older. The latter, of concrete and lacking the beauty of the other's granite, is the one chiefly used, party because it does not dry out like Creux harbour. Access to both from the shore is by short tunnels, hewn through a headland, and nearby horse-drawn carriages (if ordered in advance) and tractors await the incoming vessel.

SARK

Le Bec du Nez
Corbée du Nez
Pêcheresse
La Grune
Eperquerie landing
Les Boutiques
Les Fontaines Bay
Grand Creux
Eperquerie Common
Noire Pierre
B A N Q U E T T E BAY
Le Fort
La Banquette
Petite Moie
Saignie Bay
Grève de la Ville
Les Autelets
Port du Moulin
Tintageu
Pte Robert
Grande Moie
Pegane Bay
La Seigneurie
Lighthouse
Port à la Jument
Moie Batard
Moie de Mouton
Sch.
Ch.
Maseline Harbour
BRECQHOU
Givoude
Chapel
Le Manoir
Harbour Hill
Tunnel
Mill
Prison
Collinette
Creux Harbour
Les Burons
Havre Gosselin
S   A   R   K
Les Dents
Victor Hugo Cave
Monument
Dos d'Ane
Les Laches
Moie des Orgeries
Petite Derrible Bay
Port ès Saies
Derrible Bay
Pte Derrible
Pte Château
Grande Grève
Dixcart Bay
La Conchée
Pigeon Cave
Vermondée Bay
Caverne des Lamentes
B A L E I N E BAY
Moie de la Fontaine
LITTLE   SARK
Moie Fano
Les Hautes Boues
Old Mill
Baleine
Pot Bay
Hotel
Moie de la Bretagne
Barracks
Balmée
Rouge Cane Bay
Port Gorey
Pignon landing
Disused mines
Brenière
Moie de Port Gorey
Souffleur
Sercul
Pierres du Cours
Bretagne Uset
Demies
N
L'Etac de Sark
½   1 mile
1 km

Map 5 Sark

The Village

It is a lovely walk uphill to the village, about a mile (1½km) away.
Pasengers may ride in a 'toastrack' bus drawn by a tractor, they may
travel in trailers or carriages, or they may walk. To avoid the flow of
traffic it is suggested that a path be used, a short distance uphill on the

left, which takes the pedestrian to the summit via the cliffs of Les Laches.

Most attractive hostelries near the hilltop await the traveller and close by is the village. Here are several shops, some of them specialising in tourist wares, banks, refreshment places and dwellings. The settlement has no special name and it lacks character. Many buildings are of tasteless design and insubstantial. Yet the shops are well stocked, service is cheerful and certainly the village is the island's focal point.

St Peter's Church, built in 1820, has little architectural merit, but its grey stone and homely interior have charm. Nearby is a school which also serves as the place of assembly of Chief Pleas, Sark's parliament, and the Seneschal's Court. These meetings are worth attending. Beside the school is the Island Hall, unattractive in looks but very useful. Cinema shows, dances, meetings and exhibitions are held there, as well as remarkably good flower, produce and handicraft shows. In this vicinity are kept the fire engine and ambulance, each tractor-drawn.

The Coast

A lane running from the summit of the harbour hill, La Collinette, to La Forge will take the visitor to Derrible Bay, a spectacular place. The descent is steep, though good, the bay can only be approached when the tide permits and the climb back is rather formidable, but the effort is most rewarding. The sands are broad, bathing is good and, most important, one may visit Le Creux Derrible. This great cave has an aperture in its roof and from the top, over the cliffs, it is easy to reach the brink of this huge 'chimney' and to gaze down upon the beach 180ft (54m) below. There are other caverns in this wonderful bay, a fine view of which can be enjoyed from the Hog's Back, a headland separating the bays of Derrible and Dixcart.

To reach Dixcart, the way from the village passes another school and its neighbour, the minute prison. Occasionally, this is used but terms of incarceration are brief. A few hundred yards further along is the mill, no longer in use. During their occupation, the Germans considerably marred its appearance.

In the valley below the school and mill are two attractive hotels and beyond them is Dixcart valley, a delightful approach to the bay. From a point above the bay, near La Jaspellerie, is a cliff path running south and this is the best approach to La Coupée, the isthmus joining Big Sark with Little Sark. On the east face a sheer precipice drops to the sea; on the west is a good path running down to the extensive sands of La Grande Grève.

The main road to Little Sark traverses La Coupée, but is comparatively dull, though traffic, apart from numerous cyclists, is light. Cycles
may be hired, like carriages and, while there are tractors about, the
absence of other motor traffic is most refreshing.

Little Sark

Over La Coupée is Little Sark, an entity in itself. On the east is
Le Pot, a rugged inlet, unsuitable for bathing, but scenically fine. On
the other side of Little Sark is the cove of Les Fontaines, fine for diving.
An extremely attractive little hotel stands beside a delightful collection
of buildings and tea gardens. Near the so-called Barracks is a path
leading to the lovely and famous Venus' Bath, where one can bathe
when the tide is not covering it.

Close by is another great rock pool of equal beauty : the Pool of
Adonis. There is a good path leading past the air shafts of the old silver
mines above Port Gorey and by following it the way down to both
pools will be seen. The descents are easy but the tide needs watching.

The West

Back in Big Sark is Dos d'Ane, a valley running towards inaccessible
Port ès Saies and there is a pleasant field path just north of it, running
to Beauregard. Here is a hotel, some impressive houses, a duckpond and
ancient cliffside cottages. A track runs to the Pilcher Monument and
below it the path winds down to Havre Gosselin. Here there is deep,
clear water and the diver will be in his element.

North of Havre Gosselin a fine headland overlooks the Gouliot
passage and the glorious isle of Brecqhou, not open to visitors. Below this
headland are the Gouliot caves, a most remarkable series of caverns
requiring a low spring tide to expore them thoroughly. There is nothing
like them in the other islands, though Les Boutiques, in northern Sark,
are nearly as singular. They are easier to reach than Les Gouliots,
though their entrance is rather concealed.

Port à la Jument is reached by a path extending from the hamlet of
Le Port, near the old burial ground. At a low spring tide the huge cave
below Moie de Mouton can be reached by the energetic. North of this bay
is Port du Moulin, approached by a wooded valley beside La Seigneurie
grounds. In the bay is a natural arch (resembling the one at Dixcart) and
at low tide one can reach the towering rocks of Les Autelets.

Above Port du Moulin is 'The Window in the Rock', an artificial

aperture from which much of the north coast is visible. Above it is a beautiful cliff path and north is l'Eperquerie. Here the heights decrease and a lovely open common takes one either to Les Boutiques or, eastwards, to l'Eperquerie landing, above which is a crumbling fort. Here, as well as along the cliffs, ancient cannon lie in the turf.

La Fontaine Bay is near and to the south are the settlements of Le Fort and La Tour. There is a path down to Banquette landing, but probably more popular is Grève de la Ville, reached by a zigzag track. At Point Robert there is a lighthouse, open to visitors and reached by lanes from Rue Lucas.

The grounds of La Seigneurie are very lovely and they are open to the public at stated times. However, one may not enter the Seigneur's stately residence, though it is visible from the gardens. The wooded setting of the house is extremely attractive.

La Société Sercquiaise is interested in Sark's antiquities, history, folklore and natural history and is doing much to preserve the island's heritage. It organises lectures and field meetings and visitors are welcome. The Sark Music Society is more active in winter than in summer, but the Sark Driving Society is livelier in the season than out of it. The annual horse show is admirable, like the flower shows held during the summer. Another seasonable attraction is the cattle show.

A Sark holiday need not be a feat of incessant activity. Many are content to bask in the sun, laze on a beach, fish, paint, take photographs or spend time in under-water swimming. There is scope for all in Sark.

Brecqhou

Across the often turbulent Gouliot passage lies Brecqhou (160 acres, 65 ha), seldom open to the public. Access is not always easy, for great seas from the west sweep into Le Port, where the modern landing stage is sited, while Jacob's Head, the alternative landing, involves crossing the tide race and climbing steep cliffs.

Formerly, Brecqhou was known as Ile des Marchands, from the Le Marchants, owners in the fourteenth century. Brecqhou means 'Isle of the Breach', the deep water separating it from Sark. The island resembles Sark in its geology and has spectacular caves, most only accessible by boat. Farming has been carried on for centuries, for Brecqhou has seldom been uninhabited. Recent owners have been wealthy and the great house and helicopter pad are a far cry from the simple farmhouse which stood there until 1933. Ownership of Brecqhou carries with it a seat in the Sark Chief Pleas.

Plate 41 *St Peter Port quayside as it appeared before the Old Harbour in the foreground was turned into a yacht marina. Relatively modern buildings face the water, though the town church is medieval and is deemed to be the finest in the Channel Islands* (E. Sirett)

Plate 42 *Farmworkers' cottages, Grand Île, Chausey, with a lighthouse in the background* (M. Marshall)

Plate 43 *Les Casquents lighthouse, 9 miles off Alderney. It is one of the most important of the Channel beacons, with its powerful light, fog signal and radio beacon. For nearly 200 years a light of sorts has been shown there*

Plate 44 *St Helier, seen from Fort Regent, Jersey's leisure centre. The bus station is at the Weighbridge, adjoining the harbour and close to the shops. Below the wooded Westmount are the sands of St Aubin's bay and from this point a causeway leads to Elizabeth Castle* (States of Jersey Tourism Committee)

Plate 45 *Gannets by the hundred on the slopes of Les Etacs, or the Garden Rocks, with the Alderney coast beyond. The birds were first noticed there, and on Ortac, in the summer of 1940, just before the German occupation. The rock is easily climbed by those visiting it by boat* (Victor Coysh)

Plate 46   *The Elephant Rock, Chausey Islands* (M. Marshall)

Plate 47   *An aerial photograph of Jethou, with Herm on the left. Between them is La Percée Passage. These islands are three miles from Guernsey*

11

Vignettes— the Smaller Islands

Victor Coysh

Herm

Physically, Herm resembles Guernsey in miniature, with low ground in the north and cliffs in the south. Three miles (nearly 5km) across the Little Russel from Guernsey, it is extremely popular as a day resort, yet the hundreds present have no adverse effect upon its quiet charm and endearing beauty. Herm has been the property of the States of Guernsey since 1946 and its tenant ensures that its appeal remains unspoilt, at the same time running the island as a prosperous tourist centre and a thriving agricultural unit.

Several prehistoric burial chambers prove that Herm has been occupied by man for centuries. In the middle ages it was owned by the Abbey of Mont St Michel and transferred later to a Cherbourg monastic order. It is believed that a small settlement of monks was established in Herm, who might have been responsible for the building of St Tugual's chapel in the middle of the island. A secular population was also there and remained when it was in the hands of Cordelier friars. Herm was transferred from the see of Coutance to that of Winchester in 1499, to which it still belongs.

In Elizabethan times and for many years later, Herm was the pleasure ground of Guernsey's governors, who hunted its red deer and pheasants. In the nineteenth century mining was carried out on a small scale and traces of the copper mine survive. Considerable quarrying took place, for Herm's granite is excellent and some of it was used in the building of Guernsey's New Harbour in the last century. Abandoned quarries are to be seen on the west coast.

When it was Crown property, Herm's tenants included a number of Trappist monks, who were there from 1881 to 1884. Seven years later the German Prince Blücher was tenant and remained there until the First World War, when he was interned. Another distinguished tenant was the writer, Compton Mackenzie, who rented Herm from 1920

until 1923, when he moved to Jethou.

During the German occupation Herm was sparsely inhabited and the Germans garrisoned it for a time, though it was not fortified. In 1943 a British commando force landed there, found no Germans and left. It was cultivated and farmed for Guernsey's benefit until the end of the war, when it was offered by the Crown to the States, who bought it for the benefit of Guernsey's residents and visitors.

Herm is reached from Guernsey in less than thirty minutes and several excellent ferry launches are available. When there is sufficient water, landing is at the attractive little harbour, otherwise it is at La Rosière steps, nearby. Between them is the well-appointed White House Hotel, adjoining an excellent restaurant. Close by is a delightful shopping centre, a tourist's magnet, with a pub beside it.

At the summit of the wooded road is St Tugual's chapel, ancient and appealing in its simple beauty. Its neighbour is the former mansion, and adjacent was the island farm. In 1975 a new agricultural centre was built a few hundred yards south of it and between the two sites is the tenant's attractive residence, beside the former mill tower and near the old oxen shoeing stocks.

From the harbour it is easy to reach any part of the island on foot: indeed, there is no other form of transport. Still, Herm is only $1\frac{1}{4}$ miles from north to south and half a mile at its widest, there is an excellent path running round the coast and helpful signs inform one of the time it will take for the walker to reach the boat from various parts of the island.

The favourite walk is northward, to Shell Beach. No traffic hinders the pedestrian, there are broad views seaward, high ground lies on the other hand and ahead is the common, haunt of birds, famed for wild flowers (especially dwarf roses in early summer) and attractive to the archaeologist, for here are several cists, though some are rather over-grown.

Three heights add to the character of the scene: Le Monceau, which has been quarried; Le Grand Monceau, overlooking the Shell Beach, and the comely Petit Monceau, a little hill on whose eastern slope are prehistoric tombs. At its foot, actually on the beach, is another. North-ward is a stone obelisk, La Pierre aux Rats, marking the site of a menhir demolished by quarrymen and later replaced because it is used as a seamark.

The Shell Beach is remarkable for the variety of rare and lovely shells to be found there, though really fine specimens are uncommon as the result of years of collectors' activities. The sand is shelly, the water

crystal clear and the bathing good. Refreshments are available and many visitors spend the day there. But even more lovely is Belvoir Bay, a little way southward; it can also be reached by a valley from Herm's summit, or by cliff path. One may eat and drink here and the sands, translucent water and sheltered situation make Belvoir one of the choicest places in the islands. From here one looks across the Great Russel to Sark.

It is worthwhile to continue over the cliffs southward. The walk is bracing. At the southern end are the remains of Le Creux Pignon, a gully flanked by sheer cliffs. A little to the west of it, and fenced in, is the copper mine's entrance. From this position one may look across La Percée passage to Jethou or down to the moored boats at La Rosière landing, easily reached by cliff path. From the steps there is a road to the hotel.

Major A. G. Wood has been Herm's tenant since 1949 and he has initiated several enterprises, including the issue of 'stamps' (more properly 'carriage labels'), which are much sought after by collectors. Other industries included pottery and the making of shell figures. Today, apart from tourism, the farm is the most important industry and considerable quantities of milk are exported to Guernsey throughout the year.

Between Herm and Jethou is La Pierre Percée, a rock pierced by an artificial hole. Here, probably, barges were secured when engaged in loading stone quarried in Herm and Jethou.

Jethou

Herm's loftier though much smaller neighbour has practically no sea-level territory, for its bulk rises almost directly from the foreshore to a maximum height of 268ft (about 100m). Its area is just under 100 acres (about 40 hectares). The flat summit is partly cultivated, but much of the island comprises woodland and scrub.

The so-called Fairy Wood is a, cliffside hanger on the north and behind the residence, facing Guernsey, three miles (4.8km) away, trees extend from beach to summit. Here, in bygone days, it is said that the bodies of pirates and other rogues were hung in chains as a warning to passers-by. In more recent years a signal staff stood there.

Jethou is Crown property and the present tenant does not open it to the public, though this was not previously the case. From the landing stage the way leads past a boathouse and other buildings to the residence, an old house with modern additions, looking onto the Little Russel.

The walled gardens are charming and in the middle of the lawn is a venerable and magnificent mulberry tree. There is an abundance of wild flowers on the island and the bluebells in the Fairy Wood make a wonderful sight, especially when gorse, primroses and other blooms are in flower.

A path runs around the island's base and another encircles the summit, with connecting links here and there. The lower path is about 30ft (9m) above sea level. Additionally, there is a road extending from the harbour to the hill-top, via the house and used by a Land Rover.

The most notable physical feature of the island is the great *creux*, or cave, on the east side. At low water it can be reached from the shore opposite the lofty islet of La Grande Fauconnière, if one scrambles northward along the beach. A gully leads to a capacious cavern with a vast open 'chimney', whose sides are sheer. It can only be inspected at low tide.

Overlooking the cliff opposite the islet is a raised beach. Above, the hillside is terraced, suggesting bygone cultivation, and higher still are walls of enormous boulders, enclosing small fields and resembling those of Herm. Some believe these stones came from prehistoric remains and suggest that an upright monolith in the Fairy Wood is a menhir, but archaeologists are sceptical of this and declare Jethou has no megaliths to show today.

Two islets lie off Jethou: Crevichon on the west and La Grande Fauconnière facing Sark, on the east. Both are accessible at low water and each is noted for its nesting birds, in particular gulls. The former is easier to climb than the latter, through which runs a rocky tunnel. Each islet is surmounted by a whitewashed daymark, that of La Grande Fauconnière being more ornate than Crevichon's. In the last century Crevichon was quarried and the work spoilt its symmetry. Its highest point is 108ft (30m) above sea level, 8ft (2.5m) lower than the top of the other islet.

Robert, Duke of Normandy, in 1031 gave Jethou to his shipmaster, Restald, who presented it to the Abbey of Mont St Michel when he became a monk. The island became a Crown possession when Henry VIII seized alien-owned property and, like Herm, it was once the Guernsey governor's hunting ground, with deer, pheasants and rabbits as the quarry.

Compton Mackenzie's novel, *Fairy Gold,* had Herm and Jethou for its setting and during his tenancy of the smaller island he made several improvements to the house. The Germans left Jethou alone, though one of their aircraft, shot down by their own gunners, damaged the residence

and outbuildings. Its remains still exist on Crevichon.

At one time both Herm and Jethou could be rented from the Crown by one tenant, but this arrangement ceased when Lt-Col M. Fielden held them in 1867. He was in the habit of smuggling brandy from France to England and used Jethou as a storage depot. In order to stop further smuggling, the Crown insisted that the tenants should be different persons.

Alderney's Outliers

Two miles (about 3km) from Braye harbour Burhou lies across the Swinge, its green contours and rocky outcrops rising only a few feet above its rocky beach. Until the Germans destroyed it during target practice, a stone cottage stood on the southern shore, but today only its ruined walls remain and within them a wooden hut has been erected. This may be rented on application to the Alderney States, though campers must take their drinking water with them.

Calm weather is essential before the Swinge can be crossed and when this is so day trips to Burhou are made in summer. They afford sufficient time to explore the place and to observe its bird life, but to taste of its real atmosphere, to savour the solitude 'away from it all' and to experience the magic of night there, one should live on the island for a few days. Unhappily, it is proving so popular among visitors that bird life is suffering and, while there are still puffins, guillemots, razorbills, shags and gulls to watch among other birds, numbers are not as numerous as they were even ten years ago.

Burhou itself is 1,200yd (1,080m) long and about 400yd (360m) wide. These dimensions include Little Burhou, an islet separated from the main island at high water. It is curious that many of the plants found in the larger are absent in the smaller isle. Everywhere the soil is burrowed by rabbits, puffins and shearwaters, making it friable and likely to collapse under one's feet. Coarse grass, bracken and wild flowers grow there, but trees, gorse and scrub are absent.

Great reefs of rock surround Burhou and sometimes seals bask there. The Renonquet reef lies northward and in 1901 the destroyer *Viper* was lost there in dense fog during manoeuvres, fortunately without loss of life. Several other wrecks have occurred around Burhou, one of the most recent being that of the big Turkish merchantman *Edirne*, which stranded there in 1950 and later sank. In 1906 Burhou claimed the large *Leros*, a German steamer and six years later the ss *Rhenania* also came to grief there.

Ashore, the character of Burhou is experienced from the moment of landing from flat rocks, for there is no harbour. The quietude may be broken by the birds' cries and the endless sound of the sea, but the absence of man-made noise is a relief, while the prospect of Alderney, Les Casquets, the gannetry of Ortac and the open sea is eternally attractive.

Ortac, 80ft (24m) high, has a massive, square appearance suggestive of a giant haystack. It stands between Burhou and Les Casquets and is the second of Alderney's gannetries, the other being Les Etacs. Its crown is white, thanks to the birds, which fly above the huge rock unceasingly during their summer residence there, and to see them dive after fish is a remarkable sight. If one is able to charter a boat, a visit to the gannetry is an experience to remember and the climb to the top is not difficult. Neither are the birds aggressive, though their great size and savage aspect can be rather daunting.

Les Casquets

Nine miles (4.8km) north-west of Alderney are the Casquets, high and mighty rocks on which stands one of the most important lighthouses around the shores of Britain. A hazard to Channel shipping for centuries, the rocks today are the mariners' friend, since the beacon warns them of their peril. In poor visibility the fog signal and radio beacon further inform vessels of the Casquets' position, thus aiding them in their passage up or down Channel.

For about 250 years there has been a light of sorts on Les Casquets, for in 1709 the lieutenant-governor of Alderney, Thomas Le Mesurier, petitioned the Queen in Council to build lighthouses there and he was successful. One Le Patourel leased the rocks for sixty years and maintained a coal fire on the rocks as a shipping warning. The flames were fanned by bellows and their keeper must have lived in a hut nearby. Les Casquets were leased by Peter Le Mesurier, governor of Alderney in 1785, and he built three lighthouses, named Donjon, St Peter and St Thomas. They succeeded the open fire and in 1790 revolving lamps were installed. The three lamps shed a wider gleam in 1855 when the towers were increased in height, but in 1877 the other towers were shortened when a single lamp replaced the three.

An Alderney family lived on the rocks for several years in the last century, in the days before keepers were relieved regularly. The Houguez family were quite content to make this inhospitable place their home, preferring it to Alderney, which they found too noisy on the rare

occasions they went there! At that period it must have been a quiet island, yet the Houguez family found it too lively, preferring the sound of the sea and the voice of the wind in their lonely outpost.

Still, life in Les Casquets was not as primitive as that on the rock lighthouse of Les Hanois, off Guernsey's south-west coast, for the space surrounding the pillar is very limited. The Casquets, on the other hand, are relatively spacious, allowing ample room for cottages to house the keepers, buildings for storage and a small garden, filled with earth imported from Alderney. Here vegetables were once grown, though today the plot is not cultivated.

Originally, the link with Alderney was by sailing craft. In more recent years motor vessels were used, but even these were subject to weather conditions and keepers were often stranded on the rock for many days if conditions made departure too hazardous. Again, the relief might well arrive off the rocks, only to find that landing was impossible. There are two landing places but today they are rarely used since relief is now made by helicopter, which lands on a pad either at Alderney or on the Casquets. Only really heavy gear would necessitate the use of boats. The lighthouse is maintained by Trinity House, which has been associated with the Casquets for about a century.

Today, a light of 2,850,000 candle power is housed in St Peter's tower, 120ft above high water. It is visible for 17 miles (27.2km) and is powered by electricity, generated on the rock. Until 1953 oil was used. St Thomas' tower accommodates the radio beacon's charging plant and the electricity plant for the buildings. In the Donjon tower is the fog signal and beside it is the old tower where, at one time, a warning bell was housed. A spacious yard gives room for the keepers to take a little exercise.

Before any sort of light was there, the Casquets must have claimed countless ships and even after the introduction of a warning, wrecks continued to occur there. Today they are still by no means uncommon, despite sophisticated systems to aid the mariner. Happily, although the Germans occupied the lighthouse, its equipment was not damaged and a commando raid on its small garrison in 1942 did not cause damage, though when the lighthouse was attacked by the RAF its lenses were chipped. Traces of this damage could be seen until recently, but visitors are unlikely to notice this since the lighthouse can only be inspected by written permision from Trinity House and access is difficult for the merely curious.

Off Les Casquets the battleship *Victory* was lost with all hands in 1744, when Admiral Sir John Balchen and a thousand others perished.

There were no survivors. In 1899 the *Stella*, bound from Southampton to Guernsey, struck one of these rocks and foundered quickly. Of the 200 aboard, 102 were lost. The mail packet sank in dense fog, a factor apparently ignored by her master, since she was travelling at speed when the disaster occurred.

Alexander Deschamps, author of *Sailing Directions for Guernsey, Jersey* etc in 1824, noted that the Casquets are 'steep and clean, with 25 and 30 fathoms all round: a line-of-battle ship may lie alongside them, on the south side particularly: between the rocks to the westward and the lights is deep water and ships may pass among them all. The velocity of the tide causes the sea to ripple and the mariner might be alarmed, but all is safe and clean. Ships unable to weather on either side may close on board of them to the length of an oar in perfect safety; the passage to the westward is half a mile wide, but keep as close to the Casquets as possible: there is nothing under water to be dreaded. . . .'

It is doubtful whether the twentieth-century mariner would feel quite so confident in approaching these dreaded rocks at such close quarters, unless conditions were ideal.

Lihou Island

Off Guernsey's west coast is the isle of Lihou, a lonely place reached more or less dryshod by means of a paved causeway when the tide is sufficiently low, and allowing a stay of two or three hours at a low spring tide. Otherwise, communication is by private boat, used by the tenant and his guests only. Lihou has an area of roughly 18 acres (7.2 hectares), is treeless, green and rocky.

The island enjoys an atmosphere far more peaceful than that of Guernsey, since the only powered vehicle to be seen there is the tenant's Land Rover. Those in quest of solitude go there, together with ornithologists, seashore naturalists and those in quest of the elusive ormer, when that delectable univalve is obtainable. For a period in summer a camp is held in connection with the Lihou Youth Fellowship, a body concerned with Christianity and the study of prehistory, history and natural history.

On its south coast are the ruins of the Priory of Our Lady, an unlikely place for a religious house. It was never of great consequence, yet it was founded in 1156 under the jurisdiction of the Abbot of Mont St Michel. The prior of Lihou must have had a small body of monks to supervise and its history is not a stirring one. Yet in 1302 a monk was murdered

by the prior's servant and in the ensuing confusion another man was killed—surely the most exciting moment in the little island's history. Even during the occupation the Germans did not fortify it, though the fine farmhouse was destroyed when they used it for target practice by heavy guns at L'Erée. It has since been rebuilt and is now the residence of the tenant.

When the priory's life had ended its buildings were allowed to decay and indeed were almost demolished in 1793 for fear that they might be used by French invaders. Happily, the Germans did not further demolish the ruins, though a derelict watch-house was destroyed. After the monks had gone, Lihou was let to various persons who farmed there, though islanders retained their right to gather *vraic* (seaweed) for agricultural manure or fuel. They could also fish from its shores and these rights have survived.

In the last century *vraic* was collected for another use: the manufacture of iodine in Guernsey. On Lihou beach wooden frames existed up to the time of the German occupation where the seaweed was dried and prepared for export to the larger island.

An easy path encircles the island and it runs past the residence and priory ruins. At the western end is a superb rock pool, deep enough for swimming and diving, but rather masked by a high outcrop of rock. Beyond the pool is the islet of Lihoumel, itself engirdled by more masses of granite. The whole area is a maritime deathtrap, for this vast area of rock is quite concealed at high water. The path continues north and east, back to the causeway. An offshoot runs south to the headland of Lissroy, below which is a deep and crystal clear rock pool curiously named 'the Nuns' Bath', despite the fact that Lihou priory was a masculine house!

Away to the south, off Pleinmont Point, is Les Hanois, a reef of rocks on which stands a lighthouse, built in 1862 following numerous wrecks, including that of the frigate *Boreas*, which struck the rocks in 1807 with great loss of life. The lighthouse is a graceful pillar of Cornish granite 117ft (35m) high and its light is visible from 16 miles (25.5km) off. There is also a powerful fog signal. Keepers are relieved by means of helicopter from the Guernsey airport, their married quarters being at Pleinmont.

Other Islands

Les Ecrehous

These lie north of Jersey, between the island and Cape Carteret, on the Normandy coast and extend nearly two miles (3.2km) from north to south, comprising a reef nine square miles (777 hectares) in area when uncovered at low water. Intricate channels lead through masses of rock and shingle banks to the largest island, Mâitre Ile, at the south end of the group. In the centre is Blanque Ile and Marmoutier is at the northern extremity. The last two are only separated at high water.

The highest point of Mâitre Ile is 60ft (18km) above sea level and on a slope lie the ruins of the chapel of Our Lady, built in 1203. The priest's house has long since gone and today the scanty remains are the haunt of sea birds, abundant on the Ecrehous. They are good fishing grounds and for centuries have been visited by Jersey fishermen, who have always regarded them as part of Jersey.

Smugglers also used the rocks and the French considered them their property. From time to time disputes arose (as they did regarding the ownership of Les Minquiers) and matters came to a head when the question of ownership was brought before the Hague Tribunal in 1953. After a lengthy hearing both groups were awarded to Great Britain.

A collection of substantial stone buildings huddles on the top of Marmoutier, creating an impressive picture and of greater character than the more modern structures on Les Minquiers. At Les Ecrehous they include a States of Jersey Customs house, with the island arms on its wall. There is another house on Mâitre Ile, but there is no permanent residence on any of the group, which is inhabited only in summer. Still, from time to time hermits have dwelt there for quite long periods.

Les Minquiers

Between Jersey and St Malo, this reef, colloquially known as 'The Minkies', covers an area of 190 square miles (49,000 hectares) greater than Jersey, although this is only apparent at low tide. Otherwise but nine islets are visible, of which Mâitresse Ile alone is inhabited and then only in summer. Yet, as at Les Ecrehous, traces of early man have been found at this remote spot, suggesting that they were then part of the French mainland. No medieval remains are to be found on Les Minquiers, whose buildings comprise a Jersey Customs house and some

cottages. They were erected when granite was hewn for the building of Fort Regent, Jersey, at the end of the eighteenth century.

Access to the reef is difficult and its approaches are buoyed. Today, it is mainly visited by the occasional yachtsman, though for centuries Jersey regarded the Minquiers as its own and fishermen sometimes contested possession with Frenchmen. In 1953 sovereignty was awarded to Great Britain.

Those who succeed in reaching these islets are privileged, for there is no regular service and strangers are likely to have them to themselves. Those who do succeed in visiting them will savour the strange atmosphere of these obscure places, revel in the bird life, and will probably feel elated at visiting Channel Islands which are virtually unknown to the majority of islanders and tourists.

12

The Chausey Islands

Michael Marshall

The Chausey Islands, Channel islands belonging not to the British Crown but to the Republic of France, lie twenty-five miles south-east of Jersey and eight miles west of Granville on the Normandy coast. Communication between Jersey and the port of Granville is by the summertime daily boat service of the Vedettes Armoricaines (a two-hour crossing) and between Granville and Chausey by Vedettes Vertes Granvillaises (a one-hour crossing) in the *President Quoniam* or *La Belle Malouine*.

The archipelago consists of fifty-three islets and islands, the largest of which is Grande Ile—larger than Herm but smaller than Sark. The islands have picturesque and curious names: La Genetaie, La Houllée (a word of Scandinavian origin meaning hill), Le Colombier, Richeroche, La Conchée, Plate-Ile. Eight of the islands are thickly covered with vegetation.

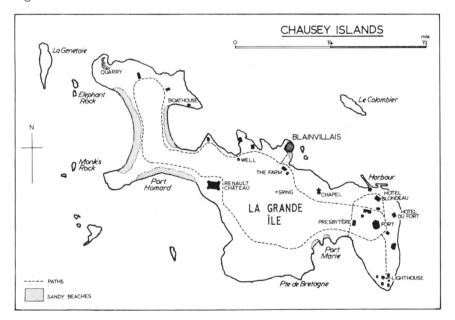

Map 6 The Chausey Islands (*after Frances Jane Marshall*)

The origin of the name Chausey is thought to be the word 'calsoi' (from the Latin *calcis* meaning chalk stone). When Richard II the Duke of Normandy in 1022 gave the islands to the monks of Mont Saint Michel they were called Calsoi, and muddy deposits of calcium are still to be found on the northern coast of the main island near the Elephant Rock and the Monks Rock.

The rise and fall of the tide in the Chausey area is 40ft—the greatest in Europe. At low water spring tide an area of fifteen square miles of rock, sand, gravel, varech beds and pebble is exposed, a paradise for the marine biologist and the amateur shrimper. In the Roman era and until the year AD 709 these shallows are thought to have been joined to the mainland of Normandy, the sea level being lower at that time. Two Roman roads are believed to have traversed Chausey, while another led from Portbail to Jersey across land not at that time inundated by the sea.

The first mention of Chausey occurs in the archives of the great abbey of Mont St Michel. There is mention of a sixth-century religious foundation built by some of the Celtic monks who later went to Sark, and centuries afterwards a Benedictine priory was founded on Grande Ile in 1120. Franciscans succeeded the Benedictines in 1343.

It was from Chausey that Bruel de la Roche set forth in the year 1549 to attack Sark and it was from Chausey again in 1780 that de Rullecourt embarked on his almost successful invasion of Jersey, where he was killed at the battle of Pierson Square. The Sound at Grande Ile was always a suitable anchorage for small warships, sheltered from the north-west and north-east, and a small protecting fortress was built on Chausey by order of Henri II of France in 1558, for which there was no lack of stone.

Chausey granite, a beautiful pale blue colour, is well known in Normandy and in all the Channel Islands. Quarrying at Chausey began about 1450 when stone was cut to construct the lower church at Mont St Michel. Subsequently, this fine stone has been employed in the ramparts of Granville (circa 1640), the *digue* at Cherbourg, the basin walls at Fécamp and Dieppe, the St Helier Hospital in Jersey in 1765, and more recently for the reconstruction of the old walled town of St Malo after the ravages of the Second World War, when 12,000 tons of granite were excavated in two years by M. Caron and his team of quarrymen. All exploitation ceased in 1951.

Following their occupation by the Franciscan or Cordelier order, the islands were held as fiefs of the French Crown by the Regnier family (the ancestors of the royal house of Monaco) and the Pimor family, but in 1802 they became part of the commune of Granville, and the rights

of the Pimor family were assumed by the Harasse family. Later they passed by inheritance to Mademoiselle Hédouin, who started a soda-ash chemical fertiliser enterprise there by the burning of dried seaweed which continued to the end of the nineteenth century.

In 1846 the French government acquired from the Pimor family an area of land amounting to one-third of Grande Ile, where they planted firs and on which they erected a lighthouse. In 1866 a vast and forbidding new fortress was constructed entirely of the silver-blue granite, pentagonal in shape, with a moat 45ft deep. This grim edifice held 300 German prisoners-of-war in 1914, but like many Victorian forts in Guernsey it never fired its guns in anger. Today the casemates are used to accommodate the families of fishermen, who operate from Chausey in the summer months.

Of the fifty-three islands, only two are inhabited: Anneret, which is about the size of Lihou, with two dwelling houses upon it, one belonging to a fisherman from Granville, the other owned by M. Pierre Letenneur, and Grande Ile.

On Grande Ile there are eighty-two houses and cottages, including the small fishermen's huts known as the Blainvillais: on the government-owned land at the southern end stand about ten attractive whitewashed summer houses held on leases of ninety-nine years, and two medium-size hotels: The Hotel Blondeau and The Hotel du Fort

Fig 22   Fishermen's huts, Blainvillais, Chausey Islands (*Frances Jane Marshall*)

et des Iles, both of which are freehold. There are also a provision shop and ship's chandlers, a cafe-bar, a sailing club building held freehold by the commune of Granville, and a lifeboat station, which occupies the southern side of the harbour slipway.

The rectory (*Presbytère*), that snug little cottage home of the much respected Abbé A. Delaby, priest of the islands, also stands upon French government land and has a front garden leased out to summer campers by that jovial, kindly, much loved, bearded man.

The remainder of Grande Ile is owned by La Société Immobilière des Iles, a trust company founded in 1910 upon the decease of Mademoiselle Hédouin, whose principal shareholders are Major E. Crosnier, a former infantry officer, M. Durand, or Marin Marie as he styles himself, an accomplished painter and expert yachtsman and lawyer, and M. Henriet, a telemechanical engineer who has recently acquired the interest of the widow of the late Louis Renault and is now owner of the Renault Château to the north of the island. The buildings and the substantial farm and pasture land owned by the trust company are leased to suitable tenants. Almost no new buildings have been erected in the last fifteen years. A small fishermen's chapel, adorned with six modern stained glass windows depicting fishing scenes, stands with its cross on a rocky gorse-covered hillock.

In winter the population of the island is a mere twenty, whereas in the summer it totals some six hundred, including two hundred who are either seasonal workers in the tourist and yachting industry or wives and families of fishermen who come to join their husbands for the season. More than 100,000 tourists visit Chausey annually and it is not unusual to observe three hundred yachts and fishing smacks anchored in the Sound at one time.

Plant life abounds everywhere despite the summer invaders. Wild flowers are profuse : gorse, goat's beard, wild radish, burnet rose and wild pear, and in the cottage gardens there are many apple and fig trees. Pine trees, elms and poplar are also numerous on the main island.

Standing in the lush green fields behind the farmhouse on Grande Ile, even after three months of drought, one is astonished by the good fresh-water springs, the fertility of the land, the giant poplar trees and the silence of another age. Here is a group of islands with no roads at all, no motor vehicles, and where the cattle wade in the sea to reach their distant grazing ground—a place with a character of its own— a place in the bay of Avranches.

Notes to this chapter are on page 244.

Notes, References and Sources

Chapter 1
(Pages 17–39)
Geology: John Renouf

1   Adams, C. J. D. 'Geochronology of the Channel Islands and adjacent French mainland', *Journal of the Geological Society*, 132 (1976), 233–50

2   Roach, R. A. 'Outline and guide to the geology of Guernsey', *Report and Transactions of the Société Guernesiaise*, 18 (1966), 751–76

3   Roach, R. A., Adams, C. J. D., Brown, M., Power, G., and Ryan, P. 'The Precambrian stratigraphy of the Armorican Massif, North-west France', *International Geological Congress, Montreal*, 24 (1972), 246–52

4   Renouf, J. T. 'The Proterozoic and Palaeozoic development of the Armorican and Cornubian provinces', *Proceedings of the Ussher Society*, 3 (1974), 6–43

5   Renouf, J. T. and Squire, A. D., *Provisional notes on the geology of Alderney*, Alderney Society (1972)

6   Gibbons, W. *The rocks of Sark* (Manche Technical Supplies, 1975)

7   Squire, A. D., 'Discovery of late Precambrian trace fossils in Jersey, Channel Islands', *Geological Magazine*, 110 (1973), 223–26

8   Mourant, A. E., 'The geology of eastern Jersey', *Quarterly Journal of the Geological Society of London*, 89 (1933), 273–307

9   Naylor, D. and Mounteney, S. N. *Geology of the north-west European continental shelf* (Graham Trotman Dudley, 1975), chapters 2, 3 and 4

10 Blake, D. M., Elwell, R. W. D., Skelhorn, R. R., and Walker, G. P. L., 'Some relationships resulting from the intimate association of acid and basic magmas', *Quarterly Journal of the Geological Society of London*, 121 (1965), 31–49

11 Wells, A. K. and Wooldridge, S. W. 'The rock groups of Jersey with special reference to intrusive phenomena at Ronez', *Proceedings of the Geologists Association*, 42 (1931), 178–215

12 Sutton, J. and Watson, J. 'The Alderney Sandstone in relation to the ending of plutonism in the Channel Islands', *Proceedings of the Geologists Association*, 81 (1970), 577–84

13 Squire, A. D. *The sedimentology, provenance and age of the Rozel Conglomerate, Jersey*. (Unpublished B.Sc. dissertation, Chelsea College, London, 1970)

14 Doré, F. 'La transgression majeure du Paléozoïcque dans le nord-est du Massif armoricain', *Bullétin de la Société Geologique de France*, 14 (1972), 79–93

15   Floyd, P. A. 'Geochemistry, origin and tectonic environment of the
     basic and acidic rocks of Cornubia, England'. *Proceedings of the
     Geologists' Association,* 83 (1972), 385–404
16   Renouf, J. T. 'Geological report for 1972', *Annual Bulletin of the
     Société Jersiaise,* 21 (1973), 145
17   Mourant, A. E. 'The raised beaches and other terraces of the Channel
     Islands', *Geological Magazine,* 70 (1933), 58–66

Chapter 2
(Pages 40–63)
Prehistory and Archaeology : David E. Johnston

References

Daniel, G. E. *The Prehistoric Chamber Tombs of France* (Cambridge,
     1958)
———. *The Megalith Builders of Western Europe* (London, 1963)
Finlaison, M. B. *A Preliminary Archaeological Survey for the Town of St
     Helier* (Jersey, 1975)
Giot, P.–R. *Brittany* (London, 1960)
Greaves, M. *The Grandmother Stone* (London, 1972)
Hawkes, J. *The Archaeology of the Channel Islands, 2: The Bailiwick of
     Jersey* (Jersey, 1938)
Kendrick, T. D. *The Archaeology of the Channel Islands, 1: The Bailiwick
     of Guernsey* (London, 1928)
Latrobe, G. & L. *Revised and Enlarged Guide to Sark,* 4 ed (Guernsey,
     1968)
Piggott, S. *Ancient Europe from the Beginnings of Agriculture to Classical
     Antiquity* (Edinburgh, 1965)

Chapter 4
(Pages 90–113)
Flora and Fauna : Nigel Jee

1   Brehaut, R. N. Zoology Report, *Trans :* Société Guernesiaise, 1974,
     382
2   Ranwell, D. S. 'The Dunes of St Ouen's Bay, Jersey', *Bull : Société
     Jersiaise,* 1975, 385
3   Le Sueur, F. 'Changes in the Flora of Jersey, 1873–1973', *Société
     Jersiaise Centenary Bulletin,* 1973, 36
4   Ibid, 38
5   Barrett, B. W. 'The Sandhill Snail – in Jersey', *Bull : Société Jersiaise,*
     1975, 409

BIBLIOGRAPHY

Bisson, A. J. *A List of the Birds of Guernsey* (Guernsey, 1976)
Conder, P. J. *A List of the Birds of Alderney* (Alderney, 1972)
Jee, N. *Guernsey's Natural History* (Guernsey, 2nd ed, 1972)

Le Sueur, F. *A Natural History of Jersey* (Phillimore, 1976)
McClintock, D. *The Wild Flowers of Guernsey* (Collins, 1975)
Rountree, D. *Birds of Sark* (Guernsey, 1972)
  Report and Transactions, Société Guernesiaise (Guernsey, annually since 1882)
  Annual Bulletins, Société Jersiaise (Jersey, annually since 1875)
  Birds in Jersey, Société Jersiaise, a systematic List (Jersey, 1972)

Chapter 5
(Pages 114–137)
Farming and Horticulture : Peter J. Girard

Bibliography and Sources
Ashby, E. 'The Cattle of Britain—Jersey', *Agriculture,* vol LXI, no 7 (October, 1954)
Blake, R. E., Sarre, J. W. 'Some Aspects of Guernsey Farming', *Agriculture* (December, 1954)
Cortvriend, V. V. *Isolated Island* (1945)
Coutanche, Lord. 'The Government of Jersey during the German Occupation', *Bulletin of Société Jersiaise* (1965)
Coysh, V. 'Mills of Guernsey' (article)
Cruickshank, C., *The German Occupation of Channel Islands* (1975)
De Guerin, Basil C., *History of the Royal Guernsey Agric and Hortic Society* (1947)
Duncan, J. *History of Guernsey* (1841)
Dury, G. *The Land of Britain—The Channel Islands,* Land Utilisation Survey (1950)
Ewen, A. H., and De Carteret, Allan R. *The Fief of Sark* (1969)
Falle, R. A. Information concerning Law of Inheritance in Jersey
Girard, P. J. Symposium on : 'Early Crop Production in the British Isles'; 'Early Crop Production in Guernsey' (University College of Wales, Aberystwyth, 1966)
Le Cornu, C. P. 'The Potato in Jersey', *Journal of Royal Agric. Society of England* (1870)
——. 'The Jersey Dairy Industry' (essay), *Royal Jersey Agric and Hortic Society Journal*
Le Maistre, Dr. F. 'La Bergerie St Ouen, and notes concerning Sheep', *Bulletin of Société Jersiaise* (1975)
——. *Dictionnaire Jersiais-Francais* (1966)
  Mollett Diary, Priaulx Library
  Official Documents, Royal Court Library (Guernsey)
Prentice, E. Parmelee. *American Guernsey Cattle* (1942)
Priaulx, T. F. 'How Guernsey Came to be Enclosed', *Bulletin of Guernsey Farmers' Association* (1962)
  Recueil d'Ordonnances, Tome 1, 'Banon', Guernsey Greffe
  Report. Commissioners of King James 1, Priaulx Library

Sharp, Eric W. Information
  Short History and Guide to Alderney. Alderney Publicity Committee
  (1963)
Small, T. 'The Control of Potato Blight in Jersey', *Agriculture*, vol XLIII,
  no 12 (1937)
———. 'Tomatoes in Jersey', *Agriculture*, vol LVIII, no 12 (March, 1952)
Small, T., Dunn, E., and Thomas, G. E. 'Potato Root Eelworm in Jersey',
  Agriculture, vol LVII, no 5 (August, 1950)
Speer, J. G. 'Pommage', *Bulletin of Société Jersiaise* (1970)
  Statistics and Reports. Guernsey Growers' Association
  Statistics and Reports. Guernsey Tomato Marketing Board
  Statistics and Reports. Royal Guernsey Agric and Hortic Society
  Statistics, Information and Reports. Royal Jersey Agric and Hortic
  Society
  Statistics, Reports, etc., from Guernsey, Jersey and Alderney. Secretaries
  of States Committees covering Agric and Hortic
Timmer, A. 'Agriculture in Guernsey during the German Occupation'
  (paper)
Warren, J. P. *Our Own Island* (1926)

Chapter 6
(Pages 138–149)
Architecture in Jersey: E. J. Leapingwell

Rybot, Major N. V. L., DSO. *Gorey Castle (Le Château Mont Orgueil)
  Jersey* (States of Jersey, 1933)

Chapter 12
(Pages 236–239)
The Chausey Islands: Michael Marshall

Barthelemy, G. *Les Iles Chausey* (Publication Pelican Tartonne, 1973)
Gibon, Comte de. *Les Iles Chausey Archipel Normand* (1918)
Jourdan, Abbé. *Les Iles Chausey* (1950)
Marshall, Michael. 'The Chausey Islands': *Transactions of La Société
  Guernesiaise*, pp 747–50 (1965)

Acknowledgements

For illustrations kindly provided I am grateful to the States of Jersey, Guernsey and Alderney, as well as to the Guernsey Press for the loan of Sark photographs and other material. Help has also been forthcoming from Mrs Joan Stevens of Jersey and from Mr A. V. Soffe of Alderney, who has allowed me to use his photograph of Ortac. The co-operation of contributors is gratefully acknowledged and I should like to say a sincere 'thank you' to the photographers whose work has been reproduced here and to others who, in various ways, have helped me.

VICTOR COYSH
Editor

Index